TOP 150
UNUSUAL
THINGS TO SEE
IN ALBERTA

Debbie Olsen

FIREFLY BOOKS

A FIREFLY BOOK

Published by Firefly Books Ltd. 2022
Copyright © 2022 Firefly Books Ltd.
Text copyright © 2022 Debbie Olsen
Photographs copyright © as listed on page 267

First printing

Library of Congress Control Number: 2022934045

Library and Archives Canada Cataloguing in Publication
Title: Top 150 unusual things to see in Alberta / Debbie Olsen.
Other titles: Top one hundred fifty unusual things to see in Alberta
Names: Olsen, Debbie, 1965- author.
Description: Includes index.
Identifiers: Canadiana 20220188009 | ISBN 9780228103721 (softcover)
Subjects: LCSH: Alberta—Guidebooks. | LCSH: Curiosities and
    wonders—Alberta—Guidebooks. | LCGFT: Guidebooks.
Classification: LCC FC3657 .O43 2022 | DDC 917.12304—dc23

FSC MIX
Paper from responsible sources
FSC® C111080

Published in the United States by
Firefly Books (U.S.) Inc.
P.O. Box 1338, Ellicott Station
Buffalo, New York 14205

Published in Canada by
Firefly Books Ltd.
50 Staples Avenue, Unit 1
Richmond Hill, Ontario L4B 0A7

Cover and interior design: Hartley Millson

Printed in China

Canada We acknowledge the support of the Government of Canada.

Disclaimer: This book is for information purposes only. The author and publisher have tried their best to ensure the accuracy of the information in this book. If possible, call ahead to the location or consult a local authority to make sure the location is open to visitors. The author and publisher are not responsible for any thefts, problems, injuries or accidental misfortunes from use of the information contained in this book.

DEDICATION

To my grandparents, Josie and Oswald Bengry, who taught me that "unusual" is a good thing. And to my husband, Greg Olsen, who has spent a lifetime exploring and appreciating the unusual side of Alberta with me. It's not about the adventure, but who you experience it with.

    – D.O.

CONTENTS

INTRODUCTION
TOP 150 UNUSUAL THINGS TO SEE IN ALBERTA

Alberta is a weird and wonderful place. It's filled with natural and humanmade attractions that aren't found anywhere else in the world. *Top 150 Unusual Things to See in Alberta* is a collection of some of the most unique, entertaining and downright odd places and things you can find in the province. This book is packed with interesting facts, trivia and even a few recipes. You'll discover hidden travel gems and also learn fascinating stories about places you may already know and love.

The unusual sites are grouped into four geographic regions: South of Calgary, Edmonton to Calgary, the Alberta Rockies and North of Edmonton. Sprinkled throughout are fun features, including Unusual Festivals and Events, Unusual Foods Invented in Alberta and Unusual Bathrooms for Regular People, which is devoted to Alberta's most exceptional biffies.

In these pages you'll learn about a lake that regularly disappears, an ancient medicine wheel that is one of the oldest religious monuments in the world, a Cold War bunker in the side of a mountain, a museum dedicated to gophers, a restaurant that was built inside a decommissioned water tower and many more weird and wonderful

attractions. Some of these places need to be seen to be believed.

Most of the listings are easy to find and open to the public, but there are a few that are challenging to reach, including the Athabasca Dunes Ecological Reserve, the World's Largest Beaver Dam in Wood Buffalo National Park and the Castle Mountain Hut's outhouse — a true loo with a view. For example, you need climbing skills to be able to personally experience the scenery from the toilet at Castle Mountain Hut. As for the others, you'll have to read those listings to see what it takes to get to each of them.

Be careful when you go out exploring. Visit the destination website or call to make sure the site you're planning to visit is open before you head out. If you're driving to a remote spot, make sure your car is in good working order and that you have a spare tire and know how to change it — some remote areas of the province do not have cellphone service. This book contains helpful tips on how to travel to many of the unusual sites listed.

Whether you are referring to a destination or a person, being unusual is a good thing, and exploring the unusual side of Alberta is an adventure you won't soon forget.

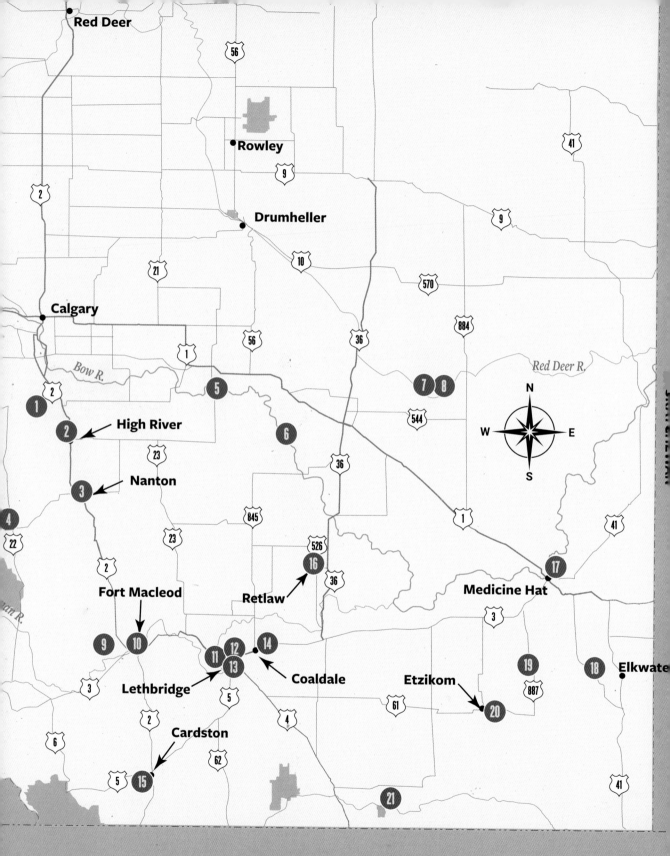

Red Deer

Rowley

Drumheller

Calgary

Bow R.

High River

Nanton

Fort Macleod

Retlaw

Lethbridge

Coaldale

Cardston

Etzikom

Medicine Hat

Elkwater

Red Deer R.

U.S.A.

SOUTH OF CALGARY

1 OKOTOKS ERRATIC (BIG ROCK)

Address Highway 7, Black Diamond, AB, T0L 0H0 | **Telephone** n/a | **Website** alberta.ca/okotoks-erratic-big-rock.aspx

The World's Largest Known Glacial Erratic

The Okotoks Erratic.

A 16,500-tonne quartzite rock sits on the flat prairie landscape 10 kilometres southwest of Okotoks off Highway 7. It looks completely out of place, because it is. The rock originally came from an area close to Mount Edith Cavell, a mountain more than 450 kilometres northwest in what is now Jasper National Park. The Okotoks Erratic, or Big Rock as it is otherwise known, is a glacial erratic.

Glacial erratics are common on the Alberta prairies, but Big Rock is exceptional. Erratics occur when rocks are dislodged and fall on top of a glacier. When the glacier moves, the rocks get a piggyback ride. Eventually the melting ice deposits the rocks where they don't belong.

In Alberta there are thousands of glacial erratics that make up a formation called the Foothills Erratics Train. It is 930 kilometres long and 22 kilometres wide and contains thousands of quartzite boulders and pebbles that lie on the Prairies. Big Rock is the crown jewel of the Foothills Erratics Train.

Scientists believe that a massive landslide occurred in the Tonquin Valley between 12,000 and 17,000 years ago. The landslide deposited millions of tonnes of quartzite and quartzitic conglomerate of the Gog Group onto the top of a valley glacier. The Gog Group is an identifiable volume of rock found in the Canadian Rockies, the Caribou Mountains and the central Purcell Mountains. The glacier became part of the Cordilleran ice sheet, which collided with the Laurentide ice sheet. During the last Ice

Another view of the large glacial erratic.

Age these ice sheets moved south, and when they began to melt they left erratics behind. Since the rocks are from an identifiable formation, it is possible to measure the approximate distance they travelled from their origin, which in the case of the Okotoks Erratic is hundreds of kilometres.

Big Rock has been on the prairie for thousands of years. Blackfoot People (or Niitsítapi) consider the site sacred and have long used it for ceremonial purposes. Their name for the erratic is derived from their word for rock, *okatok*, and that is also how the nearby town of Okotoks got its name. The massive erratic appears to be split in half and there are many legends about it. According to one Blackfoot legend, the split in the rock and its movement from its original location were the doing of the supernatural trickster Napi. One summer day Napi rested on the rock and gifted his robe to the rock. When the weather changed, Napi asked that his coat be returned, but the rock refused. Napi took the coat back, and the rock was angry and began rolling after him — moving from its original location. Napi asked several animals for assistance to stop the rock from chasing him. A bat succeeded in hitting the rock and breaking it into two pieces causing it to stop where it is today.

2 MAGGIE'S DINER, TACK and FEED

Address 123 3rd Avenue Southwest, High River, AB, T1V 1R3 | **Telephone** n/a | **Website** n/a

Heartland and Alberta's Filming Industry

The exterior of Maggie's Diner, Tack and Feed — a set used in the television series *Heartland*.

If you've ever watched the television series *Heartland*, you've heard of and seen Maggie's Diner, Tack and Feed. Located in High River, Maggie's Diner is one of the only permanent set locations for the acclaimed television show. It's a must-see destination for diehard *Heartland* fans.

Heartland is the longest-running one-hour scripted drama in Canadian television history, and it's popular in Canada, the United States and around the world. When Maggie's Diner, Tack and Feed isn't being used for filming, you can peek through the windows and look inside. It's impressive to see all the little details that go into creating a set.

The exterior of the Museum of the Highwood.

Props and costumes from *Heartland* at the Museum of the Highwood.

Alberta and Hollywood

Alberta has been the filming location for a large number of Hollywood blockbusters. Movies on the extensive list include *Jumanji: The Next Level* (2019), *Brokeback Mountain* (2005), *The Revenant* (2005), *Cool Runnings* (1993), *Unforgiven* (1992), *Inception* (2010), *Interstellar* (2014), *Legends of the Fall* (1994) and all three of the original *Superman* movies starring Christopher Reeve.

There's merchandise in the tack and feed store, and menus and other items in the restaurant.

Maggie's Diner is located in downtown High River, but it isn't the only place in town where you can see filming locations. The local tourism board produced a "Famous People, Famous Places" map that identifies a number of filming sites for *Heartland* and other television shows and movies, including *Fargo* (2014–present) and *Superman III* (1983). Unfortunately, the ranch, Heartland, cannot be seen. It is located 45 minutes northwest of High River on private property that is not open to visitors.

A short walk from Maggie's Diner, the Museum of the Highwood is also worth a stop. The "On Location: Film in the Foothills" exhibit includes props and costumes on loan from the *Heartland* series. There are also props and information about other productions that were filmed in High River.

BOMBER COMMAND MUSEUM OF CANADA

Address 1659 21st Avenue, Highway 2 South, Nanton, AB, T0L 1R0
Telephone (403) 646-2270 | **Website** bombercommandmuseum.ca

Home of Nanton's Rare Avro Lancaster FM159

The Bomber Command Museum of Canada is an aviation museum in Nanton that houses an impressive collection of aircraft and other World War II Royal Canadian Air Force (RCAF) artifacts. The museum preserves the history of the people who served in the Royal Air Force Bomber Command during World War II and the activities of the British Commonwealth Air Training Plan in southern Alberta.

Nanton's Rare Lancaster
The main landmark of Nanton has long been an Avro Lancaster FM159 World War II bomber plane. In 1960 Howard Armstrong, Fred Garrett and George White purchased the Lancaster bomber from RCAF Vulcan for $513. It had no propellers or engines, and it took two days to move it across farm fields from Vulcan to Nanton. The three men then went to RCAF Station Fort Macleod, which was scrapping Lancasters, and they purchased four engines and four propellers for $45 each.

The Bomber Command Museum of Canada's rare Avro Lancaster FM159.

The Bomber Command Museum has an impressive collection of vintage aircraft.

The plane was donated to the Town of Nanton because these men wanted a piece of history in their town that would pay tribute to the young Canadians who flew these planes and lost their lives in the war. The plane was on display outdoors for 25 years before the museum was established. The Lancaster is one of the most iconic aircraft of World War II. Even though there were 7,377 of these aircraft built, the bomber in Nanton is believed to be one of only 17 fully intact planes left in the world.

Thousands of volunteer hours have gone into restoring Nanton's Avro Lancaster FM159. The four engines are operational, and it is a taxiable aircraft, which makes it even rarer. Some estimates put the bomber's value at between $4 million and $6 million — though the town has no intention of ever selling it.

When the Museum Became Something More

The museum was opened in 1986 with the primary objective of protecting and restoring Nanton's Avro Lancaster FM159 airplane. It was initially called the Nanton Lancaster Society Museum but changed its name to the Bomber Command Museum of Canada in 2010. Today there are many artifacts, educational displays and airplanes on show inside the museum and the adjacent airport hangar. Canada's Bomber Command Memorial sits outside the museum honouring all the Canadian pilots and crew who gave their lives from 1939 to 1945.

The World's Most Democratic Train Robbery

It was a cold winter in 1907, and Nanton was running out of coal. A Canadian Pacific Railway (CPR) train with seven cars of coal arrived in town on February 5, but citizens were told the coal was not for them. As the train tried to leave, local resident Ira Shoop jumped on the caboose and ran along the boxcars, putting on the brakes. Shoop was arrested but was later released because the jail had no heat. As the train crew tried to leave again, a crowd of residents set the brakes on all the cars. Since it was lunchtime, the CPR official, the train crew and the constable went for lunch. While they were gone, the citizens of Nanton held a meeting on the station platform. A motion was passed to rob the train. It was agreed that each rural resident would take 1 ton of coal and each town resident would take 0.5 ton, and they agreed they would pay the CPR $6 per ton. Residents lined up alphabetically and took their rations of coal. By the time the authorities returned, the robbery was already in progress. Money was collected and given to the CPR agent. The CPR wasn't happy about it, and the North-West Mounted Police investigated, but the robbers were ultimately exonerated and no charges were laid.

A 1947 Mercury farm truck at Bar U Ranch.

There are many historical buildings that can be explored outside and in at Bar U Ranch.

4 Bar U Ranch National Historic Site

Address Township Road 17B and Township Road 17A, Longview, AB, T0L 1H0
Telephone (403) 395-3044 | **Website** pc.gc.ca/en/lhn-nhs/ab/baru

Learn about Canada's Ranching Industry

This Parks Canada national historic site is the only place that focuses on the importance of the ranching industry in Canada. Located near Longview, the Bar U Ranch was one of the leading corporate ranching operations in the country for nearly 70 years. Two of the ranch's owners, George Lane and Patrick Burns, were members of the Big Four who financed the first Calgary Stampede in 1912.

The ranch was founded in 1882 by Fred Stimson as the North West Cattle Company. At its peak the ranch had 63,184 hectares of deeded and leased land, 10,410 cattle and 832 horses. In 1902 George Lane and his business partners renamed the ranch the Bar U and made it world famous as a centre for breeding cattle and purebred Percheron horses. Lane operated the ranch until 1927. Burns and his company modernized the Bar U and operated it until 1950.

A number of famous people were associated with the Bar U Ranch. John Ware, Alberta's legendary black cowboy, worked at the ranch from 1882 to 1884. In 1891 Harry Longabaugh worked as a horse

A tent and cook wagon were essential in the days when cattle drives were commonplace.

breaker before he found more lucrative work as an outlaw known as the Sundance Kid. Charles M. Russell, the famous cowboy artist, did a series of paintings at the Bar U.

One of the reasons the Bar U was selected as a historical site to commemorate the ranching industry in Canada is because it has the largest collection of historical ranch buildings in the country. A visit to the ranch is a chance to see what life was like for the cowboys who worked there a century ago. There's a harness repair shop, blacksmith shop, saddlehorse barn, post office, dairy barn, bunkhouse, cookhouse and more.

Visitors can see livestock and farm animals, enjoy a wagon ride, try their hand at roping, explore the historical buildings, and meet interpreters who tell the stories of the ranch and the people who helped to make it famous.

The site is open to visitors between mid-May and late September.

DID YOU KNOW?

There are more cattle than people in Alberta. The province has the most beef cattle in Canada and the second-largest total farm area after Ontario. Agriculture has long been one of the most important industries in Alberta.

5 BLACKFOOT CROSSING HISTORICAL PARK

Address Box 1639, Siksika, AB, T0J 3W0 | **Telephone** (403) 734-4423; (403) 734-5171 | **Website** blackfootcrossing.ca

The Mystery of Canada's Only Earthlodge Village

For thousands of years Blackfoot Crossing has been an important gathering place for the Siksika Nation and other Indigenous Peoples, and it is the site where Treaty No. 7 was signed in 1877. Today it is the site of Blackfoot Crossing Historical Park, an impressive facility dedicated to promoting and preserving the Siksika Nation's language, culture and traditions. A state-of-the-art museum is located inside the 5,760-square-metre interpretive centre, and there are wonderful trails that lead to a tipi village and a mysterious earthlodge village.

What's truly unique about the museum is that it imparts information from the perspective of a Siksika person. You'll find interpretive panels with legends as told by elders and displays about language and culture from members of the Siksika Nation. The names of these contributors are right on the displays. It is fascinating and enlightening to learn about history from an Indigenous perspective.

The exterior of Blackfoot Crossing's main building.

Look carefully to see ancient stone tipi rings on the land at Blackfoot Crossing.

You can step back in time and sleep in a real Blackfoot tipi at Blackfoot Crossing.

Blackfoot Crossing has an on-site restaurant where you can taste Indigenous foods and a gift shop that sells crafts and locally made products. Dance and craft demonstrations take place frequently, and indoor guided tours with a local Siksika interpreter can be booked in advance. Enjoy more time for exploration by camping overnight in a tipi.

Earthlodge Village National Historic Site

There's a mystery at Blackfoot Crossing, and it's been around since about 1740. The Blackfoot name for the builders of the site was "Earthlodge Village." These builders created a complex of earthwork features on a grassy flat. There was a fortification ditch and 11 earthlodge dwellings that encircle a central open area. Even though these underground structures lie in Blackfoot territory, they were not built by Blackfoot people. They were built by an unidentified Indigenous group who may have come to trade, escape smallpox or flee European encroachment. Whatever their reasons, the Earthlodge Village represents a unique meeting of two cultures.

There has been much speculation over who built these structures and lived at this site and for how long. Some believe the people who built the village may have originated from the Missouri River region in North and South Dakota. Indigenous Peoples from that region were known to build residential earthlodge dwellings, but they were different than the structures found at Blackfoot Crossing. Their earthlodges were large timber-framed structures covered with sod and dirt and surrounded by ditches and palisades that were used for defensive purposes. The structures at the Earthlodge Village at Blackfoot Crossing are much smaller, and the palisade was placed inside the ring of dwellings rather than outside them. It's doubtful we will ever know for certain who built these unique dwellings and why.

If you hike to Earthlodge Village at Blackfoot Crossing, there isn't much to see unless archaeologists are working at the site. You can see depressions in the ground and not much more. That said, it is the only site of its kind in Canada and it remains a great mystery.

6 INISKIM UMAAPI (MAJORVILLE MEDICINE WHEEL)

Address Vulcan County, AB, T0J 0B0
Telephone n/a | **Website** hermis.alberta.ca/ARHP/Details.aspx?DeptID=1&ObjectID=4665-0042

Canada's Stonehenge

The central cairn of Iniskim Umaapi.

Iniskim Umaapi, commonly known as the Majorville Medicine Wheel, is one of the oldest religious monuments in the world, and yet few people ever get there. It is a geoglyph, a large hand-built design on the ground that was constructed with stones and is located in traditional Blackfoot territory. There is a central cairn linked to a large surrounding circle by 28 spokes. It sits on a high hill surrounded by rolling prairie. To many First Nations Peoples, this structure and others like it are sacred sites, and when you stand in the circle of ancient stones, you can sense that there is something special about it.

It has been estimated that the first stones were placed approximately 5,000 years ago, about the same time as the first phase of construction of Stonehenge, which sits on Salisbury Plain in Wiltshire, England. Like Stonehenge, this stone circle is a mystery. It was built thousands of years ago and no one is quite certain why. It may have been built by ancestors of the Blackfoot People (or Niitsítapi) or another Indigenous group.

In his book *Canada's Stonehenge*, Gordon R. Freeman, professor emeritus at the University of Alberta, postulates that Iniskim Umaapi is really part of a vast, open-air sun temple with a precise 5,000-year-old calendar. He believes the stone circle was used to mark the changing seasons and the phases of the moon. He described it as "the most

The view surrounding Iniskim Umaapi is breathtaking.

DID YOU KNOW?

Medicine wheels are found across the Northern Plains in Montana, Wyoming, Saskatchewan and Alberta. European settlers called them medicine wheels because they are circular and in some respects resemble giant wagon wheels. Alberta has more medicine wheels than any other province or state. There are 57 documented stone circle geoglyphs in Alberta, and Iniskim Umaapi is the oldest of them all.

intricate stone ring that remains on the North American Plains." Freeman spent years studying this stone circle and other geoglyphs around the world.

Archaeological studies indicate that Iniskim Umaapi has been used continuously for at least 4,500 years, and there are many offerings on the stones. When Blackfoot People visit, they often bring offerings of sweetgrass, sage, willow, cloth, tobacco, food, prayer and song. This action symbolically links them to their ancestors. Even if you are not Indigenous, it is considered respectful to leave a small offering at the site or to simply take a moment to sit or stand among the rocks and quietly meditate.

Iniskim Umaapi is not easy to find. It is surrounded by Crown land and the winding dirt roads leading to it are not well maintained. The stone circle sits on a high hill in the region, and on a clear day you can see for about 100 kilometres in every direction. The general store and post office of Majorville, from which the stone ring gained one of its names, is long gone. The closest town is Lomond, approximately 30 kilometres south. The best way to get there is with the assistance of a Siksika guide. If you contact Blackfoot Crossing Historical Park (403-734-4423), you may be able to arrange for someone to guide you to the circle and explain the significance of it.

The badlands scenery of
Dinosaur Provincial Park is
both unique and unforgettable.

7 DINOSAUR PROVINCIAL PARK

Address 48 kilometres northeast of Brooks, AB (see website for detailed driving instructions)
Telephone (403) 378-4342 | **Website** albertaparks.ca/parks/south/dinosaur-pp

A Nature and Dinosaur Lover's Paradise

Hidden away in the otherworldly landscape of this UNESCO World Heritage Site is the highest concentration of late Cretaceous Period fossils in the world. This provincial park has awe-inspiring badlands scenery and fascinating seasonal interpretive programming, including dinosaur digs, bus tours, fossil prospecting, guided hikes and educational theatre programs. In fact, some areas of the park can only be accessed on guided tours.

When you're in the middle of the lunar-like landscape, it's hard to imagine this place as a subtropical paradise, but millions of years ago this park was filled with palm trees and ferns. Dinosaurs roamed here on the edge of a great inland sea. Today this area contains fossils of every known group of Cretaceous dinosaurs. More than 300 specimens have been extracted from the park's Oldman Formation, including more than 150 complete skeletons, which now reside in more than 30 major museums.

Many fossils still lie waiting to be uncovered, and the opportunities for palaeontological discovery at this site are great.

Dinosaur Provincial Park also protects 26 kilometres of riparian habitat along the banks of the Red Deer River. Visitors can hike the Cottonwood Flats Trail and enjoy a leisurely walk along the riverside under a canopy of cottonwood trees — a tree that is getting harder to find in Alberta. Cottonwood trees require natural flooding in order to reproduce. Since the water level in many rivers is controlled by dams, this type of habitat has become rare in Alberta.

Located near the town of Brooks, the park stretches along the Red Deer River and provides diverse habitat for a wide variety of animals, reptiles, amphibians and birds. You might see pronghorn antelope, mule deer, bobolink, lark bunting, Brewer's sparrow, yellow-breasted chat and more, depending on where you are and when you're travelling. More than 165 species of birds have been recorded in the park, with 64 species nesting regularly. There is a significant number of breeding birds of prey, including golden eagle, ferruginous hawk, prairie falcon, merlin, marsh hawk and kestrel. You may see snakes in the particularly arid parts of the park, but most are harmless. The only venomous snake found in this area is the prairie rattlesnake and it is extremely rare to see one. It's common to see pincushion and prickly pear cacti in arid areas as well.

There are wonderful trails to explore and excellent campground facilities for tents and RVs. The park also offers comfort camping facilities in the form of semi-permanent canvas-walled tents with wood floors, real beds and handmade furnishings.

Dinosaur Provincial Park offers terrain and experiences that are unique in the world. It's truly an unforgettable place.

JOHN WARE CABIN

Address Dinosaur Provincial Park, 48 kilometres northeast of Brooks, AB (see provincial park website for detailed driving instructions) | **Telephone** (403) 378-4342 | **Website** albertaparks.ca/parks/south/dinosaur-pp/information-facilities/nature-history/john-ware/

And Other Sites That Honour Alberta's Legendary Black Cowboy

John Ware was one of the first black men to enter Alberta. He was a phenomenal cowboy who triumphed over prejudice and became a Canadian legend. In 2012 Canada Post issued a John Ware commemorative stamp to recognize his legacy and his contributions to Canadian history.

Ware was born into slavery around 1845 on a cotton plantation in Georgetown, South Carolina. When emancipation was declared, he left and began working on a ranch in Fort Worth, Texas. It was there he honed his skills as a cowboy. In 1879 he was hired as part of a cattle-driving team to move 2,400 head of cattle from Texas to Montana. Three years later he helped drive a herd of 3,000 cattle from Montana across the border to Bar U Ranch near High River, and Ware so impressed the cattle-driving team that he was offered a job at the ranch when he arrived. He stayed at Bar U until 1884.

In 1885 Ware participated in a cattle roundup outside Fort Macleod, and the *Macleod Gazette* described him as "not only one of the best natured and most obliging fellows in the country, but he is one of the shrewdest cow men, and the man is pretty lucky who has him to look after his interest. The horse is not running on the prairie which John cannot ride." Ware furthered his legend by pioneering the rodeo sport of steer wrestling in Alberta and winning his first competition at the Calgary Summer Fair of 1893.

Ware bought his first ranch in 1890 near Millarville. In 1892 he married Mildred Jane Lewis in Calgary's Baptist Church. John and Mildred, their five children, and 300 head of cattle moved from the Calgary area to a spot northeast of Duchess in 1900.

Ware became a well-known cattleman who was widely respected not only as a cowboy and a rancher but also as a human being. In the spring of 1905 his wife, Mildred, died of pneumonia, and Ware died a few months later when his horse stepped in a badger hole and fell on top of him. At the time Ware's funeral in Calgary was the largest in the city's history. John and Mildred's five children were raised by their grandparents and the ranch was sold. Since his death, many legends have been told about John Ware, one of the great heroes of the Canadian West. Here are some of the Alberta sites that celebrate this remarkable man:

John Ware Cabin

Located in Dinosaur Provincial Park, this cabin is associated with the last five years of Ware's life. Over many years the cabin fell into disrepair. With the help of volunteers and organizations, such as the Brooks Kinsmen Club, the Dinosaur Natural History Association, Alberta Environment Protection, Alberta Historical Resources and Old Bones Productions, the cabin was restored

John Ware Cabin in Dinosaur Provincial Park.

The Ware Memorial Cairn near Millarville.

and moved several times. In 1988 Parks Canada began the process of restoring the cabin, and it was ultimately moved to Dinosaur Provincial Park. New interpretive displays were installed and it was officially unveiled on Parks Day in 2002. The cabin is open on weekend afternoons during July and August and by special appointment.

John Ware Memorial Cairn and John Ware Ridge

Ware's first ranch was in the Millarville area near Turner Valley, and a cairn was placed on the original site. The Ware Memorial Cairn is a little tricky to find. It's about an 11-minute drive from Millarville and is located just off Range Road 204A. It stands 1.5 metres tall and is easy to miss — even though it's marked on Google Maps as John Ware Memorial. A barbed wire fence separates the cairn from the road, but you don't

have to cross the fence to see it. John Ware Ridge is 10 kilometres southeast of the memorial cairn. You can see the high ridge from the original Ware property.

Ware Creek Provincial Recreation Area

Ware Creek Provincial Recreation Area and the Ware Creek Day Use Area are located near the less-travelled Sheep River Provincial Park in Kananaskis. Both sites are located about 17 kilometres northwest of the John Ware Memorial Cairn. In the provincial recreation area, you can hike along Ware Creek and hike up Mount Ware.

John Ware's Gravesite

Ware is buried at Union Cemetery in Calgary. His stone marker simply reads, "Father," "John Ware," and "September 11, 1905." Mildred's grave is similarly marked

and lies next to his. Another four-sided stone sits beside the graves, and one side reads, "In memory of John Ware, born May 14, 1850, died September 11, 1905. In life beloved, in death lamented." It should be noted that there are many different estimates on his date of birth. Ware was illiterate, and he never wrote down his own history. Because he was born into slavery, it is almost impossible to find accurate birth records.

John Ware School, John Ware Building and 4 Nines Dining Centre

John Ware School is a junior high school located at 10020 19 Street Southwest, Calgary. The Southern Alberta Institute of Technology also has a John Ware building, which includes a cafeteria called the 4 Nines. Ware's cattle brand was registered around 1885 as "9999" and, like him, it became legendary.

9 HEAD-SMASHED-IN BUFFALO JUMP WORLD HERITAGE SITE

Address 275068 Secondary Highway 785, Fort Macleod, AB | **Telephone** (403) 553-2731 | **Website** headsmashedin.ca

One of the World's Oldest and Best-Preserved Buffalo Jumps

A viewing point at Head-Smashed-In Buffalo Jump World Heritage Site.

In southern Alberta, about 22 kilometres southwest of Fort Macleod, is a historical site that was used by the Plains People for nearly 6,000 years. Head-Smashed-In Buffalo Jump is one of the world's oldest and best-preserved buffalo jumps, and it was recognized as a UNESCO World Heritage Site in 1981.

Buffalo jumps were common on the northern plains, and they were one of the most productive methods developed for hunting plains bison. It was a communal hunting system that involved many people. About 10 kilometres west of the cliff is a system of 500 stone cairns that were part of the hunt. People would build fires or wave blankets to guide the stampeding herd toward the cliff. As the bison got closer to the cliff, skilled warriors would direct them down elaborate drive lanes, forcing the herd over the cliff. Injured bison were finished off by other warriors positioned near the bottom of the cliff, and the carcasses were butchered and processed at a nearby camp.

Skeletal remains measure up to 11 metres deep at the base of the cliff. The butchering camp was spread over several kilometres and contains the remains of meat caches, cooking pits and about a metre of butchered bison bones. The Blackfoot revered the bison and used every part of the creature for food, tools, weapons, clothing and shelter. The bonebeds reveal an ancient and remarkably stable way of life.

Most people assume the site gets its name from the plains bison that were driven off the cliff, but that is not the case. According to legend, a young Blackfoot warrior wanted to watch the bison fall over the cliff from below. Unfortunately he stood too close and was crushed beneath the enormous weight of the animals. When others came to do the butchering, they found his body underneath the bison. His skull had been smashed in.

When you visit the site, you can walk the clifftop trail to look

The buffalo jump.

The exterior of the site's interpretive centre.

over the actual buffalo jump, explore the artifacts and displays in the seven-level interpretive centre and participate in one of the interpretive programs or events. Head-Smashed-In Buffalo Jump tells a key story of the Indigenous People of the North American Plains, and there's no other place like it.

10 THE FORT MUSEUM

Address 219 25th Street (Jerry Potts Boulevard), Fort Macleod, AB, T0L 0Z0
Telephone (403) 553-4703 | **Website** nwmpmuseum.com

Birthplace of the Musical Ride

During the summer, a re-enactment of the original NWMP Musical Ride happens several times per day.

H ave you ever seen the Musical Ride in person? Most Canadians have not had the opportunity to watch a live performance of this iconic display of horsemanship, but at the Fort Museum of the North-West Mounted Police (NWMP) in Fort Macleod, a re-enactment of the original Musical Ride is performed several times a day in the summer months. It is the only on-site NWMP Musical Ride in Canada.

The RCMP Musical Ride has become an iconic symbol of Canada, but it had its beginnings with the NWMP in Fort Macleod. There were

Horse riders put on an incredible show at the Fort Museum.

Did an Out-of-Control Moment Inspire the Musical Ride?

In 1875 Frances Dickens, a member of the NWMP, gave an account of the incident he felt may have inspired the first musical ride. He described a moment when his horse became startled and galloped out of control. He rode with his eyes closed through a line of lancers without hitting anyone and then lost control a second time and rode through the line again. "There is some talk at HQ of organizing the Force's best horsemen into something to be called The Musical Ride," he said. "This is taking the form of a sort of equine Roger de Coverley, and I fear that I may have been responsible for starting the madness ... Some fool saw the intersection as clever, when put to music."

no members of the public in attendance for the first recorded NWMP riding performance in 1875. The ride was executed under the direction of Sergeant Major Belcher as a relief from other drills and duties. One of the original movements was called the Cavalry Drill, and it is still performed as part of the museum's Musical Ride.

Dedicated to preserving the history of the NWMP, this unique museum was built as a replica of the original fort that was constructed in 1874. The museum has eight buildings, more than 9,000 artifacts and an extensive archival collection.

It takes at least 45 minutes to view the NWMP Musical Ride at the Fort Museum. It begins with inspecting the troops, at which point visitors are given the chance to take photos. The performance itself lasts about 20 minutes. You should also leave time to explore the historical buildings and artifacts.

11 HIGH LEVEL BRIDGE

Address Scenic Drive South and 3rd Avenue South, Lethbridge, AB | **Telephone** (403) 394-2403 (Tourism Lethbridge)
Website tourismlethbridge.com/major-attractions/high-level-bridge

The Longest and Highest Trestle Bridge in the World

A train crosses High Level Bridge.

There are trestle bridges all around the world, but none are longer or taller than the High Level Bridge in Lethbridge. When it was constructed by the Canadian Pacific Railway (CPR) between 1908 and 1909, it was considered one of the engineering wonders of the world. Today it is an iconic landmark of the city.

Also known as the Lethbridge Viaduct, this engineering marvel was built to replace 22 smaller

What Is a Viaduct Anyways?

A viaduct is a high bridge that carries a road or railroad over an area that is difficult to cross, such as a deep valley. A viaduct typically uses a series of short spans supported on arches, piers or columns.

The trails and parks around the viaduct make for great exploration.

wooden trestle bridges, reduce the number of curves, cut 8 kilometres off and reduce the grade of the original route between Lethbridge and Fort Macleod.

DID YOU KNOW?

Renowned American engineer C.C. Schneider of Philadelphia was hired as a consulting engineer on the Lethbridge Viaduct. Schneider was one of the engineers hired to erect the Statue of Liberty in 1886.

This route also connects to the Crowsnest Pass, which was once a major coal-producing region of Alberta. Before the bridge was built, trains had to reduce their loads before they wound their way into and out of the Old Man River Valley, and this decreased the amount of coal that could be transported and, in turn, railway profits.

The High Level Bridge cost over $1.3 million to build, which was a staggering sum in the early days of the 20th century. John Edward Schwitzer, assistant chief of engineering for the CPR, oversaw the construction of the bridge. It took 900 railway cars

to transport the materials needed to build it, including 645 railway cars that transported over 11,000 tonnes of steel girders from the Canada Bridge Company in Ontario to the banks of the Old Man River Valley. A 100-man crew built the bridge in about 10 months using a custom-built railway crane.

The High Level Bridge has stood the test of time. It has handled heavy trains and strong winds for more than a century. Trains still cross it regularly. Although you cannot walk on the bridge, there are plenty of great spots to capture a selfie with it.

The Water Tower Grill & Bar is
one of Lethbridge's most unique
dining experiences.

12 WATER TOWER GRILL & BAR

Address 103 Mayor Magrath Drive South, Lethbridge, AB, T1J 4Y8
Telephone (403) 715-2552 | **Website** thewatertowergrill.ca

Lethbridge's Most Unique Dining Experience

Since it opened in 1959 a 58-metre-high green water tower has been a landmark in Lethbridge. It had a capacity of 1.9 million litres and provided many residents with pressurized potable water. When the city built a water treatment plant, the water tower was decommissioned in 1999.

The city planned to demolish the tower at a cost of $150,000. In early 2000 an article ran on the front page of the *Lethbridge Herald* asking the public for ideas of how to possibly salvage the landmark. Douglas J. Bergen came up with the idea to turn the water tower into a restaurant. After consulting engineers examined the structure and determined it was strong and sturdy, the city sold the water tower to Mr. Bergen in 2003.

It cost $2 million to renovate the structure and install windows, an elevator and three floors. In 2004 the restaurant opened, boasting some of the best views in Lethbridge. The restaurant has had three different owners since

The Water Tower Grill & Bar boasts some of the best views of Lethbridge.

it opened. At first it was called Ric's Grill, then it was the Water Tower Grill, which was owned by the Vintage Group from Calgary. In 2020 it reopened as the Water Tower Grill & Bar.

This restaurant is quite possibly the world's only restaurant inside a water tower. It's one of the most unique dining places on the planet, and the views from the inside are arguably the best of any restaurant in Lethbridge.

DID YOU KNOW?

Water towers are landmarks in many North American communities. They are used to store water and provide pressure to circulate it to the surrounding community. Water towers assist with everyday water needs and provide life-saving water for firefighting response.

13 NIKKA YUKO JAPANESE GARDEN

Address Corner of 9th Avenue South and Mayor Magrath Drive South, Lethbridge, AB, T1K 0C6
Telephone (403) 328-3511 | **Website** nikkayuko.com

A Japanese Oasis on the Prairies

A view of the Nikka Yuko garden.

The beautiful Nikka Yuko Japanese Garden was built to celebrate Canada's centennial, to honour the friendship between Japan and Canada, and to recognize the contributions to the community of Lethbridge by citizens of Japanese ancestry. Prince and Princess Takamado of the Imperial Family of Japan officially opened the garden in 1967. Princess Ayako of Takamado attended the 50th anniversary of the garden in 2017. Nikka Yuko Japanese Garden is a designated provincial historic resource.

Many people of Japanese ancestry helped to build Alberta. After World War II, southern Alberta had the third-largest *Nikkei* population in Canada. Nikkei is a word derived from the Japanese term *nikkeijin*, which refers to Japanese people who emigrated from Japan and their descendants.

The gardens are a 1.6-hectare paradise of perfectly pruned trees, water features, pathways and peace designed by Dr. Masami Sugimoto and

Another Amazing Japanese Garden

If you like Japanese gardens, you may also enjoy the Kurimoto Japanese Garden at the University of Alberta Botanic Garden. The 2-hectare garden was created in the *kaiyou* (strolling garden) style and has an entrance gate, lanterns, a pagoda, a teahouse and other structures. It was opened in 1990 and named after Dr. Yuichi Kurimoto, the first Japanese national to graduate from the University of Alberta's Faculty of Arts in 1930.

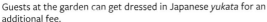

Guests at the garden can get dressed in Japanese *yukata* for an additional fee.

The Friendship Bell is made of bronze and was cast in Kyoto, Japan.

DID YOU KNOW?

The Town of Jasper was the first Alberta community to be paired with a Japanese community. On July 4, 1972, the towns of Jasper and Hakone became sister cities. Today there are 16 communities in Alberta that have sister cities in Japan. The objective of establishing sister-city status with another city is to promote friendship, education and tourism.

Dr. Tadashi Kubo of Japan. Most of the structures in the garden were built in Kyoto, Japan, including the pavilion, the shelter, bridges and gates. They were taken apart and shipped to Lethbridge, where they were reassembled. The garden uses concepts of Japanese garden design, including the principles of *wabi-sabi* (beauty in age/simplicity), *shakkei* (borrowed view) and *miegakure* (hide and reveal). The core purpose of this authentic Japanese garden is to restore your inner harmony and evoke a sense of calm and tranquility.

Visiting the gardens is a chance to experience Japanese culture in harmony with the southern Alberta landscape. There is a great deal of symbolism throughout the garden, and there are festivals, events and experiences that can be enjoyed there. You can dress in a traditional Japanese *yukata* (light, unlined kimono), participate in a traditional tea ceremony in the tea pavilion, enjoy a meditation class and much more.

The name Nikka is a combination of two Japanese words: *Ni* (from *Nihon*, meaning Japan) and *ka* (from *Kanada*, or Canada). *Yuko* translates to "friendship" and refers to the friendship between Japan and Canada.

14 ALBERTA BIRDS OF PREY CENTRE

Address 2124 16th Avenue, Coaldale, AB, T1M 1J8 | **Phone** (403) 331-9520 | **Website** burrowingowl.com

Alberta's First Privately Licenced Raptor Rescue

The exterior of the Alberta Birds of Prey Centre.

Alberta's first privately licenced raptor rescue and conservation facility is located 10 minutes east of Lethbridge. The Alberta Birds of Prey Centre is a unique attraction where visitors can see and learn about birds of prey. You can have a live owl perch on your arm, watch a trained eagle or hawk fly free using ancient falconry methods and participate in interpretive programs.

This unique nature attraction is run by a non-profit organization dedicated to conserving nature by rescuing, rehabilitating and releasing injured birds of prey back to the wild. These birds have come to the centre from all over

Canada — including the arctic regions. The facility is also involved in the captive breeding and releasing of endangered species, studying wild raptor populations and educating the public about these predators to increase ecological awareness.

In addition to visitors being able to see birds of prey up close, the centre is located on a 28-hectare restored native wetland area, so you can also see many native wetland birds at this site. There is also a pond and a flock of domesticated ducks. Guests can purchase food in the gift shop and feed the ducks — an activity that is a particular highlight for children.

Whenever possible, injured and orphaned birds are

DID YOU KNOW?

The burrowing owl is one of the most endangered birds in Western Canada, and population numbers have severely declined since 1987. Burrowing owls are unlike most other owls: they are only about 23 to 28 centimetres tall, are active during the day and eat insects (though they're also known to feast on small mammals, amphibians, reptiles and other birds). The female is smaller than the male, and the owls live in burrows that other animals have abandoned. The Alberta Birds of Prey Foundation's burrowing owl breeding program is working to help this endangered species. Offspring from the program have been released in all three of Canada's Prairie provinces.

A daily raptor show allows trainers to exercise the birds and provide information about the species. A bald eagle is pictured here.

You can get acquainted with a burrowing owl and other birds of prey.

rehabilitated and returned to the wild. Sadly, some severely injured birds can never be returned to the wild, so they live permanently at the site. This means there are always birds to see.

Facilities include a visitor centre with a gift shop as well as a natural history building that houses a massive eagle aviary, interpretive displays and nature photography displays courtesy of the Lethbridge Photography Club. Visitors can see great grey owls, burrowing owls, snowy owls, saw-whet owls, ferruginous hawks and other species at the facility.

The Alberta Birds of Prey Centre is funded entirely by donations and admission fees and does not receive government subsidies. The Alberta Birds of Prey Foundation, which operates the centre, was founded in 1982 by Wendy Slaytor and Colin Weir. With limited resources and run by dedicated volunteers and just a few key staff, this small facility often exceeds the expectations of visitors.

It is open from May through mid-September.

15 REMINGTON CARRIAGE MUSEUM

Address 623 Main Street, Cardston, AB, T0K 0K0
Telephone (403) 653-5139 | **Website** remingtoncarriagemuseum.ca

North America's Largest Collection of Horse-Drawn Vehicles

A statue of Don Remington stands outside the Remington Carriage Museum.

Carriages on display in the museum.

With more than 330 carriages, wagons and sleighs, the Remington Carriage Museum is the largest museum of its kind in the world. This unique museum in Cardston tells the story of horse-drawn transportation in North America. Along with all the carriages, wagons and sleighs, it has interactive displays, horses, a working restoration shop, activities and events throughout the year.

The museum began with the donation of 48 carriages from Don Remington, a Cardston man who restored and collected horse-drawn vehicles for 33 years. He had many remarkable carriages in his collection, including an open landau carriage that Queen Elizabeth II used during her 1980 visit to Alberta.

What Is a Surrey with the Fringe on Top and How Can You See One?

"The Surrey with the Fringe on Top" is a show tune from the 1943 musical *Oklahoma!*, the first musical written by Richard Rodgers and Oscar Hammerstein II. In the 1950s the song was also played by several jazz musicians, such as Miles Davis, the iconic trumpeter who became one of the most influential musicians in 20th-century music. The song is about a doorless, four-wheeled horse-drawn carriage that was popular in the late 19th and early 20th centuries. Surreys had a variety of tops, including a fringed canopy. There are several surreys with fringes on the tops at the Remington Carriage Museum.

Remington provided the magnificent carriage and acted as a footman to Her Majesty.

Also in the collection is a 1910 hansom cab once owned by Cornelius Vanderbilt, the 19th century railroad baron. His descendants once offered to purchase the carriage, but the museum was unable to do so as one of the conditions of the carriage's original donation was that it and the other carriages could never be sold.

The museum provides a thorough overview of horse-drawn transportation. Along with the fancy carriages are other more utilitarian vehicles, including those used in agriculture and industry, such as a wooden tank wagon that was once used to clean the streets.

The restoration shop is an interesting stop because you can watch the shop foreman and restoration experts at work and talk to them as they rebuild and restore carriages. Three breeds of horses can be seen in the stables adjacent to the museum. There are Clydesdales to haul the heavy wagons, American quarter horses for the buggies and sleighs and rare Canadian horses for light carriage work. You can reserve a carriage ride when you visit the museum.

There are several abandoned buildings in Retlaw with handwritten interpretive signs that explain how the building was originally used.

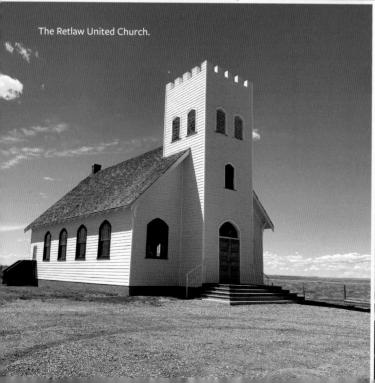

The Retlaw United Church.

The Retlaw Cemetery.

16 RETLAW

Address Retlaw, Municipal District of Taber, AB | **Telephone** n/a | **Website** n/a

The Ghost Town Where "Walter" Is Spelled Backward

There's something hauntingly beautiful about ghost towns — and it's not ghosts. Empty streets and crumbling buildings stand as a testament to the power of time and a reminder of how fleeting life can be. Even communities that were once home to dozens of shops and hundreds of people living busy lives can succumb to economic challenges and dwindle to ghost town status. Such is the case with Retlaw, a ghost town 13.5 kilometres west of Vauxhall.

When the Canadian Pacific Railway (CPR) arrived in 1913, the community that used to be named "Barney" became "Retlaw" in honour of Walter R. Baker, a CPR official. "Retlaw" is "Walter" spelled backward, and the community was expected to be a major centre of commerce. The town had a CPR railway station, four grain elevators, a hotel, a bank, a blacksmith's shop, a pool hall, two churches and several other businesses.

Walter R. Baker must have been special because naming one town after him wasn't enough.

Each of the communities near Retlaw began with a letter of his given name. There was Retlaw, Enchant, Travers, Lomond and Armanda. The last station, which was never built, was to be named Waldeck. The first letters of each little community once again spelled Walter backward.

So what exactly happened to Retlaw? The community is in a dry region of Alberta that suffered from frequent crop failures, and over time people moved away. The nail in the coffin came when the province of Alberta built an irrigation canal near Vauxhall in the 1920s. People moved where the water was so that they could have more consistent crop production.

If you visit the Retlaw ghost town, start at the cemetery. Inside an unlocked small white building, you'll find a binder compiled by the Retlaw Historical Society that contains information about births, deaths and marriages in Retlaw. Next, head to downtown Retlaw. As you walk around, you can read handwritten interpretive signs created by the historical society and see the remains of some of the buildings. The most impressive structure in town is the beautifully restored Retlaw United Church.

Are You a Ruin Gazer?

If you like visiting ghost towns, you might be a ruin gazer. The term is used to describe people with a fascination for exploring abandoned places, and ghost towns are prime sites for this kind of tourist.

17 MEDALTA in THE HISTORIC CLAY DISTRICT

Address 713 Medalta Avenue Southeast, Medicine Hat, AB, T1A 3K9
Telephone (403) 529-1070 | **Website** medalta.org

Western Canada's Ceramic-Producing Centre

At one time Medalta produced 75 percent of Canada's stoneware. Today it is a fascinating industrial museum — both inside and out.

Medalta Potteries manufactured ceramics from 1916 to 1954 and is today a fascinating industrial museum. The company was the first Western Canadian company to ship manufactured goods east of Manitoba. At one time it produced 75 percent of Canada's stoneware and was a household name. Medicine Hat was an industrial powerhouse, and clay products and pottery were long one of the most important industries in the city. Many homes in Canada had ceramic items, bricks, tiles and dinnerware manufactured by the Medalta factory.

Today Medalta is a national historic site that has been converted into an industrial heritage museum.

It's a fascinating place to tour and learn about the history of this industry. You can tour the century-old factory, see the kilns, look at an impressive collection of products once made in Medicine Hat, take pottery classes and enjoy other hands-on experiences. The artist-in-residence program attracts pottery and clay artists from around the world, and their artworks are on display inside the museum.

The Gas City

Sometimes you read a city slogan and you wonder what the town's forefathers were thinking when they came up with it. There was a time when Medicine Hat imagined that travellers and business investors

Pottery kilns at Medalta.

Examples of Medalta pottery.

would find "The Gas City" appealing. The slogan still appears on the city's welcome sign, and it doesn't refer to what you think it does. In the early 1900s "The Gas City" slogan really worked. Located above an enormous natural gas field, Medicine Hat lured manufacturers with free land, free water and cheap gas for heat, light and power. The city became an important manufacturing centre. Some residents were so committed to their tagline that in 1910 they petitioned to have the city name changed to "Gasburg,"

and they almost won. If not for Rudyard Kipling, British author of *The Jungle Book*, Medicine Hat might now be Gasburg.

Kipling had a special place in his heart for the uniquely named southeastern Alberta city, so he wrote a letter to the local newspaper: "This part of the country seems to have All Hell for a basement, and the only trap door appears to be in Medicine Hat ... And you don't even think of changing the name of your town. It's all your own and the only hat of its kind on Earth."

Origin of the Name Medicine Hat

Medicine Hat is a unique name that originates from the Blackfoot word *saamis,* pronounced "sa-mus." It is a word describing the eagle tail feather headdress worn by a spiritual leader known as a medicine man. There are several legends associated with the name, but they all conclude with a medicine man losing his headdress in the river and the surrounding area becoming "the site of the Medicine Hat."

18 CYPRESS HILLS INTERPROVINCIAL PARK

Address 8304 Highway 41, Cypress County, AB, T0J 1C0 (Alberta Visitor Centre)
Telephone (403) 893-3833 | **Website** cypresshills.com/alberta/alberta-home

Canada's First Interprovincial Park, a *Nunatak* on the Prairies

Birdwatching is excellent from the Elkwater Lake Boardwalk in Cypress Hills Interprovincial Park.

anada's first interprovincial park was created in a place that contains areas virtually untouched by the last Ice Age. In the southeast corner of Alberta, about an hour's drive from Medicine Hat, the Cypress Hills have been called "an island of forest in a sea of grassland." Millions of years ago during the last Ice Age, the top 100 metres of the plateau literally were an island, or *nunatak*, in a sea of ice. The word *nunatak* is derived from the Inuit word *nunataq*, which is used to describe glacial islands.

Head of the Mountain, a peak on the Alberta side of the interprovincial park is the highest point between the Rocky Mountains and Labrador. The fact that the soil and vegetation were not scraped away by glaciers has resulted in a region with unusual geology and plant life. The high elevation and unique geology allow this area to support a

Breathtaking views from Cypress Hills Interprovincial Park.

wide variety of ecosystems and diverse plant and animal life. At least 18 species of orchid grow here — more than anywhere else on the Prairies. It's common to see elk, mule deer, white-tailed deer, bison, pine martens and cougars in the park. It's also one of the best birdwatching locations in Canada, with more than 220 recorded species. The interprovincial park straddles an area on the southern border of Saskatchewan and Alberta and this also makes it unique.

For thousands of years this area has been an important gathering place for Indigenous Peoples, who were the first to appreciate its unique characteristics. According to some legends, the Creator placed the first man and the first woman of Turtle Island (North America) in the Cypress Hills. Considering what scientists know, this unique untouched region might well have been one of the first habitable places in Alberta after the glaciers of the last Ice Age retreated.

Cypress Hills Interprovincial Park is a dark-sky preserve that accommodates a wide variety of all-season recreational activities. There are many campgrounds, and Alberta Parks also offers furnished comfort camping cabins and huts equipped with soft beds and kitchen facilities. At the Elkwater townsite, you'll find Elkwater Lake Lodge and Resort as well as a few shops and restaurants.

The Alberta side of the park is a year-round recreational wonderland. Summer activities include hiking and cycling on more than 50 kilometres of trails, wildlife watching, birding, frisbee golf, minigolf and water activities. There are two designated swimming areas with sandy beaches, a food concession and playground facilities. In the winter there are over 40 kilometres of groomed cross-country ski trails, a snow slide, a toboggan hill, an ice-skating trail, an outdoor hockey rink, a downhill ski resort, fat biking trails, snowshoe trails and winter events. The visitor centre rents skis, skates, snowshoes and kick sleds in winter and fishing gear, canoes, kayaks, paddleboards, paddleboats, mountain bikes, tandem bikes and child cabooses in summer. Guided nature walks and other interpretive programs can also be booked at the visitor centre.

DID YOU KNOW?

In August 2001 an amateur astronomer named Vance Petriew, who was attending the Saskatchewan Summer Star Party in Cypress Hills Interprovincial Park, discovered a comet. The comet was officially named Comet Petriew (P/2001 Q2) after its discoverer.

19 RED ROCK COULEE NATURAL AREA

Address 49 km southwest of Medicine Hat, AB, off Highway 887
Telephone (403) 528-5228 | **Website** albertaparks.ca/parks/south/red-rock-coulee-na

Alberta's Overlooked Geological Gem

The otherworldly landscape of Red Rock Coulee Natural Area.

Just off a dusty gravel road in the southeast corner of Alberta lies a fascinating landscape that looks like it belongs on another planet. Forty-nine kilometres southwest of Medicine Hat, massive red, spherical rocks as big as 2.5 metres in diameter are scattered across 324 hectares of prairie landscape. These gigantic stones look unusual because they are. They are some of the largest concretions in the world.

The concretions at Red Rock Coulee were formed in a prehistoric sea. As organisms died, they left behind shells, leaves and bones on the sandy sea floor. The decaying organic matter released calcite and iron oxide, which began to cement the sand and

This site contains some of the world's largest concretions.

clay particles together. The precipitation of mineral cement filled in the spaces between sand particles. As circulating water deposited more layers of matter, the concretions became more compact and grew larger. Eventually when the sea dried up, the former sea floor was exposed to forces of erosion like rain and wind. Concretions are formed in place because they resist erosion more than the surrounding landscape.

The enormous lichen-covered concretions at Red Rock Coulee are admired by geologists, hikers and photographers alike. When you walk among them and view them against the big prairie sky, they are simply magical. Though this is a popular hiking area, there are no trails, and there are also no bathrooms or other facilities. There's an aging interpretive sign, barbwire fences and little else. On a positive note, there usually aren't many other people at this special place, and having it all to yourself makes it even more remarkable.

The Pronghorn – One of Alberta's Most Unusual Animals

Keep an eye out for pronghorns as you drive to Red Rock Coulee. They are commonly seen in this part of Alberta. Though its scientific name, *Antilocapra americana*, translates to "American antelope goat," pronghorns are neither antelopes nor goats; they are more closely related to giraffes. The pronghorn can run at speeds of up to 92 kilometres per hour, making it the fastest land animal in North America and the second-fastest in the world, next to the cheetah. Though the cheetah is the fastest sprinter, the pronghorn can maintain high speeds over longer distances. Some scientists have theorized that pronghorns once shared the grasslands with long-extinct predators resembling cheetahs, and that is how they evolved to run at such high speeds.

20 ETZIKOM MUSEUM and HISTORIC WINDMILL CENTRE

Address Highway 885, Etzikom, AB, T0K 0W0 | **Telephone** (403) 666-3737 | **Website** facebook.com/etzikommuseum

The "Powerful" History of Alberta's Windmills

There are almost as many windmills as people in the tiny hamlet of Etzikom, 85 kilometres southwest of Medicine Hat. Unless you count the visitors. Several thousand people stop by every year to visit the Canadian National Historic Windmill Interpretive Centre and the adjacent Etzikom Museum. The windmill centre is a unique outdoor museum with antique windmills and interpretive signs that tell the story and history of wind power in Canada.

One of the signs at the centre reads, "It wasn't the gun that won the west, it was the windmill." Windmills played an important role in settling the arid Alberta prairie. They were used to pump water for irrigation, refill steam-powered locomotives and power other activities.

The Post Mill is one of the most unusual windmills in Etzikom. It looks like it came from Holland, but it really came from Martha's Vineyard, Massachusetts. It is a replica of the first known windmill in North America

The Post Mill looks like it came from Holland, but it really came from Martha's Vineyard.

Alberta's Wicked Winds

St. John's, Newfoundland, tops the list of Canada's windiest cities, but Lethbridge is a close second. Calgary is the windiest large city in the country. The position of the jet stream over Alberta is responsible for the famously strong winds. When the wind comes across the mountains of southern British Columbia and drops down the steep east slopes of the Rockies to the prairies, it funnels through and accelerates. Strong winds that sometimes seem like a curse aren't all bad — they are also responsible for warm chinooks in winter.

There are almost two dozen windmills of all shapes and sizes in Etzikom, and guests can wander through and photograph them all year long.

and was built by Peter and Gerry Tailer. The giant house-like windmill has a moveable staircase that can be used as a lever to turn the entire structure toward the direction of the wind. This type of windmill was originally used to grind flour. After it was donated by the Tailers, it had to be completely dismantled to transport it to Etzikom and then reassembled on-site.

There was a time when there were many windmills like the Post Mill in Canada — including one built in 1825 in Fort Douglas, Manitoba, that is in downtown Winnipeg today. Most of the windmills have been all but lost.

There are almost two dozen windmills in Etzikom, each with its own unique story, and interpretive signs help relate the history and stories of many of them.

There are also a few antique farm implements scattered among the windmills.

Next to the windmills is the Etzikom Museum, which is housed inside the community's former school building. The classrooms now house a wide variety of artifacts that offer a glimpse into the history of the Canadian Prairies. There's a recreated general store, a boarding house, a prairie school, a post office, a blacksmith's shop, a barbershop and a typical rural prairie home.

The Etzikom Museum is only open in summer and during business hours. The windmills can be seen all year long.

21 ÁÍSÍNAI'PI (WRITING-ON-STONE PROVINCIAL PARK)

Address Range Road 130A off Highway 500, Aden, AB, T0K 0A0
Telephone (403) 647-2364 | **Website** albertaparks.ca/parks/south/writing-on-stone-pp

Amazing Indigenous Rock Art

A view over the Milk River.

A mysterious energy is concealed in the fascinating landscape of Áísínai'pi, also known as Writing-on-Stone Provincial Park. You feel it when you walk among the sandstone hoodoos and gaze at the Sweet Grass Hills that hug the horizon. It's intangible and yet it's not. The Blackfoot People (or Niitsítapi) believe that all things within the world — even rocks — are charged with supernatural power. To them this land is sacred and the hoodoos are home to powerful spirits.

The Blackfoot called this place Áísínai'pi, which means "it is pictured/written." This was a place young warriors came to fast and pray on vision quests — some recording their spirit dreams as pictographs and petroglyphs.

Tucked away in the southeast corner of Alberta, near the Montana border, this UNESCO World Heritage Site contains the largest collection of rock art on the North American Plains, dating back thousands of years. Historians believe First Nations

Examples of rock art found at Áísínai'pi.

Coulees and hoodoos dominate the landscape of this unique park.

DID YOU KNOW?

According to Blackfoot oral traditions, people have camped along the Milk River near Áísínai'pi for thousands of years. Archaeological evidence from the surrounding prairies show that people have lived on this land for at least 10,000 years. The earliest archaeological evidence in Áísínai'pi itself is 3,500 to 4,500 years old.

Peoples created rock art to depict historical events like hunts and battles and important ceremonial events like vision quests. But according to Blackfoot legend, the rock art at Áísínai'pi comes from the spirit world. It is a place they still return to for spiritual guidance.

Rock art is the big attraction here, and even though access is restricted, park interpreters can take you to places where you can view it.

The unusual terrain of the park supports some rare species of plants and animals. Pronghorns roam the grasslands, raccoons and beavers can sometimes be seen in the Milk River or in ponds, and bobcats and mule and white-tailed deer can be found in the coulees. It's not uncommon to see bull snakes and prairie rattlesnakes in the park, so it's important to stay on trails and watch where you are walking and sitting.

Visitors can enjoy a wide variety of activities in this park. The Milk River is a marvellous place to paddle a canoe or float in a tube, and there is a small beach area along the river's edge that is lovely on a warm summer day. The campground is equipped with RV and tent sites as well as comfort camping facilities that include permanent shelters with private decks and comfortable beds.

Writing-on-Stone Provincial Park is unique in the world. One visit and you'll know why it is considered a sacred landscape.

UNUSUAL BATHROOMS FOR REGULAR PEOPLE

I f you can't sit on your own throne, you should find the best alternative possible. Holding it in is not good for anyone. Fortunately, there are quite a few fantastic biffies to choose from in Alberta. From 2012 to 2021 an Alberta bathroom was declared the best restroom in Canada more times than any other province's. Alberta's toilet culture is alive and well and something to be proud of. Here are some exceptional bathrooms that not only provide relief, but in most cases offer an exceptional potty break experience.

 ## CANADA'S BEST RESTROOM

Cintas Canada's Best Restroom Contest showcases the best public washrooms in Canada and awards $2,500 in Cintas products and services to the winner. Every year five finalists are selected based on cleanliness, visual appeal, innovation, functionality and unique design elements. Once the finalists are selected, the vote goes to the public. The bathroom that receives the most votes is crowned Canada's Best Restroom. Over the years there have been a lot of Alberta winners. Look up the list of winners and if you find yourself near an award-winning restroom, make a pit stop — you won't be disappointed. Among Alberta's numerous champions is a quartet of bathrooms that gave the province an impressive four-year winning streak, from 2018 to 2021:

BEAVERHILL SHELL

2021 **Borden Park**
11020 75a Street Northwest, #102, Edmonton, AB, T5B 2C5

2020 **Westview RV Park**
243019C Highway 13, Wetaskiwin, AB, T9A 1W8

2019 **Beaverhill Shell**
9024 Beaverhill Road, Lac La Biche, AB, T0A 2C0

2018 **St. Albert Honda**
875 St. Albert Trail, St. Albert, AB, T8N 3X9

23 BANFF'S $2-MILLION SOLAR-POWERED OUTHOUSE

Address Lake Minnewanka, Banff National Park, AB

Lake Minnewanka Outhouse

You may have been to Banff, but have you stopped to enjoy the park's $2-million solar-powered outhouse? In 2008 Parks Canada installed a new environmentally friendly public bathroom at Lake Minnewanka. Made of concrete, the facility has a lifespan of 100 years. Solar panels on the roof provide electricity and heat the water system. A septic field disperses the effluent, which saves the cost of pumping and trucking it out. The bathroom is decorated with funky eco art and it's open from May through Thanksgiving. The only thing that stinks about this bathroom is the price. At a total cost of $1.8 million, it has been estimated that it will take 500 years to break even on the cost of this facility. You'll find this biffy beside the parking lot at the edge of Lake Minnewanka in Banff National Park.

24 A LOO WITH A VIEW

Address Goat Plateau, halfway up the south face of Castle Mountain, Banff National Park, AB

Castle Mountain Hut

The Castle Mountain Hut, operated by the Alpine Club of Canada, is an overnight accommodation with an exceptionally unique outhouse. It is an aspirational toilet for most people. It takes climbing skills to get to the Castle Mountain Hut, but those who make it can enjoy one of the most exhilarating views in the Canadian Rockies ... while they sit on the biffy. This is one occasion when you'll want to sit back, relax and really focus on the beauty that surrounds you. Exhibitionists will be pleased to know that the hut can be seen from the Trans-Canada Highway (Highway 1). It's a small white speck on the sixth buttress from the east.

UNUSUAL FOODS INVENTED in ALBERTA

According to Travel Alberta, there are seven signature foods in the province: beef, bison, Saskatoon berries, Red Fife wheat, canola, honey and root vegetables. Alberta is famous for these foods, but it is also revered for several food items that were invented in the province, some of which have become Canadian culinary icons.

THE Caesar Cocktail | CALGARY

If Canada had a national cocktail, it would be the Caesar, or the Bloody Caesar as it is also known. It's the most popular mixed drink in Canada, and Canadians are said to drink more than 400 million Caesar cocktails annually — though it is unclear how this statistic could be accurately calculated. The drink is unique to Canada (it never really caught on anywhere else). You'll find it on almost every restaurant and bar menu, and it was invented in Calgary.

The Caesar was first created in 1969 by bartender Walter Chell for the grand opening of the Calgary Inn's new Italian restaurant, Marco's. Chell spent several months perfecting the drink and is said to have drawn his inspiration from spaghetti alle vongole, a pasta dish that is made with clams. Chell hand mashed clams and mixed the clam liquid with tomato juice and spices. The cocktail caught on quickly in Calgary and soon spread to the rest of Canada. The Mott's company developed Clamato, a mixture of clam and tomato juices, around the same time the Caesar was invented. The company only sold 500 cases of Clamato in 1970, but sales dramatically increased as the Caesar cocktail became more popular. The Calgary Inn is now the Westin Calgary. If you want to have a Caesar at the place where it was born, the closest you can get is the hotel's Liquid Lounge. There are many different variations of the Caesar cocktail today, and National Caesar Day, an unofficial holiday, is celebrated each year in May.

THE CAESAR COCKTAIL

Mott's Classic Caesar Cocktail Recipe

Ingredients
Celery salt
1 oz. (29 ml) vodka
2 dashes hot sauce
4 dashes Worcestershire sauce
3 grinds fresh cracked salt and pepper
Ice
4 oz. (118 ml) Mott's Clamato The Original
Celery stalk
Lime wedge

Directions:
1. Rim a tall glass with celery salt.
2. Add the vodka, hot sauce, Worcestershire sauce and fresh cracked salt and pepper.
3. Add ice then pour in Mott's Clamato The Original.
4. Stir the cocktail and garnish with a celery stalk and a lime wedge.

GINGER BEEF

PUFFED WHEAT SQUARES

TABER CORN | TABER

Taber is known as the Corn Capital of Canada. Taber corn is so famous in Alberta that it sells at a premium price. And Albertans are not only willingly pay for it, they also eagerly anticipate it. When the first cobs of Taber corn are ready for sale at roadside stands, it makes the news.

Since Taber corn sells at a high price, some vendors have tried to pass off fake Taber corn as the real thing. Like buying a fake designer purse, however, fake Taber corn doesn't quite cut it. A vendor selling real Taber corn will have a certificate of authenticity.

Sunny days and cool Alberta nights in the Taber area result in the sweet, crisp cobs that have become a beloved summer treat. Those who really love corn should attend Cornfest, the town of Taber's annual summer festival.

GINGER BEEF | CALGARY

Several restaurants and chefs have claimed to be the inventor of ginger beef, but the most widely accepted origin story attributes the creation of the dish to George Wong, a chef from northern China, who worked in the mid-1970s at Calgary's Silver Inn Restaurant. The sweet and spicy dish is now a staple at most Chinese restaurants in Canada.

Ginger beef is made from lightly battered deep-fried strips of beef served with a sweet sauce containing ginger, garlic and hot peppers. It is commonly served with julienne carrots and slices of onion. In 2020 CBC's *Calgary Eye-opener* sent restaurant reviewer Elizabeth Carson and two food aficionados to find the best ginger beef in the city. After several taste tests, the team of judges felt the best ginger beef in Calgary was still found at the Silver Inn Restaurant, which is located at 2702 Centre Street North.

PUFFED WHEAT SQUARES | RED DEER

Sweet and sticky puffed wheat squares are a Canadian delicacy invented by Alan J. Russell, a Red Deer–based candymaker who opened a candy shop in 1913 on Ross Street. With the start of World War I, Russell had to become inventive with his recipes as food supplies were in tight demand. He swapped out sugar for molasses and traditional grains for puffed rice and wheat. The original puffed wheat square was born when Russell answered a call from the Quaker Oats Company to submit ideas for a new candy bar. Russell adapted the original recipe over time as ingredients became more accessible. Today the puffed wheat square, also known as the puffed wheat cake, is a beloved treat in Alberta and the other Prairie provinces, but it is virtually unknown in other parts of Canada.

Puffed Wheat Squares

Ingredients
6½ cups puffed wheat cereal
½ cup margarine
1 cup brown sugar
½ cup corn syrup
3 tablespoons cocoa

Directions:
1 Grease a 9 in. x 9 in. (23 cm x 23 cm) pan.
2 Put puffed wheat cereal into a large bowl.
3 Melt margarine in a heavy saucepan over medium-low heat and then add the brown sugar, corn syrup and cocoa.
4 Stir margarine mixture with a wooden spoon until the mixture comes to a full boil. Let it boil for one minute, then remove from heat.
5 Pour mixture over puffed wheat and stir well until the cereal is evenly coated.
6 Press the cereal mixture into the greased pan.
7 Cool, cut into squares and store in an airtight container.

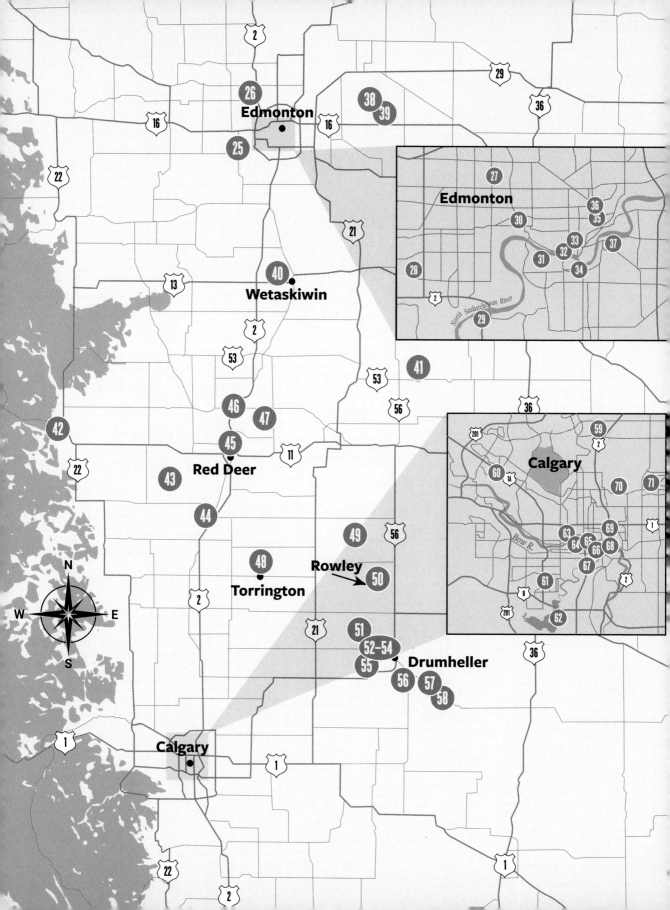

EDMONTON TO CALGARY

25 UNIVERSITY OF ALBERTA BOTANIC GARDEN

Address 51227 Highway 60, Parkland County, AB, T7Y 1C5
Telephone (780) 492-3050 | **Website** botanicgarden.ualberta.ca

Exploring the Province's Largest Botanic Garden

A serene view over the Aga Khan Garden at the University of Alberta Botanic Garden.

When the University of Alberta Botanic Garden was established on donated land in 1959, it was simply called the Botanic Garden and Field Laboratory of the University of Alberta's Department of Botany. It was viewed as a site for agricultural research. No one imagined that the garden would one day become a tourist attraction.

Over the years the garden has seen a few name changes. When it was damaged by severe flooding in the 1970s, a donation from the Devonian Foundation helped to repair the damages and expand the garden. In recognition of the donation, the name of the garden was changed to the Devonian Botanic Garden. In 2017 the garden was renamed again to the University of Alberta Botanic Garden.

Today the garden is a 97-hectare plant-lover's paradise with many highlights, including a unique Indigenous Garden (which features plants traditionally used by Indigenous Peoples), a Japanese garden, an indoor tropical garden with colourful butterflies,

The Aga Khan Garden is a contemporary interpretation of an Islamic garden suited for a northern climate.

The Kurimoto Japanese Garden.

exploring the garden. It's so large that it's difficult to see it all in one visit.

The University of Alberta Botanic Garden is open during the warmer months and for some special events during the winter. Whenever you visit, it never disappoints. There is always something new to discover in these beautiful gardens, which showcase many different cultures and a wide variety of plants while also providing an important space for research.

North America's Largest Islamic Garden

Opened in 2018 the Aga Khan Garden is one of the newest and most interesting garden areas to explore. It was made possible with a $25-million donation by His Highness the Aga Khan, the hereditary Imam, or spiritual leader, of the Shia Ismaili Muslims. It is the most northerly Islamic garden in the world, and for many Canadians it is a rare opportunity to experience this style of garden. Although the structure and style is inspired by traditional Islamic gardens, this contemporary interpretation features native plants and fruit trees rather than date palms, olive trees and pomegranates, which do not survive northerly climates. The garden is meant to be an expression of culture and cooperation.

extensive natural areas and North America's largest Islamic garden. The botanic garden is located a few kilometres west of Edmonton and a few kilometres north of the town of Devon.

Besides an amazing collection of plants, there are bridges, walkways, water features, gazebos, benches, natural areas and beautiful stone landscape features that all add to the enjoyment of

26 FATHER LACOMBE CHAPEL

Address 5 St. Vital Avenue, St. Albert, AB, T8N 1K1 | **Telephone** (780) 459-7663 | **Website** fatherlacombechapel.ca

Alberta's Oldest-Surviving Building

Father Lacombe Chapel in St. Albert.

On top of Mission Hill in what is now St. Albert sits the oldest-surviving building in Alberta. The Father Lacombe Chapel was built in 1861 by Father Albert Lacombe and members of the Métis community to service the newly established St. Albert Roman Catholic Mission. The chapel was built using a classic fur-trade construction technique called "post on sill." This technique uses slotted vertical posts into which the wall pieces are slipped and then held together with wooden pegs. This type of construction allowed the building to be easily moved, and over the years it was relocated twice. It now sits in a prominent location on Mission Hill, overlooking the Sturgeon River.

The building served as a chapel in the community until 1870, when it was replaced by a larger church building. The original chapel likely survived because it was used for storage. In 1929 the building was converted into the Father Lacombe Museum, and in 1977 it was declared a provincial historic site.

A thriving French-speaking Métis settlement grew in the area around the chapel. It soon became one of the largest Métis communities in Western Canada. The Grey Nuns arrived in 1863, and a hospital, an orphanage and a school were soon established. The Grey Nuns Hospital in Edmonton traces its roots to the first nuns who came to the area.

Those who visit the Father Lacombe Chapel can experience a guided tour with a costumed interpreter from May through Labour Day. You can tour the chapel only or take a full tour that also includes the grotto and the cemetery and learn the history of Mission Hill. Along the way you'll learn more about Father Lacombe and his role as a spiritual leader, a peacemaker and a negotiator. You'll also learn about the history of the surrounding Métis community and the St. Albert Roman Catholic Mission.

Take a stroll along St. Albert's Founders' Walk to learn more about the area's fascinating history. You'll find the paved trail right across from the chapel with interpretive signs and historic stops along the way. There's even a wild rhubarb patch.

This statue of Father Lacombe sits near the Father Lacombe Chapel. It is a reminder of the Métis Mission and, later, the Franco-Albertan farming community that once existed here.

Other Places in Alberta Named after Father Albert Lacombe

Two cities in Alberta were named for Father Lacombe: St. Albert and Lacombe. Three schools in Alberta also bear his name: Father Lacombe High School in Calgary, Father Lacombe Catholic School in Lacombe and Albert Lacombe Catholic Elementary School in St. Albert.

TELUS WORLD of SCIENCE – EDMONTON

Address 11211 142nd Street Northwest, Edmonton, AB, T5M 4A1
Telephone (780) 451-3344 | **Website** telusworldofscienceedmonton.ca

Canada's Largest Planetarium Dome Theatre

TELUS World of Science – Edmonton first opened in 1984 as a replacement for the Queen Elizabeth II Planetarium, the first public planetarium in Canada, which had been in operation since 1960. The original Queen Elizabeth II Planetarium was designated a municipal historic resource by the City of Edmonton in 2017, and it has been restored and will open to the public in 2022. Even today the planetarium is an important part of TELUS World of Science – Edmonton, and the new Zeidler Dome is the largest planetarium dome theatre in the country and the only dome theatre in the world with 10K resolution. It's a wonderful place to learn about astronomy and the night sky.

As important as the planetarium is, the science centre has much more to offer. Over the years the facility has had several name changes and undergone many expansions. Today it is home to Alberta's largest IMAX® screen, hundreds of hands-on exhibits, cool technology, science

Young or old, you will find lots to discover at TELUS World of Science – Edmonton.

The exterior of TELUS World of Science – Edmonton.

experiments and more. Its many cutting-edge attractions and displays inspire discovery. Kids and adults can step inside a giant laboratory, learn to program a robot, watch a live science show, explore the permanent exhibits and check out rotating special exhibitions.

Gallery of Gross and Other Exhibits

In all there are five permanent exhibit galleries to explore, and Body Fantastic is one of the most fun and interesting on offer. The displays help visitors learn about the inner workings of the human body. Those who chuckle at bathroom humour will undoubtedly enjoy the Gallery of Gross, with its "different" sights, sounds and smells.

Whether learning about weather systems by creating lightning and tornadoes, discovering fossils or pretending to pilot an airplane, visitors will find something unusual to experience at Edmonton's science centre.

Tons of interactive displays keep kids engaged and curious.

DID YOU KNOW?

The science centre hosts DARK MATTERS 18+ events for adults. The events feature music, a bar and grown-up science experiments.

28 WEST EDMONTON MALL

Address 8882 170th Street Northwest, Edmonton, AB, T5T 4J2 | Telephone (780) 444-5321 | Website wem.ca

North America's Largest Enclosed Shopping Mall

The Ship, a replica of the *Santa Maria*, is also available for event rentals.

West Edmonton Mall is North America's largest enclosed shopping mall as of 2021, with more than 800 retail shops, numerous entertainment venues and attractions, and over 100 dining venues. The mall spans the equivalent of 48 city blocks, and it's one of the top tourist destinations in Alberta, visited by millions of people every year.

When the mall opened in 1981, it was the largest indoor shopping mall in the world. It was revolutionary in the sense that its creation changed an ordinary shopping complex into a world-class destination with entertainment venues and exceptional attractions. At one time West Edmonton Mall held at least seven Guinness World Records, including the world's largest parking lot.

The World Waterpark is like a tropical oasis in the middle of Edmonton.

Get up close with penguins and other swimming creatures at the Sea Life Caverns.

DID YOU KNOW?

The Guinness World Record for the most indoor bungee jumps in 24 hours was set inside West Edmonton Mall. The total number of jumps was 225, and the record was achieved by Peter Charney at the World Water Park indoor bungee jump in November 2007. The spectacle raised money for a local charity.

There are many things in the mall that could be classed as unusual. The World Waterpark is home to the world's largest indoor wave pool, and it has more than 17 waterslides. Galaxyland, once the world's largest indoor amusement park, is now North America's largest indoor amusement park, with 27 rides and play areas — including four roller coasters.

The mall is also an accredited zoo, and the Marine Life Sea Life Caverns are home to more than 100 species of colourful fishes, sharks, reptiles, sea turtles, amphibians and penguins. There's also a sea lion encounter program that lets you meet California sea lions up close.

Other unusual attractions include a massive indoor lake with a replica of Christopher Columbus's *Santa Maria* and a hotel with fantasy rooms that feature themes ranging from igloos to Polynesia.

West Edmonton Mall may not be the world's largest indoor shopping centre anymore, but it is still one of Alberta's most unique attractions and worth seeing first-hand.

Visitors can actually stay overnight in the Hotel Selkirk on 1920 Street.

A view of Fort Edmonton Park's 1885 Street.

29 FORT EDMONTON PARK

Address 7000 143rd Street Northwest, Edmonton, AB, T6H 4P3
Telephone (780) 496-7381 | **Website** fortedmontonpark.ca

The Largest Living History Museum in Canada

After being closed for more than two years for a $165-million enhancement project, Fort Edmonton Park reopened in July 2021 as Canada's largest living history museum. That title had previously been held by Heritage Park in Calgary. Whether it's the largest or the second-largest park of its kind, Fort Edmonton Park is a unique attraction. Costumed interpreters and unique programming help bring history alive by re-enacting and recreating the past. The park depicts the City of Edmonton's history in distinct eras — the 1846 fur-trading era, the 1885 settlement era, the 1905 municipal era, and a street and midway from the 1920s. The park also opened a new and unique exhibit called the Indigenous Peoples Experience.

Fort Edmonton, also known as Edmonton House, was the name of several trading posts built by the Hudson's Bay Company from 1795 to 1914 on the north bank of the North Saskatchewan River. The park gets its name from the original fort, and so does the city for that matter.

When the park first opened in 1974, the main attraction was a recreated fort, designed to replicate the original forts built by the Hudson's Bay Company. A working steam train was added in 1977, and each of the other historic areas of the park as well as a streetcar and midway rides were gradually added as the park expanded.

Indigenous Peoples Experience — First Exhibit of Its Kind in Canada

The Indigenous Peoples Experience is the newest signature exhibit from the latest Fort Edmonton Park renovation and enhancement. One of the things that makes this exhibit special is the fact that an Elders Advisory Council, with representation from the Métis Nation of Alberta and the Confederacy of Treaty Six First Nations, was involved in its creation. This exhibit captures the vibrant history, culture and knowledge of the Indigenous Peoples of Alberta.

Park visitors can immerse themselves in Indigenous

The Capitol Theatre on 1920 Street is a recreation of Edmonton's original Capitol Theatre from circa 1929.

cultures local to the Edmonton region, with interactive and hands-on exhibits, audio-visual components, music, art and information provided by Indigenous elders, historians, educators and community members. Indigenous park interpreters also help guide visitors through this unique area of Fort Edmonton Park.

30 GOVERNMENT HOUSE

Address 12845 102nd Avenue Northwest, Edmonton, AB, T5N
Telephone (780) 427-2281 | **Website** alberta.ca/government-house.aspx

How Alberta's Lieutenant Governor Became Homeless

Government House is the former official residence of the lieutenant governors of Alberta, and today the restored and repurposed building is used by the Alberta government for ceremonial events, conferences and meetings. Visitors can also enjoy a free guided tour, see the stunning architecture and view an extensive art collection.

Alberta became part of Canada in 1905, and in 1913 Government House was opened as the official residence of the province's lieutenant governor. Between 1913 to 1938 six lieutenant governors resided there. If you visit the province's website, it says that Government House was closed as the vice-regal residence in 1938 for financial and political reasons. But that is not the whole story.

What Does a Lieutenant Governor Do?

Lieutenant governors represent the Crown in the province in which they serve. They are appointed by the governor general of Canada on the advice of the prime minister. Among the key roles of a lieutenant governor is granting royal assent to bills passed by the Legislative Assembly and signing Orders in Council as well as other cabinet documents — giving them all the force of law. Without royal assent, bills passed in the legislature cannot be legally enforced.

A Constitutional Crisis

On March 23, 1937, John C. Bowen was appointed as the sixth lieutenant governor of Alberta. Soon after taking office, Bowen found himself in the middle of a constitutional crisis when he refused to give royal assent to three bills Premier William Aberhart (Social Credit Party) had pushed through the legislature. One was designed to control bank operations in the province, another would tax banks and a third was to control the press. The Accurate News and Information Act would have forced newspapers to provide the names and addresses of their sources to the government and to print rebuttals to stories the government objected to.

Bowen believed the bills to be unconstitutional, so he reserved royal assent until the legality of the bills could be tested by the Supreme Court of Canada. It was the first time a lieutenant governor in Alberta had used the power of reservation. All three bills were later declared unconstitutional by the Supreme Court of Canada and the Judicial Committee of the Privy Council — confirming that Bowen

DID YOU KNOW?

Bowen was Alberta's longest-serving lieutenant governor, acting from 1937 to 1950. Despite this, his portrait was noticeably absent from the Alberta legislature for nearly 40 years. In 1975 his portrait was finally hung with the other lieutenant governors.

Government House is a beautiful building with a colourful history.

had taken the correct action. What was his reward? In the summer of 1938 Aberhart's government took away Bowen's official residence, his government car and his staff. Bowen defiantly stayed in the house for a while after the power, heat and telephone service had been cut off, but he eventually moved into a hotel suite. In 1942 all the fixtures and furnishings were sold at auction, and Government House was leased as a dormitory to Northwest Airlines. The building was sold in 1951 to the federal Department of Veterans Affairs (now Veterans Affairs Canada) and was purchased back in 1964, but it has never been reinstated as an official residence.

31 UNIVERSITY OF ALBERTA MUSEUMS

Address 3-20 Rutherford South, University of Alberta, Edmonton, AB, T6G 2J4 (Administration Office)
Telephone (780) 492-5834 | **Website** uab.ca/museums

Amazing Free Museums That Nobody Knows About

The University of Alberta has 30 registered museums distributed across its campus housing millions of objects and specimens. These museum collections are integral in teaching and research, and some are also open to public viewing. In-person and online exhibitions and public programs also showcase many artifacts and specimens. The best part is that these museums are free to visit.

The museum collections include fossils, meteorites, antiquities, textiles, artworks, plants, animals and much more. If you want to be a lifelong learner, visiting one of these museums in person or taking in an online exhibition is a good place to start.

The University of Alberta Museums is a Recognized Museum Leader by the Alberta Museums Association, and individual museum collections are curated by a university faculty member with expertise in the area. You need an appointment through the appropriate curator to view some of the collections, while some have regular hours open to the public. It is best to check out the University of Alberta Museums website to see what interests you and how to visit the museum collection.

University of Alberta Museums Art Collection

For many years the University of Alberta has collected works of art and historical artifacts for exhibition, research and teaching purposes. There are more than 7,000 works of art in the collection today in many different mediums. The collection includes

Dragons on the Tibetan Plateau exhibition featuring the University of Alberta Museums Mactaggart Art Collection.

paintings, drawings, prints and sculptures from both Canadian and international artists.

Many private donors have contributed to the university's art collection. Notably, Emma Read Newton, the wife of the university's fourth president, Dr. Robert Newton, donated 200 works of art in the 1950s, including works by Group of Seven founder A.Y. Jackson and Canadian printmaker Walter J. Philips. Newton and her donation have been credited as being the foundation of the University of Alberta Museums Art Collection. Since this donation, passionate individual collectors and

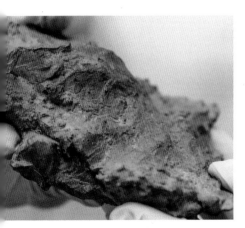

A meteorite specimen from the University of Alberta's Meteorite Collection.

The Mineralogy and Petrology Museum.

artists have continued to donate to the collection. The University of Alberta Museums Art Collection now includes influential Inuit printmakers such as Pitseolak Ashoona, international sculptors such as Anthony Caro, and prominent Canadian artists such as Emily Carr.

Starting in 2005, Edmonton philanthropists Sandy and Cécile Mactaggart donated a collection of East Asian art to the University of Alberta. The Mactaggart Art Collection, as it is now named, contains more than 1,000 rare works of art, including textiles, costumes, paintings, handscrolls, albums, engravings and other artifacts from ancient and modern East Asia. Some pieces date back as far as the 13th century and there is an impressive collection of Tibetan costumes. The Mactaggart Art Collection was certified by the Canadian government as Canadian cultural property, which identifies it as a collection of national importance.

Ground beetles from the E.H. Strickland Entomological Museum.

The Nickle Galleries at the University of Calgary

The Nickle Galleries (nickel.ucalgary.ca) at the University of Calgary also contain remarkable collections. The Nickle Numismatic Collection is one of the most important numismatic collections in Canada. It contains more than 23,000 objects, including coins, paper money, tokens, medals and pre-coinage currencies that date from the 7th century BCE. The coin collection has a particular focus on ancient Greek and Roman coins and was donated to the University of Calgary in 1980 by Carl O. Nickle. The Nickle Family Foundation and other donors have since further expanded the collection. There are also impressive collections of art, rugs and textiles in the Nickle Galleries, which are open for public viewing.

A streetcar crosses High Level Bridge in Edmonton

The view across the highest streetcar river crossing in the world.

32 HIGH LEVEL BRIDGE STREETCAR

Address 8408 Gateway Boulevard Northwest, Edmonton, AB, T6E 2G9
Telephone (780) 437-7721 | **Website** edmonton-radial-railway.ab.ca/highlevelbridge

The Highest Streetcar River Crossing in the World

Some of the beautifully restored streetcars come from other parts of the world.

Between 1913 and 1951 Edmonton Transit operated one of the most spectacular streetcar rides in North America — a route that crossed the High Level Bridge and offered amazing views of the North Saskatchewan River Valley. In 1997 the non-profit Edmonton Radial Railway Society (ERRS) reinstated that service by electrifying an old Canadian Pacific Railway line that runs from Old Strathcona to the north side of the High Level Bridge. From May to October streetcars travel the scenic route, which is the highest streetcar river crossing in the world.

Enjoying a ride on the High Level Bridge Streetcar is like stepping back in time and experiencing a piece of the past. The streetcar is a unique way to get from Old Strathcona to downtown Edmonton. The antique trolley cars, dating back to the early 1900s, have been beautifully refurbished. Each car has its own history, and some originated from other parts of the world, including one from Osaka, Japan, and another from Melbourne, Australia.

The ERRS has nine operational streetcars and 17 others in its reserve fleet. It is the largest collection of heritage electric streetcars in Western Canada. Their goal is to restore one car of each type that once operated in Edmonton. They hope to restore more streetcars from other locations as well. A visit to the Strathcona Streetcar Barn & Museum is a fascinating way to start your ride on the High Level Bridge Streetcar. The museum contains artifacts, pictures and information relating to streetcar history and the Edmonton streetcar system and has a collection of streetcars from around the world. The museum is located in the Strathcona Streetcar Barn on 103rd Street and 84th Avenue (at the north end of the Farmers' Market building). Admission is by donation.

The High Level Bridge Streetcars are operated by volunteers dressed in historical uniforms. They have a wealth of knowledge and they love to share it during the journey. Many volunteers donate their time repairing and maintaining the streetcars as well. The ERRS also has streetcars at Fort Edmonton Park dating from 1908, 1912 and 1930. Travelling on a historic streetcar is always exciting, but journeying across the High Level Bridge is a streetcar experience unlike anywhere in the world.

33 LEGISLATIVE ASSEMBLY OF ALBERTA

Address 9820 107th Street Northwest, Edmonton, AB, T5K 1E7
Telephone (780) 427-2826 | **Website** assembly.ab.ca

The Site of Alberta's First Mace

If you read this tagline and wondered what a mace is, you would have fit right in with Alberta's first legislators. When Alberta became a province of Canada, members of the Legislative Assembly forgot they needed a mace. And that is why Alberta's first mace was made with plumbing parts.

To put it simply, the mace symbolizes the authority of the Speaker and the right conferred on the Assembly by the Crown to meet and pass laws on behalf of the people. It is a ceremonial staff the Sergeant-at-Arms carries into the chamber at the beginning of each sitting. Although the mace has no constitutional significance, it is such an important symbol that the Government of Alberta cannot conduct its business unless the mace is present.

With the excitement of officially becoming a province, Premier Alexander Rutherford's government forgot to commission a mace. A few weeks before the first sitting of the Assembly in 1906, the government realized

The exterior of Alberta's Legislative Assembly.

Alberta's first mace was constructed entirely of scrap parts, including plumbing pipe and a toilet tank float.

The grounds around the Legislative Assembly are lovely in every season.

the mistake and had a pattern-maker and railway carpenter named Rufus E. Butterworth, who worked for Watson Brothers Jewellery, hastily construct one. Alberta's first mace was made entirely of scrap parts. Plumbing pipe was used for the shaft, a toilet tank float was used for the orb and ornamental decorations were made from old shaving mugs and scraps of wood. With a little red velvet and a coat of gold paint, the mace was ready to go for the rock bottom price of $150.

Despite what it's made of, the mace looks really impressive. The original plan was to use the make-shift mace for only a short time and commission a proper one soon after. In the end, Alberta's first mace was used for 50 years. It was finally replaced in 1956 in honour of Alberta's 50th anniversary as a province.

How Did the Queen React?

The government didn't tell the monarchy about the mace — for nearly 100 years. According to the Legislative Assembly of Alberta website, Queen Elizabeth II was delighted with the story of the makeshift mace during her visit in 2005 to celebrate Alberta's centenary. The mace was used again in the Chamber in 2006 to commemorate the 100th anniversary of the Assembly's first sitting. It's still on display inside the Alberta Legislature.

Tours of the Legislative Assembly of Alberta

Touring the Alberta Legislature is free and fun. The grounds are a beautiful place for a picnic, and there's also a visitor centre with a fascinating free 3D film about the history of the province. Guided tours of the interior of the legislature allow visitors to learn about Alberta's political history and the roles of the Lieutenant Governor, Premier, Speaker and Members of the Legislative Assembly. Visitors can also learn about the art and architecture of the building and view Alberta's first mace and other interesting sites, including an acoustic phenomenon called the magic spot. When you stand on the magic spot, you can hear water raining down from above even though the rotunda fountain is three floors below. There's also a door with a sign that reads, "Red Tape Reduction." If you think the legislative process is slow, just imagine how much slower it would be without a Minister of Red Tape Reduction.

34 ᐄᓃᐤ (ÎNÎW) RIVER LOT 11 ∞

Address 10380 Queen Elizabeth Park Road, Edmonton, AB, T6E 6C6
Telephone (780) 442-5311 | **Website** publicart.edmontonarts.ca/IAP

Celebrating Indigenous Art and Voices

Preparing to Cross the Sacred River by Marianne Nicolson evokes ancient petroglyphs as well as Indigenous beadwork.

What's in a name? There's a lot of significance in the name of Edmonton's Indigenous art park. ᐄᓃᐤ (ÎNÎW) is a Cree word meaning "I am of the Earth," and it recognizes the fact that the park lies on the ancestral lands of the Papaschase Cree. Long before Edmonton was a city, the land was a gathering place for Cree, Dene, Blackfoot, Salteaux, Stoney and Métis Peoples. These lands later became River Lot 11, the historic river lot that originally belonged to Métis landowner Joseph McDonald. The river lot system was used when rivers were the main transportation corridors in Canada. The long, narrow lots predate the establishment of Alberta.

This unique art park is located within Queen Elizabeth Park in Edmonton's North Saskatchewan River Valley. The art park was curated by Candice Hopkins of Carcross/Tagish First Nation of the Yukon. Hopkins is a well-known artist who has worked as a curator at the National Gallery of Canada in Ottawa, Walter Phillips Gallery in Banff and the Museum of Contemporary Native Arts in Santa Fe, New Mexico.

△ᐞᑯᑌᐤ (*iskotew*) by Amy Malbeuf, a Métis artist from Rich Lake, Alberta.

One of the turtles in Jerry Whitehead's installation *mamohkamatowin*.

Ȧσ̇ᐤ (ÎNÎW) River Lot 11 ∞ opened in 2018 and features six permanently installed artworks by Indigenous artists. Each work is a unique expression of the vibrancy of Indigenous cultures. The artists were asked to create a work "inspired by this land" and each piece is thought-provoking. The two Alberta artists represented are Amy Malbeuf from Rich Lake and Tiffany Shaw-Collinge from Edmonton. There are also two artists from British Columbia and artists from Saskatchewan and Ontario.

Each art piece contains a great deal of symbolism. The installation by Jerry Whitehead called *mamohkamatowin*, which means "Helping One Another," is a prime example. Two turtles facing in opposite directions are covered with mosaic tiles.

Artists, artisans and students layered the tiles on the turtles' backs. While the tiles were laid down, students from amiskwaciy Academy, an Indigenous public school in Edmonton, had the chance to talk and engage with elders and knowledge keepers to hear stories of the land. The installation reflects all the people, including settlers, who shaped the history of *amiskwaciy-wâskahikan*, the traditional Cree name of Edmonton.

There are lovely trails, picnic tables and places to sit and ponder. In 2019 Ȧσ̇ᐤ (ÎNÎW) River Lot 11 ∞ park was selected as one of the 50 best international public art projects by the Americans for the Arts Public Art Network. Of the park, they said, "If the role of public art is to form a map of where a community

or city has been, and where it's going, then Ȧσ̇ᐤ (ÎNÎW) River Lot 11∞ is a momentous signpost on that journey."

The Ancient Indigenous Burial Ground in Edmonton's River Valley

There is an ancient once-forgotten and desecrated First Nations burial site in the Edmonton River Valley. Located at 101st Street and 96th Avenue, the Rossdale Burial Site contains the remains of First Nations, Métis, and non-Indigenous inhabitants of the Hudson's Bay Company Fort Edmonton fur-trading post. In 2006 human remains that had been removed from the site when the Rossdale Power Plant was built were reburied. A memorial was installed in 2007. Interpretive signage tells the story of the site.

35 ART GALLERY OF ALBERTA

Address 2 Sir Winston Churchill Square, Edmonton, AB, T5J 2C1 | **Telephone** (780) 425-5379 | **Website** youraga.ca

The Oldest Cultural Institution in Alberta

The swirling exterior of the Art Gallery of Alberta.

Inspired by the flowing colourful lights of the aurora borealis, the swirling glass, zinc and steel on the exterior of the Art Gallery of Alberta (AGA) make the building itself a work of art. The AGA was founded in 1924 and is the oldest cultural institution in the province. Alberta's premier art museum is located on Sir Winston Churchill Square in downtown Edmonton.

A view from the inside of the gallery.

The silver exterior of the building, which was designed by architect Randall Stout, not only evokes the aurora borealis, but it is also meant to reflect it when the northern lights dance in the Edmonton sky. The 7,900-square-metre AGA has three light and airy floors of exhibition space that display more than 6,000 regional, national and international artworks.

The AGA's collection was built primarily through donations and grants. The Ernest E. Poole Foundation gifted the gallery almost 100 works by some of Canada's pre-eminent artists, including pieces by Paul Peel, Emily Carr, James Wilson Morrice, Cornelius Krieghoff, A.Y. Jackson, Jack Bush and Jean-Paul Riopelle. The AGA also has an impressive collection of works by contemporary Albertan and Canadian artists such as Jane Ash Poitras, Allen Ball, Catherine Burgess, George Littlechild, Lyndal Osborne and Peter von Tiesenhausen, to name a few. There is also an extensive photography collection by historical and contemporary Canadian artists.

Exhibitions and educational programs make art accessible to all age groups and ensure there is always something new to see at the Art Gallery of Alberta.

36 ROYAL ALBERTA MUSEUM

Address 9810 103a Avenue Northwest, Edmonton, AB, T5J 0G2
Telephone (825) 468-6000 | **Website** royalalbertamuseum.ca

The Largest Museum in Western Canada

The exterior of the Royal Alberta Museum.

The Royal Alberta Museum (RAM) is Western Canada's largest museum and one of the top museums in the country. There are more than 7,600 square metres of exhibition space in this 38,900-square-metre facility in downtown Edmonton. It houses an incredible collection of artifacts that helps visitors understand Alberta's remarkable landscapes, wildlife, culture and history. It's a journey that goes from the Ice Age to First Peoples and beyond.

The RAM first opened in 1967 as the Provincial Museum of Alberta. In 2005 Queen Elizabeth II visited Alberta, and the museum was renamed the Royal Alberta Museum in her honour. In 2018 the RAM moved into a new building in downtown Edmonton, which has twice as much space as the previous facility. The total combined cost of the new building with its expanded galleries and moving fees was estimated to be about $375.5 million.

The museum has an impressive permanent collection of remarkable artifacts and displays, and it also regularly hosts special programs and exhibitions. Here are a few of the most unusual things to see at the RAM.

DID YOU KNOW?

The Natural History Hall contains fossils and information about the animals that once lived in Alberta.

The Human History Hall includes a substantial collection of artifacts from Indigenous Peoples.

The Bug Gallery

Invertebrates make up 97 percent of the animal kingdom, and yet we seldom talk about them. The Bug Gallery has a collection of live insects, spiders and other invertebrates from Alberta and other places around the world. This gallery helps visitors see insects in a controlled environment and learn about metamorphosis, insect behaviour, conservation, diversity and other issues.

The Natural History Hall

The Natural History Hall contains fossils, a fantastic collection of gems and minerals and information and displays about the last Ice Age and the animals and plants found in Alberta.

The Human History Hall

This hall examines the deep questions of who the people of Alberta are and where they came from. It shares the history of Alberta through its people and includes a substantial collection of artifacts from Indigenous Peoples, through the arrival of Europeans and the formation of the province to contemporary stories of Albertans today. The museum has about 18,000 objects of Indigenous origin in its collection, from the mid-1800s to the present. The museum works with Indigenous Knowledge Holders to ensure the collection is cared for and displayed in a culturally sensitive and respectful way. The bulk of the artifacts are of Plains Cree (Nêhiyawak), Blackfoot Peoples (Niitsítapi), Dene and Métis origin. The Human History Hall is divided into six sections and contains personal accounts of real people, including heartbreaking narratives about Indigenous Peoples after European contact and settlement.

The distinctive glass pyramids of the Muttart Conservatory.

The arid region pavilion at the Muttart Conservatory.

37 MUTTaRT CONSERVATORY

Address 9626 96A Street, Edmonton, AB, T6C 4L8
Telephone (780) 442-5311 | **Website** edmonton.ca/attractions_events/muttart-conservatory

Glass Pyramids Filled with Plants

You can't drive past the four glass pyramids in Edmonton's North Saskatchewan River Valley without noticing them. The unique design of the Muttart Conservatory was conceived by architect Peter Hemingway. Each glass pyramid contains thousands of plants from a specific climate zone. One pyramid is devoted to tropical plants, another to temperate plants and a third to plants from the arid region. The fourth pyramid changes with the seasons and features specialty shows. Walking into a warm, vibrant, flower-filled glass pyramid on a bleak winter day feels like you've been transported into another world.

The Muttart Conservatory is owned and operated by the City of Edmonton, but $500,000 in seed money came from the Muttart Foundation, which was established by philanthropists Dr. Gladys Muttart and Mr. Merrill Muttart. Additional funding came from the province of Alberta and the City of Edmonton. The conservatory first opened its doors in 1976.

The glass pyramids were placed in a flat area of the river valley with no mature trees. This makes the structures stand out more, and the lack of tall trees allows the maximum amount of natural light to enter the glass domes.

The arid region pyramid showcases an amazing display of cacti, and the temperate region pyramid contains species found in Alberta as well as plants from Australia and some regions of Asia. One of the largest collections of orchids in North America can be found in the tropical region pyramid, along with a fascinating corpse flower, lush ferns and other species, like banana trees and flowering plants.

The Muttart Conservatory offers a variety of classes for adults and children and plays host to events throughout the year. There's also an on-site restaurant called the Culina Muttart Café.

Putrella — The First Corpse Flower to Bloom in Western Canada

One of the conservatory's star attractions in the tropical pyramid is *Amorphophallus titanum*, a plant commonly known as titan arum and also called a corpse flower. The tropical plant grows in the wild in Sumatra, an island in Indonesia. One of the tallest flowering plants in the world, it can grow from a small shoot to 9 metres tall in a few weeks. It blooms very rarely and only for a short time, but when it does it's the world's smelliest flower. It emits a putrid stench that smells like rotting meat to attract carrion beetles to pollinate it. When the plant bloomed for the first time in 2013, staff nicknamed it Putrella. More than 8,800 people came to see and smell it in bloom.

The flowering of a corpse flower is a special event indeed as it flowers once every seven to nine years.

Plains and wood bison roam freely in Elk Island National Park, which makes for wonderful photo ops.

Elk Island National Park is home to beautiful hiking trails.

38 ELK ISLAND NATIONAL PARK

Address 54401 Range Road 203, Fort Saskatchewan, AB, T8L 0V3
Telephone (780) 922-5790 | **Website** pc.gc.ca/en/pn-np/ab/elkisland

Where Bison Came Back from the Brink

Bison were brought back from the brink of extinction in the only completely fenced national park in Canada, which sits about an hour's drive east of Edmonton.

For centuries bison were central to the cultures of the Indigenous Peoples of the Great Plains. Until the late 1800s North America's prairies teemed with millions of plains bison. As a result of western settlement, industrialization, indiscriminate slaughter and agricultural activities, plains bison numbers declined catastrophically, and the species was nearly lost forever.

Attempts were made to preserve the species, and one of the most successful bison conservation efforts took place in Alberta. In 1907 the Canadian government purchased 410 plains bison from a rancher named Michel Pablo and had them shipped to Alberta from Montana and placed in what was then known as Elk Park. As the herd grew, bison were transported to other national parks and conservation areas in Canada and the United States. Some researchers estimate that 80 percent of the plains bison living today descended from this original herd.

Elk Park became Elk Island National Park in 1913. It is Canada's only entirely fenced national park and one of its smallest at 194 square kilometres. It's also one of the few places where you can see plains and wood bison roaming and learn about the conservation efforts that brought these species back from extinction.

The park is home to the densest population of hoofed mammals in Canada. Plains bison, wood bison, elk, moose, mule deer and white-tailed deer are commonly spotted in the park. Other mammals — like tiny pygmy shrews, porcupines, beavers, coyotes and the occasional black bear, timber wolf and lynx — may also be seen.

More than 250 bird species can be found in the park throughout the year. In 1987 trumpeter swans were introduced, and the population of this threatened species is healthy and growing. Other notable bird species include red-necked grebes, double-crested cormorants, red-tailed hawks, American bitterns, American white pelicans and great blue herons.

There are more than 80 kilometres of trails in Elk Island National Park that can be hiked in summer or winter. Cross-country skis and snowshoes can also be used in winter.

The park is part of the Beaver Hills Dark Sky Preserve, and that makes it a good spot to spread out a blanket and gaze at the stars. An annual star party is held in early September, where you can learn more about the planets and solar system. The annual Bison Festival in mid-August features live entertainment, bison products, traditional dancing, demonstrations, educational programming, kids activities and voyageur canoe rides.

Elk Island National Park is a special place for many reasons, but the park's role in conservation makes it unique in the world.

39 UKRAINIAN CULTURAL HERITAGE VILLAGE

Address 195041 Highway 16 East, Lamont County, AB | **Telephone** (780) 662-3640 | **Website** ukrainianvillage.ca

The Story of Alberta's Early Immigrants

The Ukrainian Cultural Heritage Village offers an immersive experience of late-19th-century Alberta.

A horse-drawn wagon rides along a dusty road, passing a young woman wearing a headscarf as she works in her garden harvesting beets. Nearby a group of children gather around an outdoor table to enjoy a lunch of homemade soup and bread. This kind of scene would have been commonplace in many small Ukrainian settlements in Alberta in the late 19th century, but today you can only find it at a living history museum like the Ukrainian Cultural Heritage Village, about 50 kilometres from downtown Edmonton.

Alberta was once home to the largest Ukrainian settlement in Canada, and even today about 10 percent of Albertans can trace their ancestry back to Ukraine. Sites like the Ukrainian Cultural Heritage Village help tell the story of these early immigrants.

The Ukrainian Cultural Heritage Village is an open-air museum that allows guests to step back in time and explore life as it was in early settlements. Following a wide, treed path, you will be transported back in time to the early settlement days of 1892 to 1930. Costumed interpreters play the roles of various pioneers who lived at that time, thus opening a window into history.

There are more than 40 restored heritage buildings on the site, including farmhouses, churches, a one-room school, a grain elevator and a blacksmith's shop. The farmyards have heritage gardens and raise heritage livestock.

There's also a visitor centre with a gift shop and food kiosk, and the cultural village hosts a variety of programs and events throughout the year to celebrate Ukrainian culture, as well as a fall harvest event to showcase the region's agricultural history. You don't have to be Ukrainian to appreciate this unique living museum.

You can learn from costumed interpreters about what it was like to live in early settlements.

Big Ukrainian Attractions

The Ukrainian Cultural Heritage Village isn't the only Ukrainian attraction in Alberta. Go on a road trip to see the giant Ukrainian sausage in Mundare, the world's largest pysanka (Ukrainian Easter egg) in Vegreville and the world's largest perogy in Glendon.

REYNOLDS-ALBERTA MUSEUM

Address 6426 40th Avenue, Wetaskiwin, AB, T9A 2G1 | **Telephone** (780) 312-2065 | **Website** reynoldsmuseum.ca

The Largest Donation of Vintage Aircraft in Canadian History

The Reynolds-Alberta Museum in Wetaskiwin is focused on transportation, aviation, agriculture and industry from the 1890s to the present day, and it exists because of one man's passion. Stan Reynolds was a Wetaskiwin businessman and a renowned collector. His collection of vintage automobiles, motorcycles, bicycles, trucks, stationary engines, tractors, agricultural implements, aircraft and industrial equipment form the basis of the Reynolds-Alberta Museum, which opened in 1992. Reynolds donated more than 1,500 artifacts before his death in 2012 at the age of 88. His original donation of vintage aircraft combined with donations from the Reynolds Foundation totals approximately 125 aircraft. This is the largest donation of vintage aircraft in Canadian history.

Included in the museum's vast collection are some rare items. One of the many highlights of the vintage aircraft collection is a 1942 Hawker Hurricane Mark XII.

An aerial view of the Reynolds-Alberta Museum.

A 1942 Hawker Hurricane Mark XII.

A 1929 Duesenberg Phaeton Royale Model J.

A 1917 Bucyrus Class 24 dragline.

In the machinery collection is a 1917 Bucyrus Class 24 dragline, which is the world's oldest existing dragline. The museum's transportation collection includes more than 500 cars, trucks and motorcycles. Highlights of the collection include an 1898 Innes Car Chassis, a 1929 Duesenberg Phaeton Royale Model J, a restored 1933 Ford Model 40B Fordor Sedan and a 1913 Chevrolet Series C Classic Six, which is reported to be the world's oldest known Chevrolet vehicle.

DID YOU KNOW?

The Reynolds-Alberta Museum has a full-scale replica model of the 1959 Avro CF-105 Arrow aircraft. It was used in the four-hour CBC Television series *The Arrow* (1997). *The Arrow* is a docudrama starring Dan Aykroyd that highlighted Avro Canada's attempt to produce the Avro Arrow supersonic jet interceptor aircraft.

A view of the world's largest oil lamp, which sits across the road from the Donalda & District Museum.

Displays of some of the museum's marvellous oil lamps.

DONALDA & DISTRICT MUSEUM

Address 5001 Main Street, Donalda, AB, T0B 1H0 | Telephone (403) 883-2100 | Website donaldamuseum.com

The World's Largest Collection of Oil Lamps

The exterior of the Donalda & District Museum.

There are over five times as many oil lamps in Donalda than there are people. The tiny village is also home to the world's largest oil lamp, one of Alberta's many roadside attractions. When it comes to rural Alberta, some of the smallest places have the biggest attractions.

The Donalda & District Museum contains more than 1,100 oil lamps — some dating back to the 1600s and many more from the 18th and 19th centuries. It is said to be the world's largest collection of oil lamps, though there hasn't been any official designation.

The Donalda & District Museum has some Métis artifacts and other historically significant items, but the lamps are the real highlight. They come in all sizes, shapes and colours and had many different purposes. Inside this fascinating museum you'll see lamps that were used in businesses, such as darkroom photography lamps, as well as lamps that were commonly used in homes.

One of the most interesting is the courting lamp. It is a small lamp that was used when a young man came courting or visiting a young woman. A young woman's father would provide the lamp. Once the lamp went out, it was time for the young man to leave. Less-favoured suitors got smaller lamps that held less oil. It was one way a father could discourage a less-desirable young man from courting his daughter. Some suitors would put the lamp out and then relight it later to give themselves more time.

Many of the decorative lamps on display are beautiful. There are collections of Aladdin parlour lamps, bull's-eye pattern lamps, composite lamps, hand-painted vase lamps and a variety of stained-glass lamps.

Before electricity came to the Prairies, the oil lamp made it possible for people to read and study during the long, dark winters. The Donalda & District Museum tells the story of these lamps and how they were used in bygone times.

42 ROCKY MOUNTAIN HOUSE NATIONAL HISTORIC SITE

Address Off Highway 11A, Rocky Mountain House, AB, T4T 2A4
Telephone (403) 845-2412 | **Website** pc.gc.ca/en/lhn-nhs/ab/rockymountain

Learning about the Fur Trade in Canada

If you want to understand more about how the fur trade shaped Canada as a nation, Rocky Mountain House is a good place to start. The national historic site, operated by Parks Canada, contains the archaeological remains of four fur-trading forts built and occupied between 1799 and 1875 on the west bank of the North Saskatchewan River.

Thousands of artifacts have been unearthed at the site and scientists are still making discoveries here. Some of the artifacts are on display in the visitor centre.

Besides its significance as an archaeological site, this is a place where you can immerse yourself in the fur trade. You can visit a historic fur-trading fort, see artifacts, check out interactive exhibits, watch a bison herd, explore a blacksmith's shop, hike interpretive trails and much more.

This site has strong ties to the Blackfoot People (or Niitsítapi), particularly the Piikani (Peigan) Nation, as well as the Métis. You can listen to the stories of the local First Nations and Métis,

Rocky Mountain House is the place to discover the significance of the fur trade in shaping Canada.

play traditional games, learn to make bannock and participate in activities typical of Métis culture, such as beading, fiddling and jigging. You can also stay overnight in a tipi, a Métis trapper tent or a trapline cabin.

Rocky Mountain House is fun and educational for children as well. Parks Canada has created a special Kids Xplorers Guide for kids over the age of 6 and

another activity book for kids 6 and under. There's also a 1:4 scale replica fur-trading fort designed specifically for kids and a puppet show about David Thompson, the legendary explorer who visited the site.

Rocky Mountain House was established in 1799 by the North West Company, and nearby Acton House was established by the Hudson's Bay Company. It was

Rocky Mountain House National Historic Site is fun and educational for children.

Rocky Mountain House is also home to a herd of bison.

You can camp in a tipi or a trapper's tent at Rocky Mountain House.

Métis voyageurs were also part of the history of this place.

not uncommon at the time for two competing companies to both establish fur-trading forts in the same area. The area selected was near the Brierly Rapids on the North Saskatchewan River, which was historically an obstacle to navigation by canoe. It was also a site frequented by the Niitsítapi, so this made it a good location for a fur-trading post.

This site was not continuously used during the fur-trade years, and it was built and rebuilt several times on at least four different sites between 1799 and 1875. Though the fort was not used after 1875, during its existence it played an important role in the fur trade and the history of Canada. A visit today is a chance to understand and relive some of this history.

43 STEPHANSSON HOUSE

Address 2230 Township Road 371, Red Deer County, AB, T4G 0M9
Telephone (403) 728-3929 | **Website** stephanssonhouse.ca

The William Shakespeare of Iceland Was an Alberta Farmer

The charming exterior of Stephansson House.

Alberta's past is brimming with stories of the hardships and triumphs early settlers experienced as they sought to tame a wild western frontier, but few accounts are as unique as that of Stephan G. Stephansson, who, having first immigrated to Wisconsin then Dakota, brought his family to the Markerville area of Alberta in 1889. His house is a provincial historic site, and costumed interpreters offer a glimpse into the life and poetry of this great man, who only became legendary in his homeland after he left.

Stephansson was a hard-working Icelandic homesteader who was known to have suffered from insomnia. After working long, hard hours farming his homestead to support his family, he was unable to sleep at night.

As he sat up night after night, Stephansson began writing poetry in his native language to fill

Costumed interpreters bring the history of the site to life.

Stephan G. Stephansson Monument in Iceland.

Family Cemetery. As well, the Writers' Guild of Alberta has a poetry award in his name and the University of Iceland has named an endowment fund after him.

A visit to Stephansson House, about 30 minutes west of Red Deer near Markerville, is a chance to see the home of this great poet and to come to understand a little more about his life and the lives of Alberta's early immigrant homesteaders. The story of Stephan G. Stephansson is also a reminder that the challenges and trials we face can help shape us into the people we are meant to be.

Markerville Creamery Museum

This unique museum lies 7 kilometres south of Stephansson House. You can enjoy a tour of a 1930s creamery and learn about the thriving Icelandic immigrant community that Markerville once was. The Kaffistofa (café) is a good stop for coffee, lunch or an ice cream cone. It is open for the summer season only.

the sleepless hours. Over the years he produced 2,300 pages of poetry, which were published in six volumes entitled *Andvökur*, which means "Wakeful Nights." His prolific writing and the high quality of his work made him famous in his homeland, and he is regarded by many experts to be one of Iceland's greatest poets. Stephansson has been called "the poet of the Rocky Mountains," and some even regard him as the Shakespeare of Iceland. He is revered in both Iceland and Alberta. There is a monument honouring Stephansson in northern Iceland, one honouring him in Markerville and a cairn at the Christinnson-Stephansson

"Staddur a grothrarstoth" ("At the forestry station") (1917)

Monuments crumble. Works of mind survive
The gales of time. Men's names have shorter life.
Forgetful time may mask where honour's due
But mind's best edifices live and thrive.

— Stephan G. Stephansson

44 THE RCMP POLICE DOG SERVICE TRAINING CENTRE

Address Queen Elizabeth II Highway, Innisfail, AB, T4G 1S8
Telephone (403) 227-3346 | **Website** rcmp-grc.gc.ca/depot/pdstc-cdcp

The RCMP's Police Academy for Dogs

The Royal Canadian Mounted Police (RCMP) have been using police dogs to assist with their duties since 1935, when the first Police Dog Section was established with three German shepherds. Since that time, police dogs have proven invaluable in many different areas of police work. In 1965 the RCMP Police Dog Service Training Centre was established in Innisfail. This facility works to breed high-quality police dogs, train dog teams and annually validate dog teams. Under normal circumstances, visitors can stop by the centre between Victoria Day and Labour Day and enjoy regularly scheduled 45-minute public demonstrations that show the dogs participating in the training program.

Police dogs perform a variety of functions in the RCMP. In addition to aiding in the apprehension of individuals suspected of committing crimes, specially trained dogs can help find missing persons, detect narcotics, explosives and human remains,

According to the training centre, ideal police dogs need to be in perfect physical condition, have a keen hunting instinct and be of sound mind and even temperament.

You can watch dogs participating in the training program during 45-minute demonstrations.

and assist in avalanche search and rescue. Police dogs also help with crowd control and VIP protection and sometimes assist in hostage situations. Dogs sometimes attend public events and act as ambassadors for the program, highlighting the important work they do.

The RCMP uses purebred German shepherds for general duty, but other breeds are sometimes used in specialized units. Male dogs are generally favoured over female dogs, but some females are also chosen. The dogs selected must be in excellent physical condition and have personality traits that make them suited to police work. Only about 17 percent of the dogs that go through the RCMP training program go on to become members of Police Dog Units across the country. Even after they become members of a Police Dog Unit, all teams are subject to annual validations of their training.

On average, police dogs work in the field for about six or seven years and retire around the age of eight or nine. When a dog is ready for retirement, the handler is given the option of keeping the dog as a pet. If the handler cannot take the dog, it may be adopted out, but a lot of work goes into making sure the dog and the new owner are well matched.

If you want to learn more about the RCMP Police Dog Service Training Centre or find out when it offers public demonstrations, visit the website.

Name the Puppy Contest

RCMP police dog names are chosen by Canadian children in an annual contest. In 2021 more than 20,000 kids submitted entries, from which the RCMP chose 13 names to give to 13 dogs. All of the police dog names began with the letter "P" in 2021.

Each child whose name is chosen receives a photo of the puppy they named, a stuffed dog called Justice and an RCMP water bottle. If you know a child who wants to participate, entries must be submitted online at rcmp-grc.gc.ca/en/depot/name-the-puppy-contest.

45 FRANCIS THE PIG STATUE

Address Rotary Recreation Park, 4620 47th Avenue, Red Deer, AB, T4N 6C3
Telephone (403) 309-8428 | **Website** reddeer.ca/about-red-deer/history/history-of-red-deer/time-machine/francis-the-pig

Commemorating Red Deer's Fugitive Pig

The tale of Francis the Pig is a memorable part of Red Deer history.

Francis was a pig with gumption who escaped certain death and lived his life on his own terms. He is legendary in central Alberta.

In the summer of 1990 a 108-kilogram pig, known only as hog KH27, jumped a 1.2-metre wall inside a Red Deer slaughterhouse, ran through the sausage plant, pushed open a screen door and escaped. Little is known about the first weeks of his freedom, but in October pig sightings became big news. The public and news media alike began making up names for him. Of all the names used to describe the plucky pig, Francis was the one that stuck.

Francis foraged for food along the bike trails near the Red Deer hospital and was known to rummage through residential garbage as well. He sometimes startled cyclists and pedestrians when they saw him on the trails. Francis sightings and tales of his antics were regularly featured in local news reports.

As winter approached, the public became more concerned about Francis's well-being. They were worried that he would have difficulty foraging once snow covered the ground, and he might not survive cold temperatures without shelter. A tracker was hired to capture the pig, but Francis was too wily. Near the end of November the tracker finally found him on an

Francis's sculpture is part of a larger "Ghost" project organized by the city of Red Deer.

acreage just outside the city, but even though he shot him with a tranquilizer Francis managed to escape again. On November 29 the tracker located Francis again and brought him down with three tranquilizers. He was taken to a local farm where it was intended that he would live out the rest of his days in comfort and peace. Unfortunately, one of the tranquilizer darts pierced his bowel and Francis died on December 1, 1990, as a result of the wound.

Today a bronze statue of Francis the Pig is located near the Blue Grass Sod Farms Central Spray & Play Park (47A Avenue and 48th Street) on the northwest corner of Rotary Recreation Park in Red Deer. The sculpture of Francis is part of the city's "Ghost" project. The "Ghosts" are a collection of life-sized bronze statues that decorate downtown Red Deer and help tell the history of the city. Francis the Pig was immortalized along with other important historical figures, such as the city's first mayor and Reverend Leonard Gaetz, one of the early settlers and founders of the city. Red Deer's downtown Ghosts comprise one of Canada's largest collections of life-sized bronze sculptures.

Calgary's Turk Diggler

Red Deer isn't the only city in Alberta that's had livestock on the loose. In 2019 residents of Calgary's Ramsay neighbourhood began seeing a lone male turkey with brown and grey feathers wandering around. He was dubbed Turk Diggler, a name play on the fictional porn star, Dirk Diggler. Some people just called him Turk.

It's possible that Turk escaped from an event at the Stampede Grounds, but no one knows for sure. At first he stuck around the Ramsay area, but in the spring of 2020 he began venturing into other areas of the city, staring at his own reflection in glass windows. Experts theorized he was searching for a mate. His antics were a regular event on the news, and he had almost 6,000 followers on Facebook. Unfortunately, Turk died in an apparent coyote attack in July 2020. Perhaps someday he will be immortalized with his own bronze statue.

46 LACOMBE RESEARCH and DEVELOPMENT CENTRE

Address 6000 C&E Trail, Lacombe, AB, T4L 1W1 | **Telephone** (403) 782-8100
Website profils-profiles.science.gc.ca/en/research-centre/lacombe-research-and-development-centre

Home to Alberta's Only Weed Garden

A garden designed to showcase weeds is unusual. There are only a few weed gardens in Canada and just one in Alberta. It is located at the Lacombe Research and Development Centre, a federal agriculture research facility operated by Agriculture and Agri-Food Canada. It is a marvellous educational tool for staff, summer students, weed inspectors and members of the public. Anyone can stop by the centre and see the garden during the growing season.

The first weed demonstration garden was set up at Lacombe Research and Development Centre in the 1970s by Don Dew, a weed biologist. The garden was briefly terminated after Dew's retirement and then re-established in a new location in the late 1990s by Dr. Neil Harker and Robert N. Pocock.

Containing the weeds is the greatest challenge in designing a weed garden. At the Lacombe Research and Development Centre, holes were drilled deep into the soil and steel culverts were inserted. Topsoil was poured into the culverts, and the area surrounding the culverts was covered with landscape fabric and wood chips. This was done to prevent weeds from growing around the culverts and to reduce maintenance. The weed garden is organized into annuals, perennials and biennials, and each weed is identified with both its common name and its scientific name. The weed garden showcases the most common troublesome weeds that grow in central Alberta.

The weed garden is located on a small plot of land on the south side of the southernmost road of the

The weed garden can be a busy place during open houses or training days.

main research centre grounds. Follow the road west until you pass some spruce trees, and you will see a garden filled with shiny metal culverts on the south side of the road. Visitors can also inquire at the administration building (a brick building with flagpoles in front of it) for directions during business hours.

While you're at Lacombe Research and Development Centre, take a walk on the lovely grounds and explore the arboretum. A red shale path winds through an area where you can see a wide variety of beautiful trees and shrubs. There's also a paved trail that passes through the grounds with interpretive signs about agricultural research and why it is important. The paved trail is part of the Trans Canada Trail and runs from Lacombe Research and Development Centre through Blackfalds to the northern side of Red Deer.

What You Should Know about Weeds

Simply put, weeds are plants that grow where you don't want them to. Even crop plants can be weeds when they grow (volunteer) in another crop. There are annual, biennial and perennial weeds. Annual weeds germinate, flower, set seed and die all in one season; biennial weeds have a two-year biological cycle; and perennial weeds have regenerative crowns, rhizomes or rootstocks that enable them to regrow each spring without being reseeded. Some weeds are edible, and some are poisonous. Some weeds reduce crop yields and others are invasive — choking out native plants. The vast majority of troublesome weeds in Western Canada are non-native species that were intentionally and unintentionally introduced from Europe.

Weeds are hardy. Some weed seeds, like wild oat, can stay dormant in the soil for years, waiting for the right conditions to grow. Other perennial weeds, such as Canada thistle, can have roots that extend down metres into the soil.

The Weed Control Act is one of Alberta's oldest pieces of legislation. The Act defines the actions municipalities in Alberta must take regarding weed control. Many urban and rural municipalities hire weed inspectors to inspect properties and serve notices regarding the control of noxious and prohibited noxious weeds. Some summer students and weed inspectors visit the weed garden in Lacombe to see weed species firsthand as part of their job training.

We all play a role in controlling weeds and invasive species that can impact vulnerable species and cause irreversible damage to an ecosystem. You, too, can learn to recognize weed species at Alberta's only weed garden.

Weed Eating Goats to the Rescue!

There are many methods of weed control. Targeted grazing has been a popular organic option for urban municipalities in recent years. Creekside Goat Company, based in Magrath, offers trained goats that will eat invasive species such as leafy spurge, wormwood, thistle, crested wheatgrass and brome grasses. Goats are browsers not grazers, so they pick out the plants they prefer to eat. Creekside Goat Company trained the goats by feeding them invasive plant species until they developed a preference for them over other native grass species. Herding dogs and human goatherders protect the goats from predators and keep them moving through the terrain.

In some municipalities, the goats have become a tourist attraction. The City of Medicine Hat uses goats to fight leafy spurge in Police Point Park. Goat grazing nature walks are offered as one of the interpretive programs in the park for those who want to watch the goats in action and learn more about invasive weeds and why it's important to control them.

Photographers and birders alike come to Ellis Bird Farm to catch a glimpse of gorgeous bluebirds and many other bird species.

A mountain bluebird.

A tree swallow.

There are over 300 different nest boxes and birdhouses placed around the site.

ELLIS BIRD FARM

Address 39502 Range Road 260, Lacombe, AB, T4L 1W7 | **Telephone** (403) 885-4477 | **Website** ellisbirdfarm.ca

World's Largest Collection of Mountain Bluebird Nest Boxes

Surrounded by working farms, Ellis Bird Farm is a one-of-a-kind working farm, non-profit organization, conservation site and birding attraction in the countryside north of Red Deer and east of Lacombe. The site focuses its conservation efforts on purple martins, mountain bluebirds, tree swallows and other native cavity-nesting birds, and it is an excellent place to see and learn about the backyard birds of central Alberta. It's also home to the largest collection of mountain bluebird nest boxes in the world.

Ellis Bird Farm was established in 1982 to carry on the legacy of Lacombe-area conservationists Charlie and Winnie Ellis. The brother-and-sister pair turned their farm into a haven for wildlife. They rimmed their fields with 300 nest boxes for mountain bluebirds and tree swallows, built and erected houses for black-capped chickadees, purple martins and flickers, established a program for feeding overwintering bird species and planted

extensive orchards and gardens. Charlie became widely known as Mr. Bluebird — a title originally bestowed by Kerry Wood, a well-known Red Deer naturalist.

When their farm was purchased by Union Carbide Canada Limited, Charlie and Winnie operated one of the largest bluebird trails in Canada and maintained a huge bird-feeding program. They stipulated two conditions for the sale of their land to Union Carbide — that "their" birds be looked after and that the operator of the industrial site support Ellis Bird Farm, a non-profit organization dedicated to their legacy. Today a petrochemical complex (now operated by MEGlobal Canada) sits on one corner of the original Ellis homestead. The rest of the Ellis farm continues to raise cattle, crops and bluebirds.

Depending on the season and the weather, visitors can expect to see a wide variety of backyard birds, including purple martins, mountain bluebirds, ruby-throated hummingbirds,

pine siskins, American goldfinches, black-capped chickadees, tree and barn swallows, least flycatchers, yellow warblers, cedar waxwings, red-winged blackbirds and great blue herons, as well as several species of native sparrows and waterfowl. You might also see great horned owls, North American beavers, short-tailed weasels, snowshoe hares and other wildlife.

The world-class gardens at Ellis Bird Farm have been designed to attract birds and support native pollinators and are linked together with wheelchair-accessible trails. There are water gardens, a xeriscape garden (garden designed to conserve as much water as possible), a hummingbird garden and butterfly gardens. There's an excellent visitor centre and the on-site café makes a great lunch or tea stop.

If you want to see bluebirds, June is the best time to visit. The gardens are at their peak in July and August, and you should visit before mid-August if you want to see purple martins.

48 WORLD FAMOUS GOPHER HOLE MUSEUM

Address 208 1st Street Southwest, Torrington, AB, T0M 2B0
Telephone (403) 631-2133 | **Website** worldfamousgopherholemuseum.ca

One of Canada's Most Unusual Museums

What does a tiny rural hamlet with a population of under 200 people have to offer tourists? When the Alberta government came out with a tourism grant program, the community of Torrington asked that very question. Somebody joked that they had more gophers than they knew what to do with, and that quip inspired the community to apply for a grant to start one of the most unusual museums in Canada.

In 1996 Alberta's first gopher museum was opened. The museum is housed in a former one-room schoolhouse that is over 100 years old. It contains dioramas about life in Torrington using individual gophers preserved by taxidermy. Each gopher is dressed in handmade clothing and has props that were either built by hand or purchased in hobby shops.

The first dioramas were built completely from glass, and you can see two examples of those in the museum. Afterward, the museum decided to use a different approach, creating dioramas that looked

The exterior of the World Famous Gopher Hole Museum.

more like wooden shadow boxes. This allowed them to be able to paint backgrounds and light up the scenes. It's like you're looking into a gopher's hole.

The dioramas were a collaborative effort by many members of the community, but the more elaborate background scenes were created by artist Shelley Haase with assistance from Dianne Kurta, who was the museum director for over two decades. Haase lived in the Torrington area for several years when the museum was being established, and her artistry helped to create many beautiful background scenes.

DID YOU KNOW?

Torrington-born songwriter and musician Dennis Oster wrote "The Gopher Song" to celebrate the community, its beloved museum and its mascot, a giant gopher named Clem.

Who doesn't want to see rodents dressed in outfits and placed in painstakingly constructed scenes? Truthfully, there are a few haters out there. The organization People for the Ethical Treatment of Animals (PETA) is one. The museum receives its share of hate mail, which it normally displays proudly. For anyone with moral qualms, you have to remember that Torrington is a rural community and controlling the gopher population has been part of farming for decades. When the gopher population gets out of hand, the pesky rodents eat crops and create mounds that damage farm equipment.

Despite the controversy, the museum receives a lot of love, too. There were more than 10,000 visitors the first year it opened, and every year there are thousands of people from all over the world who come to look inside the gopher holes. You'll see dioramas depicting the post office, the curling rink, a yard sale, gopher Olympics, the Torrington fire department, the Old Tyme Music Jamboree and many other scenes. Look carefully at the scenes and you'll see gophers with tan-coloured fur, black fur, striped fur and white albino fur.

The museum is a non-profit entity run by volunteers and it is open in the summer months. Admission is by donation. There

Here you can enjoy a music jamboree and cheer on your favourite gopher at the gopher Olympics.

are washrooms and a small gift shop with handcrafted products made by community members.

Other Things to See in Torrington

While you're in town, make sure you tour the gopher fire hydrants, which all have names. You can also see the mural of the World Famous Gopher Hole Museum created by Wayne Schneider, who grew up near Torrington. As you drive around Torrington, you'll want to snap a picture of the community mascot, Clem, who of course is a giant gopher. Interestingly, the town mascot used to have a hat, but the hat has been stolen at least three times. After the last hat theft, it was decided Clem would remain hatless.

DRY ISLAND BUFFALO JUMP PROVINCIAL PARK

Address Highway 585, Elnora, AB, T0M 0Y0
Telephone (403) 742-7516 | **Website** albertaparks.ca/parks/central/dry-island-buffalo-jump-pp

Home to the World's Largest Tyrannosaur Bonebed

A view over Dry Island Buffalo Jump Provincial Park.

This provincial park is home to a buffalo jump that was historically used by Plains Cree beginning about 3,000 years ago, and it is also home to the world's largest tyrannosaur bonebed. It has hoodoos, badlands, a flowing river and aspen-rich woods. The only thing missing is the crowds. Finding solitude and having a natural space all to yourself are two of the best reasons to visit this unique park.

Visiting the Provincial Park

The park itself is a day-use area with several picnic spots and no official trails. Its interesting name actually has two parts. The "dry island" is a geological

Dry Island Buffalo Jump is a stunning landscape in every season.

The Red Deer River can be explored by raft, canoe or kayak.

feature of the park. Thousands of years of erosion from rain and streams has created what looks like a flat-topped island covered in prairie grasses. Amid the otherworldly landscape of the badlands, it looks like an island. Visitors to the park often make it a goal to get to the top. The other key feature is a buffalo jump, which was used by the Plains Cree many times over the past 3,000 years. Hunters herded bison and drove them over the cliff. The dead bison would provide meat for their families. This cliff is unique because it is higher than other buffalo jumps discovered in Alberta. Bison were run off a 40-metre cliff at the north end of this park. As a comparison, the cliff at Head-Smashed-In-Buffalo Jump is 11 metres high.

About 150 species of birds have been spotted in the park, and it's common to see migrating birds of prey along valley cliffs. The badlands provide ideal habitat for raptor species like the ferruginous hawk, golden eagle and prairie falcon. Marsh areas provide habitat for waterfowl and many more birds can be found in the deciduous woods.

The park has a boat launch, and it's a good spot to begin a raft, canoe or kayak journey along the Red Deer River. Fur traders and early explorers, like Anthony Henday, used the river as an important trade and exploration route. It's not uncommon to see fossils in the park and along the banks of the river; however, don't remove fossils if you find them. The placement of a fossil may tell an important tale. It's best to mark the spot and report it to staff at the Royal Tyrrell Museum of Palaeontology.

The World's Largest Tyrannosaur Bonebed

In 1910 a group of researchers from the American Museum of Natural History discovered a bonebed containing *Albertosaurus sarcophagus*, a species of tyrannosaurid theropod. The bonebed, however, was not systematically excavated, and the site was lost. In 1997 it was rediscovered, and since that time more than 1,500 specimens have been extracted. It's believed that there are at least 12, and perhaps as many as 26, individual tyrannosaurs at this site. The large number of dinosaurs at one site lends evidence to the theory that tyrannosaurs may have travelled in packs.

Rowley's distinctive grain elevators punctuate the landscape.

The buildings in Rowley feel like they've been captured in time, like the Rowley Trading Post, which operated from 1920 to 1973.

50 ROWLEY

Address Rowley, Starland County, AB | Telephone (403) 368-3816 | Website facebook.com/RowleyAlberta

How to Have Pizza in a Ghost Town

A mural featuring the town's famous pizza night and landmarks.

Thirty-nine kilometres northwest of Drumheller, the ghost town of Rowley has a present-day population of about eight people and a dozen feral cats — down considerably from its peak of 500 human residents. There are many distinctive buildings in Rowley, including the grain elevators that are officially listed on Canada's Historic Places. But the thing that makes this ghost town truly unique is its monthly pizza night.

The last Saturday of every month has traditionally been pizza night in Rowley, and in the past it has been a real party atmosphere, with many visitors in attendance. The event was started as a way for local residents to keep the town alive and help preserve its old buildings. The record attendance for pizza night is just over 700 people, set in July 2018. Check the Rowley Facebook page a few days before the last Saturday of the month for details on when locals will be holding the next pizza night event.

Rowley was incorporated in 1912 and was named after Lieutenant-Colonel Charles Walsh Rowley. In 1919 the Canadian Northern Railway came to town, and that's when Rowley really started booming. At its peak the town had a rail station, several grain elevators, a hospital, a general store, a movie theatre, a garage, a livery stable, a church, a saloon, a restaurant and many homes.

By the 1970s the economy was suffering and Rowley was declining. There were many empty houses and businesses. There was no sewage or water system and no municipal services, but local residents did not give up. Around 2005 they came up with the idea of pizza nights to help fix up the downtown buildings and make Rowley a tourist attraction.

Rowley was the film site for the 1989 Hollywood movie *Bye Bye Blues*, and the boardwalk and some of the buildings created for the movie set are still standing. The last train passed through Rowley in 1999, but the locals continued their efforts to preserve the town.

If you want to stay overnight in a ghost town, camping is allowed in a small campground on the west side of town. Payment is by donation. Rowley's community hall, church and saloon can also be booked for weddings, family reunions and other events. Funds are used to help maintain the community and its historic buildings.

51 BLERIOT FERRY

Address Highway 838 over the Red Deer River, AB, T0J 2C0
Telephone (403) 710-9422 (Carson Elliot); (403) 934-8896 (Doug Goodine) | **Website** alberta.ca/alberta-ferry-schedules.aspx

Ride a Ferry in Landlocked Alberta

Catch the Bleriot Ferry across the Red Deer River to go between Kneehill and Starland counties.

Alberta is a landlocked province, but that doesn't mean there are no ferries. The Bleriot Ferry, one of the oldest ferries in Alberta, has been in operation for more than a century. It is a cable ferry that links two sections of the North Dinosaur Trail (Alberta Highway 838) near Drumheller. The ferry is guided across the Red Deer River by cables attached to both shores. More than 100 years after it was first built, it is still the fastest way to drive between Horsethief Canyon and Orkney Viewpoint outside Drumheller.

The ferry ride is only a few minutes, but it's a memorable, scenic journey.

The Bleriot Ferry crosses the Red Deer River and connects two counties: Kneehill County on the west side of the river and Starland County on the east side. The ferry is a free service offered by Alberta Transportation, and it operates from mid-May to the end of October.

The first ferry at this site was built by area resident Andre Bleriot in 1912. Bleriot had transported lumber, household furnishings and farm supplies down the river by raft and it didn't go well. His supplies and rafts frequently got caught on sandbars, and he experienced

serious delays. This prompted him to build the first ferry. He let others use his ferry free of charge. In 1913 the Government of Alberta deemed it necessary to install a larger ferry at the same site and hire a full-time operator. When the ferry was first installed, it was known as the West of Munson Ferry. In 1966 the name was changed to Bleriot Ferry to honour the original ferrymaster.

The Bleriot Ferry has had many years of smooth operation with a few mishaps along the way. The two most memorable incidents involve an airplane and ice. In 1943 a plane crashed east of the ferry site and severed the cables. In 1951 ice broke the ferry loose and sent it downstream.

The current ferry was commissioned in 1997. It is just over 27 metres long and a little more than 10 metres wide. It can carry more than 62 tonnes — though it's never come close to that.

The Bleriot Ferry is still an important transportation link for area residents and a tourist attraction for visitors. Every year thousands of people and cars use the ferry. The journey takes only a few minutes, but it is an opportunity to enjoy a unique experience and remember a time when ferries were more common than bridges as river crossings.

Don't Pay the Ferrymaster

There is no fee to ride the Bleriot Ferry and the other ferries operated by Alberta Transportation, as the fees are covered by taxes. Alberta Transportation operates six ferries as part of Alberta's highway network: Bleriot Ferry, Crowfoot Ferry, Finnegan Ferry, Klondyke Ferry, La Crete Ferry and Shaftesbury Ferry.

52 DINOSAUR TRAIL GOLF & COUNTRY CLUB

Address 6455 North Dinosaur Trail, Drumheller, AB, T0J 0Y0
Telephone (403) 823-5622 | **Website** dinosaurtrailgolf.com

The Toughest Back Nine in North America

This unique course makes for a memorable and, at times, challenging round of golf.

The Dinosaur Trail Golf & Country Club claims to have the toughest back nine in North America. It's not an official title, but it's one that is generally accepted as fact — especially by those who have lost golf balls there. Tough or not, it's one of the most unique golf experiences in Canada.

Located in Drumheller, Dinosaur Trail is like two golf courses in one. The front nine winds along the Red Deer River and has the feel of

110

The badlands scenery that surrounds the back nine is stunning to say the least.

a parkland golf course. The back nine is set in the dramatic badlands that were formed thousands of years ago. These holes feel like you're golfing on another planet.

Simply put, the back nine is target golf. On some holes, you tee off on the top of one eroded hill to a green that sits on the top of another. Many other sandy badlands formations and gullies lie between the tee off box and the green. If you try to retrieve a ball that goes off track, you might encounter rattlesnakes, and most people opt to leave those balls where they lie. Walking this section of the course isn't really an option as it goes up and down incredibly steep terrain.

The back nine can be seen from the world-famous Royal Tyrrell Museum. It's amazing to tee off in the same kind of terrain where palaeontologists have discovered dinosaur fossils. Whether or not you agree with others that Dinosaur Trail has the toughest back nine in North America, there is no denying that there's no golf course like it anywhere else in the world.

Why Alberta's Potato Growers Love the PGA

In Alberta the abbreviation PGA has two meanings. If you're a golfer, PGA is the Professional Golfers' Association. If you're a farmer, PGA stands for the Potato Growers of Alberta. This explains why the Potato Growers of Alberta purchased pga.com as their website domain. It also explains why the Professional Golfers' Association contacted them in 1996 to ask them to relinquish it. A few months later the growers agreed to hand over pga.com, for a tidy $34,000. They were very practical with their windfall. After paying the expenses associated with switching websites, they used the surplus for research on potato starch. The current Potato Growers of Alberta website is albertapotatoes.ca, but the letters PGA are still prominently featured in their logo. You'll find this and other captivating potato stories in the Potato Growers of Alberta history book, which can be purchased on their website.

53 THE LITTLE CHURCH

Address North Dinosaur Trail and Murray Hill Road, Drumheller, AB, T0J 0Y0
Telephone (403) 823-8100 | **Website** drumhellerchamber.com/your-chamber/the-little-church

Drumheller's Tiny Place of Worship

The exterior of the Little Church.

The Little Church has been a longstanding landmark in the town of Drumheller. The standing joke is that the 3.4 metre by 2.1 metre church seats 10,000 people — six at a time.

The idea of building a little white church was conceived by Reverend E.C. O'Brien of the Pentecostal Church and approved by the local ministerial association as a place of worship and meditation.

The church was designed by Robert "Bob" Gibson and constructed by Tyvge "Tig" Seland, who is also credited with building several dinosaur statues around the town.

The church was first erected on July 9, 1958, and later reconstructed by prison inmates of the Drumheller Institution in 1991. After the church was vandalized in 2014, the Drumheller & District Chamber

The interior of the church seats six at a time.

of Commerce partnered with the Drumheller Institution to reconstruct the beloved little chapel once again in 2015.

The chamber of commerce owns and maintains the Little Church. It is open to the public and entrance is free of charge. It can be booked for weddings and other ceremonies by donation. The suggested donation is about $50. While the chamber of commerce cannot close the chapel to the public, it can put up a sign saying that the church is reserved for a ceremony and asking visitors for privacy. The reservations are also listed on the Little Church's Facebook page, so check before you visit so you don't barge in on a private celebration.

Drumheller's Little Church is located on the northeast side of North Dinosaur Trail, between the turn off for the Royal Tyrrell Museum and the Dinosaur Trail Golf & Country Club. It's a fun stop and a great photo op.

The Back to God Chapel in Bellevue

Drumheller isn't the only Alberta community with a tiny church. There's an even smaller white chapel in Bellevue. This little chapel is on the north side of the Crowsnest Pass Highway on the southeastern edge of town. A visitor information centre is near it. The Back to God Chapel was originally constructed in the 1960s. The door is always unlocked, so you can go in and see the tiny pulpit and pews.

54 ROYAL TYRRELL MUSEUM

Address 1500 North Dinosaur Trail, Drumheller, AB, T0J 0Y0 | **Telephone** (403) 823-7707 | **Website** tyrrellmuseum.com

The Mona Lisa of Dinosaurs

Not far from the town of Drumheller, in the rugged Alberta badlands, the Royal Tyrrell Museum of Palaeontology is one of the world's top palaeontological research facilities and museums. On display in the museum is one of the world's largest collections of dinosaurs, including five specimens that hold Guinness World Records. One of those specimens has been dubbed the Mona Lisa of dinosaurs.

The World's Best-Preserved Dinosaur Fossil

The Mona Lisa of dinosaurs is regarded as the world's best-preserved armoured dinosaur and perhaps the best-preserved fossil of any species of dinosaur in the world.

The specimen was discovered by Sean Funk during mining operations at an oil sands mine (Suncor Millennium Mine) on March 21, 2011. It is a nodosaur, a heavily armoured plant-eating dinosaur. Since it was a new genus and species, it was named *Borealopelta markmitchelli* after Mark Mitchell, the fossil technician who spent nearly six years removing the rock from the specimen.

Only the front of the dinosaur is preserved, but what is preserved has more detail than any other specimen ever recovered. The specimen is covered in preserved soft tissue including skin and keratinous scales. There's even pigment in the skin that provides evidence that it was reddish brown. The specimen retained its three-dimensional shape and its stomach contents, so scientists were able to determine what it ate for its last meal.

The exterior of the Royal Tyrrell Museum.

Borealopelta markmitchelli, the Mona Lisa of dinosaurs.

The museum contains an incredible collection of dinosaur fossils.

How the Museum Got Its Name (and How to Pronounce It)

The museum was named after Joseph Burr Tyrrell, a Canadian geologist, cartographer, explorer and mining consultant. In 1884 he discovered the first carnivorous dinosaur skull (*Albertosaurus sarcophagus*) near the site of the present-day museum. One of his other notable accomplishments occurred in 1916. David Thompson (1770–1857) was one of the greatest land geographers the world has ever seen. After stumbling across Thompson's biographical recollections consisting of 11 books of field notes, 39 journals, maps and a narrative, Tyrrell published them as *David Thompson's Narrative* (1916). If not for Tyrrell, the world might not have known about Thompson and his explorations.

Tyrrell retired in Ontario and lived to the age of 98. If you want to truly honour this man and his important place in Canadian history, you can start by pronouncing the museum's name correctly. Tyrrell is pronounced "TEER-ul."

Other Amazing Specimens and Activities

Besides the dinosaur Mona Lisa, there are four other Guinness World Record–earning specimens: the world's largest marine reptile, the world's most complete ornithomimid fossil, the most complete tyrannosaur skeleton and Albertonectes, a marine reptile fossil with the world's longest neck (most vertebrae).

The Royal Tyrrell Museum houses one of the world's largest collections of dinosaurs in a dozen different galleries. You can also watch technicians at work in the Preparation Lab. The museum has a wide variety of programs for kids and adults that bring the age of dinosaurs to life.

55 HORSeSHOe Canyon

Address Township Road 284, AB, T0M 2A0
Telephone (403) 443-5541 | **Website** kneehillcounty.com/2272/Horseshoe-Canyon

Fossil Hunting in Beautiful Badlands

A sunset view over Horseshoe Canyon.

There's something mystically beautiful about the region of Alberta known as the badlands. If you want a spectacular view of a badlands landscape shaped over millions of years, Horseshoe Canyon is a good place to go. Located 17 kilometres southwest of Drumheller along Highway 9, the canyon gets its name from its horseshoe shape.

It was French explorers who first described such places as "badlands." They called them "les mauvaises terres à traverser," which means "the bad lands to cross." Since the land had very little agricultural potential, the word badlands was also used by early settlers.

Horseshoe Canyon has two coulees that flow into Kneehill Creek, a tributary of the Red Deer River. Each arm of the canyon is about 5 kilometres long. There's a campground near the top of the canyon, a small campground store, a parking lot, lookout points, interpretive signs and a hiking trail that winds through the inside of the canyon. There is a small fee to park in the parking lot at the top of the canyon. These funds help support the costs of the care and conservation of Horseshoe Canyon.

Many plant and animal species have adapted to the harsh environment of the badlands. You may see

Viewing platforms offer incredible views of the badlands scenery.

seven species of sage and several species of cactus, prairie grasses, birds, garter snakes and other animals and plants.

It is not uncommon to see dinosaur fossils in the eroded badlands landscape. The first humans to find dinosaur fossils in the canyon believed the bones belonged to ancient ancestors of bison and that the badlands were an ancient graveyard.

In 2020 a 12-year-old boy named Nathan Hrushkin found a hadrosaur skeleton at the top of a hill while hiking with his father through Horseshoe Canyon. Nathan and his father took photos of the partially exposed fossils and sent them to the Royal Tyrrell Museum in Drumheller. Scientists confirmed the bones belonged to a young hadrosaur, commonly known as the duck-billed dinosaur. The fossil is about 69 million years old, and the find filled in some gaps in knowledge about the species.

If you believe you see a fossil while hiking through the canyon,

Stunning badlands scenery is the reason to visit this spot.

you should take a photo and contact the Royal Tyrrell Museum. It's important to leave fossils where they lie so that scientists can look for more bones near it. Scientists were able to recover more bones of the hadrosaur skeleton near the exposed bone that Nathan discovered.

Part of Horseshoe Canyon is owned by Kneehill County, and another is owned by the Nature Conservancy of Canada (NCC). The land the hadrosaur was discovered on was NCC land that was donated by the Nodwell family in honour of Leila Nodwell, who wished to see the canyon maintained in its natural state.

Another Horsey Canyon

Horsethief Canyon resembles nearby Horseshoe Canyon, but it is less known and less developed. It is located 16 kilometres northwest of Drumheller. There are great views from the edge of the canyon, and you can follow a steep trail from the canyon's rim to hike inside it. Over 100 years ago the canyon was used by outlaws to hide stolen livestock, which is how it got its name.

The Last Chance Saloon and Rosedeer Hotel are still operational and evidence of Wayne's former glory.

One of the 11 bridges of Wayne.

56 Wayne

Address 555 Jewell Street, Rosedale Station, AB, T0J 2V0 (Last Chance Saloon)
Telephone (403) 823-9189 | **Website** visitlastchancesaloon.com

Dine, Drink and Doze in a Real Ghost Town

In the community of Wayne, you'll find a bar with real bullet holes in the wall and a ghost town that is said to have real ghosts. You'll also find an operating hotel — possibly the only one in a Canadian ghost town.

Wayne came to be when the Red Deer Coal Company built the Rose Deer Mine in 1912. In its heyday the town had a population of more than 2,000 people. There were two schools, a hospital, several stores, a hotel and a saloon that miners affectionately dubbed the "Bucket of Blood" due to the large number of drunken brawls.

Life was hard for the miners who lived in Wayne, and many took liberties with the law, especially the prohibition laws that were in place in Alberta from 1915 to 1923.

The 11 Bridges of Wayne

You will cross 11 one-lane bridges in a 6-kilometre stretch of road that leads to Wayne. The bridges over the Rosebud River once transported coal, and you can still see the defunct railway tracks in places. The 11 bridges have become a local tourist attraction, and according to some sources these bridges once held the Guinness World Record for the most bridges in the shortest distance.

The Great Depression hit Alberta's coal mining industry hard, and the first mine in the Drumheller area closed in 1932. By the time the last mine in the area shut its doors, the population of Wayne had dwindled to fewer than 300 people. Today the hamlet has under 30 permanent residents. The only evidence of the glory days is the Rosedeer Hotel and the aptly named Last Chance Saloon, both of which are still open.

The walls of the Last Chance Saloon are decorated with old black-and-white photos of miners, antiques, numerous knick-knacks and mounted hunting trophies. There isn't a bare spot on the wall and even the roof is "decorated." There's a raccoon wearing a New Year's Eve party hat in the corner, a warthog over the door wearing a Canada flag toque and a white-tailed deer wearing several political campaign buttons.

The atmosphere at the saloon is truly unique, and enjoying a beverage and a meal in a historic Wild West saloon located in a ghost town is something you don't get to do every day. If you stay overnight in the Rosedeer Hotel, you can determine if there's truth in the rumours that the hotel is haunted.

These hoodoos have been created by millions of years of erosion.

57 DRUMHELLER HOODOOS

Address Coulee Way, Drumheller, AB, T0J 1B0 (Hoodoos Trail) | **Telephone** (866) 823-8100 (Drumheller Visitor Information Centre) | **Website** traveldrumheller.com/attractions/drumheller-hoodoos

Unique and Ancient Rock Formations

The Drumheller Hoodoos are interesting to visit in any season.

According to legend, the tall rock formations near Drumheller that are known as hoodoos are petrified giants that protect the land. At night they come alive and attack any intruders that dare to invade their territory. It's something to note if you plan to photograph the hoodoos at night.

The geological explanation of the Drumheller hoodoos is almost as amazing as the legend. At 5 to 7 metres tall, each unique rock formation was created by millions of years of erosion. The main body of the hoodoo is made of soft sandstone, and it has a harder rock on top called a capstone. The capstone helps slow the process of erosion, and the hoodoos become particularly fragile if it is removed. That is part of the reason the hoodoos near Drumheller are fenced off and people are asked not to climb on them.

Hoodoos are found around the world, and there are many different names for these unique geological formations. In addition to the name hoodoos, they have been called sand pillars, fairy chimneys, sand mushrooms, earth pyramids, goblins and other descriptive names.

If left alone, the hoodoos will erode until the base can no longer support the capstone and they eventually collapse. That process takes millions of years. Hoodoos of various shapes and sizes are found throughout Alberta's badlands, but the ones 16 kilometres southeast of Drumheller are some of the largest formations in the region.

The Drumheller hoodoos are located just off the road. There's a large parking lot and a public toilet at the site. A walking path and steel steps allow visitors to see the hoodoos from every angle. The most fragile areas are fenced off to protect these amazing structures. Wear hiking shoes if you plan to hike along the Hoodoos Trail. It can be slippery if the ground is wet from rain or snow. There are other places near Drumheller where you can also see hoodoos and badlands. Horseshoe Canyon, Horsethief Canyon and Orkney Viewpoint are three spots famed for the incredible views and unusual landscape.

58 ATLAS COAL MINE NATIONAL HISTORIC SITE

Address Box 521, 110 Century Drive, East Coulee, AB, T0J 1B0
Telephone (403) 822-2220 | **Website** atlascoalmine.ab.ca

Canada's Last Wooden Tipple

The wooden tipple at Atlas Coal Mine.

What is a tipple? It's a coal sorting structure. The seven-storey wooden tipple at Atlas Coal Mine near Drumheller is the last one in Canada. It was built in 1937.

Between 1911 and 1979 there were 139 coal mines in the Drumheller Valley. It was one of the top coal-producing regions in North America at a time when Canada was powered by coal. Working in a coal mine in the early 20th century probably wasn't very fun, but touring a coal mine today is certainly interesting and entertaining.

This national historic site includes both underground and surface workings from the Atlas No. 3 and 4 coal mines. It also includes residential buildings, a wash house, a supply house, a lamp house, a mine office and a working pre-1936 battery-powered locomotive.

Atlas Coal Mine began operating in 1936 and

Visitors can take a ride on a 90-year-old train and tour the grounds of the national historic site.

ceased coal production in 1979. It officially closed in 1984. The owner handed it over to the local historical society, and the mine reopened as a national historic site in 1987. It is now

DID YOU KNOW?

Sub-bituminous coal from the Drumheller area was used to heat homes, cook food and generate electricity. It also powered steam locomotives of both the Canadian National Railway and Canadian Pacific Railway.

locally operated and supported by visitors, with no ongoing operational support from any level of government.

At the Atlas Coal Mine, you can tour the tipple and put on protective gear and go deep into the mine to see what it was like to be a real miner. Before child-labour laws came into effect, some boys started mining as young as age 12, and the youngest miners worked on the tipple. A canvas belt carried the coal out of the mine to the tipple, where it was sorted, stored and put into railcars.

Coal mining was dangerous work — even on the tipple. Thirteen people died in the Atlas Coal Mine, including four from a gas explosion on June 24, 1941.

With a helmet and a headlamp on, you can follow an interpreter on a guided tour inside the dark mine to see mining equipment and artifacts and learn how they were used. It is a fascinating exploration of the coal mining history of Alberta. The mine is typically open for tours and visitors from May through September.

When the tour is over, head to the Last Chance Saloon in the nearby ghost town Wayne — just like the real miners did. You can still see black-and-white photos of miners on the walls of the saloon.

59 TRAVELLING LIGHT

Address 96th Avenue Northeast, Calgary, AB, T3K 6G4
Telephone (403) 268-2489 | **Website** calgary.ca/csps/recreation/public-art/96-avenue-ne.html

The Giant Blue Ring and More Controversial Public Art

Travelling Light, or the Giant Blue Ring.

"I am big, blue, and beautiful. I am also a streetlight." That's the description on the Facebook page for the Giant Blue Ring, a public art piece officially known as *Travelling Light*. It may be unusual for a public art piece to have its own social media accounts (@giantbluering), but this is no ordinary piece of art.

The Giant Blue Ring sits on the overpass at Deerfoot Trail and 96th Avenue Northeast in Calgary. Installed in 2013 it is a large blue metal hoop with streetlights on top. When word got out that the city paid $470,000 for this piece of art, there was quite an uproar. Former Calgary mayor Naheed Nenshi, who is known for his diplomacy, described the work as "awful."

The piece was meant to be a landmark that represents the universal mode of transportation — the wheel. The Berlin-based art collective inges idee, which designed and installed the art piece, placed it near the airport on the edge of a roadway where all modes of transportation and movement come together.

When it comes to *Travelling Light*, Calgarians either love it or hate it, and the Giant Blue Ring's social media sites give them a chance to express their opinions. But the art piece has become a landmark that is slowly working its way into the hearts of city residents.

More Controversial Public Art in Calgary

Travelling Light is not the first piece of controversial public art in Calgary, nor will it be the last. Art is subjective and everyone is a critic. In 2013 another piece of public art called *Wishing Well* by Po Shu Wang and Louise Bertelsen also caused controversy. The polished mirror split sphere was supposed to allow visitors to send text messages that would be converted into light and sound.

Talus Dome, which sits in the Edmonton River Valley.

The problem was, it didn't really work, and the sun reflected so strongly off the object that it allegedly burned holes through someone's jacket. The art piece that cost Calgary $559,000 was removed and put into storage for several years.

In 2018 a piece called *Bowfort Towers* by Del Geist and Patricia Leighton was also not well received. Sitting along Highway 1 near the Canada Olympic Drive exit, *Bowfort Towers* is "a celebration of the ancient geological history of the region," according to Del Geist's website. Other people didn't see it that way, though. According to some Blackfoot critics, the $500,000 public art installation looks like traditional burial scaffolds. There was a huge social media outcry from many who felt it was offensive to display Indigenous burial

scaffolds as public art on the side of a highway.

Controversial Public Art in Edmonton

Calgary is not the only Alberta city with controversial public art. In 2011 *Talus Dome* by Benjamin Ball and Gaston Nogues was installed along the Fox Drive Northwest exit onto Whitemud Drive North, in the Edmonton River Valley. At $600,000 the pile of silver balls is the most expensive piece of public art in the city's history. At the time, people compared it to everything from rabbit poop to a big bag of marbles. It is made out of 1,000 handmade steel spheres. The word "talus" describes an accumulation of gravel at the base of a cliff. It was designed to remind people of the city's relationship to the river valley.

60 BOTANICAL GARDENS of SILVER SPRINGS

Address 37 Silver Springs Drive Northwest, Calgary, AB, T3B 4N3 | **Telephone** (403) 268-2489 | **Website** bgss.ca

Alberta's Only Shakespeare Garden

The entrance to the Botanical Gardens of Silver Springs.

If you have ever doubted the power of volunteers, visit the Botanical Gardens of Silver Springs near Crowchild Trail and Sarcee Trail in Calgary. These beautiful gardens were designed, developed, maintained and are managed entirely by a volunteer group. The gardens are a not-for-profit charitable society that are supported by donations, provincial grants, the City of Calgary Parks Department and the Silver Springs Community Association, but these gardens would not exist without the time and talents of dedicated volunteers.

In 2002 the city's BP BirthPlace Forest program began planting 7,000 trees in the community of Silver Springs. Large grassy areas were left beside the trees, and a small group of volunteers saw this bare

This botanical garden also contains one of the largest outdoor labyrinths in Canada.

space as a missed opportunity and set out to beautify their neighbourhood. The first garden was planted in 2007. It was an oval-shaped perennial garden that was put in with the help of the City of Calgary Parks Department and the Silver Springs Community Association.

Today there are 12 main garden areas and six specialty garden areas encompassing 3,692 square metres of cultivated space. It's a 1.4-kilometre walk from one end of the gardens and forest to the other, so you can exercise and enjoy nature at the same time.

The best part about these gardens is that they are open year-round, and there is no admission fee to see them — though you may want to consider giving a donation to help support the gardens.

One of the Largest Outdoor Labyrinths in Canada

One of the largest outdoor labyrinths in Canada was built in 2013 using 9,000 bricks laid by volunteers. It takes about 20 minutes to meditatively walk through the 187-metre-long pathway of the labyrinth. While it can be experienced in any season, spring is the prime time. Volunteers planted 700 plugs of wild thyme around the labyrinth, and it smells and looks wonderful when the wild thyme blooms.

The Only Shakespeare Garden in Western Canada

Located at the north end of the botanical gardens, the Shakespeare Garden is the only garden of its kind west of Ontario. It features plants mentioned in Shakespeare's writing along with quotes. William Shakespeare understood the power of plants to elicit an emotional response, and he mentioned plants more than 200 times in his plays and sonnets. Roses were mentioned 95 times, oak trees 36 times, lilies 28 and the list goes on. When you walk through the garden, you may be surprised by the number and variety of plants the Bard included in his writing.

Romeo and Juliet, Act 2, Scene 2

"What's in a name? That which we call a rose by any other name would smell as sweet."
— William Shakespeare

61 THE MILITARY MUSEUMS

Address 4520 Crowchild Trail Southwest, Calgary, AB, T2T 5J4
Telephone (403) 410-2340 | **Website** themilitarymuseums.ca

Enigma, the Twin Towers and More

The exterior of the Military Museums.

The Military Museums of Calgary is the largest army, navy and air force museum in Western Canada and the second-largest military museum in the country. This sprawling facility houses a library and archives, four regimental museums, three service-specific museums and an art gallery. You could spend several days exploring this museum and its amazing collection of artifacts, which includes an Enigma machine from World War II and a steel beam from one of the Twin Towers at the World Trade Center in New York.

The museums span Canadian military history from the late 1800s through both World Wars to the Afghanistan conflict. There's also an extensive Cold War exhibit in two hangars, which also house several fighter planes. It's a good place to learn more about Canada's military.

Enigma Machine

The Enigma machine on display at the Military Museums is located in the Naval Museum. The 2014 movie *The Imitation Game* tells the story of the Enigma cryptosystem used by Nazi Germany during World War II and how cryptanalyst Alan Turing and his team managed to break Enigma's code and turn the tide of the Battle of the Atlantic. The Germans believed their Enigma cryptosystem was indecipherable to the Allies, and they used it to send top-secret messages between all branches of the military during World War II. The machines themselves were used to encode and decode messages sent by radio communications. It gave the Germans a huge advantage until Turing managed to crack the code. Deciphering Enigma is said to have shortened the war by no less than three years.

The Enigma machine at the Military Museums is a Swiss-made Type-K machine, which may have been used by the

Swiss Army and the Italian Navy during the war. Some businesses also used Enigma machines to send encoded messages. The machine looks like a typewriter and comes in a large wooden case. It has been estimated that as many as 10,000 Enigma machines were made, but no one knows how many survived.

The Twin Towers

Outside the Military Museums is a steel beam that came from the wreckage of one of the Twin Towers at the World Trade Center. It was presented to the Military Museums in memory of those who perished in the terrorist attacks on September 11, 2001. The beam is located just outside the main entrance of the museum. There are several displays on the grounds outside the museum, including an eternal flame, statues, several tanks, armoured cars, anti-tank guns and a Canadair CF-5 that is visible from Crowchild Trail.

In 2021 the Military Museums commemorated the 20th Anniversary of the 9/11 attacks with a special outdoor ceremony held beside the Twin Towers artifact. The ceremony included speeches from the U.S. Consul General and the Calgary Fire Chief. Many Canadian firefighters assisted after the attacks, which killed nearly 3,000 people and injured 25,000 more.

One of the most interesting permanent exhibits is the Enigma machine.

Realistic dioramas immerse visitors in the gritty realities of war.

The Naval Museum and Archives has the most complete collection of major ship weapons systems in Canada.

62 HERITAGE PARK HISTORICAL VILLAGE

Address 1900 Heritage Drive Southwest, Calgary, AB, T2V 2X3 | **Telephone** (403) 268-8500 | **Website** heritagepark.ca

One of Canada's Largest Living History Museums

Situated on 51 hectares of parkland on the banks of the Glenmore Reservoir, Heritage Park Historical Village was opened on July 1, 1964, and was for many years the largest living history museum in Canada. It's currently ranked the second largest, but it's not just size that makes the park special. The park's exhibits span Western Canadian history from the 1860s to the 1950s. There's a steam train, a paddlewheeler, costumed interpreters, an antique midway, a fur-trading fort, a gasoline alley museum and a historic town with many different buildings. The Prince House, located in the village centre, is one of the most unusual historic buildings in the park — mostly because it's widely believed to be haunted.

Paranormal Activity at the Prince House

Peter Anthony Prince formed the Calgary Water Power Company in 1890 and had an exclusive contract to provide Calgary with electricity. He also owned a flour mill,

The Prince House is believed to be the site of many paranormal activities.

DID YOU KNOW?

Most Canadian women got the right to vote in the 1921 federal election, but men and women in some ethnic groups were excluded. Chinese, Japanese and South Asian Canadians were finally able to vote in the 1948 federal election. Indigenous Peoples did not get the right to vote in national elections without conditions until 1960. Prior to that, First Nations had to give up their treaty rights and Indian Status to vote. During World War II at least 3,000 First Nations and 500 Chinese-Canadian soldiers fought for Canada, a country that denied them the right to vote.

This living history museum transports you back to the early days of Western Canada.

a meat-packing plant, grain elevators and a brewery. In 1894 Prince built a house for his family in the west end of Calgary — reportedly after a design he saw in *Scientific American*. The Prince House was preserved and relocated to Heritage Park in 1967, and park staff have been reporting paranormal activity ever since its arrival.

Prince was married four times, and three of his wives died in the home of natural causes — dying at home being normal in those days. Despite there being no electricity, staff have reported seeing lights coming from the third floor. There have been reports of seeing a lady in white on the second floor in the nursery, and another apparition has been spotted sweeping the back bedroom with a corn broom. There have also been unusual sounds like doors slamming and music playing. Paranormal investigators have examined the house and confirmed it is haunted. When the park occasionally gives ghost tours, the Prince House is the highlight.

The Famous 5 Centre of Canadian Women

A replica of Nellie McClung's home at Heritage Park houses the Famous 5 Centre of Canadian Women. It is used to tell the story of five brave Alberta women — Nellie McClung, Irene Parlby, Louise McKinney, Henrietta Muir Edwards and Emily Murphy — who petitioned and won the right for women to be considered "persons" under the British North America Act in 1929. The groundbreaking case was an important move forward for women to enjoy greater equality in Canadian society and allowed women to be appointed to the Canadian Senate.

The Peace Bridge has become an important pedestrian link between Sunnyside and Eau Claire.

63 PEACE BRIDGE

Address Peace Bridge, Calgary, AB
Telephone (403) 268-2489 | **Website** calatrava.com/projects/peace-bridge-calgary.html

A Calgary Architectural Icon

Calgary's Peace Bridge was designed by acclaimed Spanish architect Santiago Calatrava, and there's a reason this iconic walking and cycling bridge looks the way it does. A helicopter flight zone above the area meant the bridge could not be too high, but flood levels of the river meant it had to be high enough. Furthermore, ecological concerns prohibited any supports in the water. Calatrava's solution was a clever one — an impressive 126-metre-long, 8-metre-wide steel structure designed to support its own weight as it stretches across the Bow River. With its tube-like shape and crisscrossing pattern, it has been compared to a finger trap puzzle, one of those bamboo tubes you put your fingers in and when you try to pull them back out the trap tightens. Custom light fixtures keep the Peace Bridge aglow at all hours, and cameras on the bridge help deter vandalism.

The Peace Bridge, named as a tribute to the military, was built to alleviate congestion in

The design of the bridge is said to resemble a novelty finger trap puzzle.

Calgary's downtown core. It connects the residential community of Sunnyside on the north side of the river with the downtown community of Eau Claire on the south side.

There was some controversy over the bridge when it was first proposed. In 2008 the city council vote to proceed with the $25 million project barely passed. Months afterward, some councillors tried to introduce emergency motions designed to stop the project when the global economy went into a tailspin. Those motions failed and the project proceeded.

With such a unique design, the bridge faced many challenges and

delays in the building process. The project was originally meant to be completed by the end of October 2010. On March 24, 2012, Calgarians finally celebrated the grand opening of the bridge with a 1960s-style love-in, dance and hula hoop party. More than 2,000 people showed up for the party.

Today the bridge is a beloved architectural icon of the City of Calgary that is doing exactly what it was meant to do — alleviating downtown traffic congestion by encouraging people to walk and ride their bikes to the city's downtown business core. More than 6,000 people cross this unique bridge on foot or bicycle every day.

Water features and plenty of greenery make the Devonian Gardens a welcome tropical escape, especially in the dead of winter.

64 DEVONIAN GARDENS

Address CORE Shopping Centre, 317 7th Avenue Southwest, 4th floor, Calgary, AB, T2P 1B5
Telephone (403) 268-2489 | **Website** calgary.ca/csps/parks/locations/downtown-parks/devonian-gardens.html

Calgary's Only Indoor Park

Walking into a lush tropical oasis filled with green plants in the middle of a cold Alberta winter can feel like a small miracle. Calgary's only indoor park offers one hectare of botanical gardens with more than 680,000 kilograms of soil, 550 trees, 10,000 shrubs, 50 different plant varieties, a living wall, fountains, fish ponds and a large indoor playground. These botanical gardens are free and they can be enjoyed in every season.

The Devonian Gardens are located in the heart of downtown Calgary on the top floor of the CORE Shopping Centre. They're a popular spot for people who work downtown to take a lunch or coffee break. The gardens are considered a city park and are maintained by the City of Calgary Parks Department.

Designed by J.H. Cook Architects and Engineers, the gardens were donated to the City of Calgary by the Devonian Group of Charitable Foundations and first opened in 1977. The original construction cost was $9 million.

There are more than 550 trees in this beautiful indoor park.

After more than 30 years much of the infrastructure for the gardens had exceeded its lifespan. Leaks in the planters and other problems required repairs. The gardens underwent a $37-million renovation that included making repairs and expanding the existing gardens. They were reopened in 2012 after a four-year renovation.

The Devonian Gardens are a unique free indoor park that is lovely any time of year, but is particularly magnificent on a cold winter day.

65 CENTRAL LIBRARY

Address 800 3rd Street Southeast, Calgary, AB, T2G 2E7
Telephone (403) 260-2600 | **Website** calgarylibrary.ca/your-library/locations/cent

An Architectural Marvel

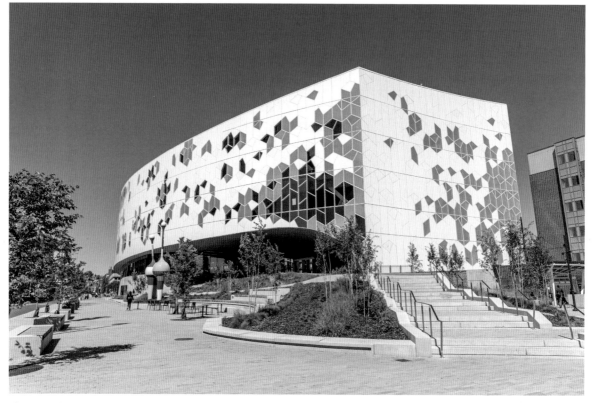

The mosaic-like exterior of the Central Library.

Opened in 2018 Central Library is the flagship of Calgary's public library system and one of the city's most important and distinctive cultural institutions. The building is an architectural masterpiece that received many awards, including an Architecture Honor Award from the American Institute of Architects, a Mayor's Urban Design Award and the Award of Excellence in Building Engineering at the Consulting Engineers of Alberta 2020 Showcase Awards.

Central Library is located one block east of City Hall in the heart of the Calgary's East Village. The 22,000-square-metre curved building was designed by American-Norwegian architecture firm Snøhetta

The interiors of the library are just as stunning as its exterior.

and Canadian firm DIALOG. The building and its surrounding plaza were constructed at a cost of $245 million.

The curved exterior is a massive eye-catching mosaic of windows that brings to mind the pattern of a snowflake. The interior is even more stunning, with a chinook-inspired red cedar archway, winding staircases, vaulted ceilings, murals and an enormous round Oculus skylight that lets in natural light. The building was built atop an existing light rail transit track, and there's a café overlooking the track at the northernmost point of the library. Visitors can watch trains pass by while they sip their drinks.

Not many public libraries are tourist attractions, but this one is. Calgary was listed in a *New York Times* article entitled "52 Places to Go in 2019," in part because of Central Library.

The interior of the library also features a unique book escalator for users who are returning books. Designed by Lyngsoe Systems, the 48-metre enclosed escalator takes books from the ground floor to the second floor. You can watch the books as they travel along this specially designed escalator.

This library is so architecturally unique that 60-minute tours are offered daily during regular library hours. Visitors can learn more details about the history and architecture of the building on these tours.

The exterior of Studio Bell.

The National Music Centre has an extensive collection of stage costumes and instruments, including a 16th-century Italian virginal.

66 STUDIO BELL

Address 850 4th Street Southeast, Calgary, AB, T2G 0L8 | Telephone (403) 543-5115 | Website studiobell.ca

Home of the National Music Centre

Opened in 2016 Studio Bell, home of the National Music Centre, was built to celebrate Canadian music in all its forms. Over the five floors of Studio Bell you'll find a huge collection of rare musical instruments, including the famous TONTO synthesizer, Elton John's songwriting piano and a circa-1560 Italian virginal, which is like a harpsichord. Studio Bell is also home to the Canadian Country Music Hall of Fame and the Canadian Music Hall of Fame. There are name plaques recognizing more than 50 legendary Canadian artists along with musical artifacts and memorabilia.

The National Music Centre has stage costumes of several famous Canadian musicians on display, and some of these will surely amuse and surprise you. Singer-songwriter k.d. lang has worn some unusual outfits over the years; she even had a dress with plastic dollar-store barns and farm animals sewn onto the yoke. This dress, along with outfits from other musicians, can be found on the fifth floor.

Studio Bell is very hands-on and interactive — it's a great place to pretend you're a rock star. There are stationary displays of rare musical instruments, but there are also many instruments you can try yourself, including drum sets, guitars, synthesizers and pianos. On the third floor, there are vocal recording booths where you can practice singing. The Soundbox on the fourth floor is especially fun for kids. They can build and play with musical instruments.

What Is TONTO?

Built in 1968 by music producers Malcolm Cecil and Robert Margouleff, TONTO is a legendary synthesizer that was used to create several of Stevie Wonder's most famous albums. It was officially known as The Original New Timbral Orchestra, and many other institutions — including the Smithsonian and Yale University — were interested in acquiring it. The National Music Centre acquired the instrument in 2013 and fully restored it so that it can continue to be used. Some consider it to be the Holy Grail of synthesizers. The Halluci Nation, formerly known as A Tribe Called Red, was the first band to produce new music using the legendary synthesizer after it was restored. Artists in residence at the National Music Centre in 2018, The Halluci Nation used the synthesizer to create electric powwow music.

The King Eddy

Located next door to Studio Bell, the King Edward Hotel was Calgary's second-oldest hotel and the longest-operating bar and hotel when it closed in 2004. In 2008 the National Music Centre acquired the King Eddy and restored it in collaboration with Calgary Municipal Land Corporation. In July 2018 it reopened as a restaurant, bar and live music venue. The building also houses CKUA Radio Calgary, the Rolling Stones Mobile Recording Studio and other National Music Centre facilities.

REaDER ROCK GARDEN NATIONAL HISTORIC SITE

Address 325 25th Avenue Southeast, Calgary, AB, T2G
Telephone (403) 268-2489 | **Website** calgary.ca/csps/parks/locations/se-parks/reader-rock-garden.html

William Roland Reader's Ode to Alberta's Gardens

Built into a steep hillside south of Calgary's downtown, Reader Rock Garden is an Arts and Crafts–style alpine rockery, a garden type that was popular in Europe and North America at the beginning of the 20th century. It features rock paths, steps and walls forming numerous planting beds that contain thousands of native and non-native plant specimens. It's also a national historic site and a free public space that is wonderful to explore.

Reader Rock Garden was laid out between 1913 and 1942 by William Roland Reader, Calgary's most influential parks superintendent. Reader served as parks superintendent for nearly 40 years, and he significantly shaped Calgary through his skill, energy and dedication. In designing the garden, Reader drew from British gardening influences popular in the late 19th and early 20th centuries and adapted them to the dramatically different environment of the Canadian Prairies.

The West Garden features a small bridge, a stream, two constructed pools and a bog garden.

140

There are many spots to sit and enjoy the beauty of Reader's vision.

Reader's restored house now features a café.

citizens to follow Reader's example in their own gardens.

For many years Reader Rock Garden was one of the most spectacular gardens in Alberta, but after the death of William Roland Reader in 1943, the garden was not maintained and so it drastically declined. In 2006 the restoration of the garden was completed, and it earned an official designation as a provincial historic resource.

In 2018 Reader Rock Garden was officially named a national historic site. It received the designation not only because it is one of Alberta's premier public gardens, but also because it was a botanical testing ground where Alberta's first gardeners discovered what plant species could grow in the soil and climate of this region. At its peak the garden was home to some 3,500 plant species, a culmination of Reader's artistic and scientific interests. It remains the signature work of a man who advocated that well-designed civic green spaces are an essential part of a well-designed city. The garden is the legacy of William Roland Reader, but so are Calgary's tree-lined streets, lovely city parks, playgrounds and many beautiful public green spaces.

The creation of the garden was driven by two factors: the encouragement of European settlement at a time when southern Alberta was considered hostile to agricultural and horticultural development, and the City Beautiful Movement, which linked civic beauty with social progress. The resulting garden was well appreciated for its beauty and design and inspired private

WILDER INSTITUTE/ CALGARY ZOO

68

Address 210 St. George's Drive Northeast, Calgary, AB, T2E 7V6 | Telephone (403) 232-9300 | Website calgaryzoo.com

Canada's Second-Largest Zoo and an Innovator of Wildlife Conservation

Canada's second-largest zoo is home to nearly 1,000 creatures representing 119 different species from five continents. One of just five zoos in Canada accredited by the Association of Zoos and Aquariums, the Wilder Institute/ Calgary Zoo is internationally recognized as one of the top zoos in the world for conservation research. The zoo is operated by the Calgary Zoological Society, an independent not-for-profit organization that was established in 1929 and is Alberta's oldest registered charity.

The 48.5-hectare zoo is organized into zones. Some include the Canadian Wilds, Destination Africa, Land of Lemurs, Penguin Plunge, Dorothy Harvie Botanical Gardens, Eurasia, the Prehistoric Park and the ENMAX Conservatory, which features a butterfly garden.

A visit to the Wilder Institute/ Calgary Zoo is a unique and fun outing for all ages and offers visitors a chance to learn about animals and the importance of

Prehistoric Park is a glimpse into Alberta's prehistoric past, when dinosaurs roamed the landscape.

conservation. The zoo also holds a variety of events throughout the year.

Wildlife Conservation

In 2021 the Calgary Zoo changed its name to the Wilder Institute/ Calgary Zoo. The Wilder Institute oversees the Calgary Zoo's conservation portfolio. The name change was part of a journey to transform from a zoo that does conservation work into a

The zoo is great for guests of all ages.

The Wilder Institute/Calgary Zoo's whooping crane breeding program has helped introduce hundreds of cranes back to the wild.

The ring-tailed lemur is one of three lemur species at the zoo's Land of Lemurs exhibit.

conservation organization that operates a zoo.

In its efforts to be a Canadian leader in wildlife conservation, the Wilder Institute/Calgary Zoo has established a large number of conservation breeding programs that take place at its off-site Wildlife Conservation Centre. Much effort has gone into the science of species recovery and reintroduction, and the zoo has made a difference in helping to save a number of species from extinction.

In the 1990s the zoo began working to save the endangered whooping crane. At the time there were only 20 left in the wild. By late 2020 there were an estimated 825 whooping cranes in the wild — thanks in part to the efforts of the zoo. The Wilder Institute/Calgary Zoo is Canada's only facility that breeds whooping cranes for release into the wild. Researchers used artificial insemination and other breeding practices to increase the number of hatchlings of this endangered species. Expertise in reintroduction has helped to increase the wild population and bring these magnificent birds back from the brink of extinction.

Some of the other species that have benefited from the zoo's conservation efforts include the burrowing owl, the sage grouse, the Vancouver Island marmot and the British Columbia northern leopard frog.

69 TELUS SPark SCIENCE CENTRE

Address 220 St. George's Drive Northeast, Calgary, AB, T2E 5T2 | **Telephone** (403) 817-6800 | **Website** sparkscience.ca

Drink Out of a Toilet and Lie on a Bed of Nails

The exterior of the TELUS Spark Science Centre.

TELUS Spark is Calgary's science centre, and it is a fun and fascinating attraction to explore — for both children and adults. Established in 1967 the centre focuses on STEAM (science, technology, engineering, art and math), an approach to learning that has been a buzzword in recent years. The science centre has many fun and fascinating exhibits and programs designed to spark a sense of wonder and curiosity about the world. In such a place, you'll find many displays that classify as unusual. Here are a few of them.

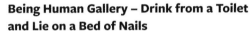
Do you dare to drink from a toilet bowl?

The Brainasium features one of the longest metal slides in Canada.

Being Human Gallery – Drink from a Toilet and Lie on a Bed of Nails

Are your everyday decisions based on logic or perception? If you can take a sip out of TELUS Spark's toilet bowl water fountain, you may be able to better answer that question. The Being Human Gallery is all about the human experience and how each human being is unique. Another interesting display in this gallery is the bed of nails. This teaches some important principles of science: if you were to step on one sharp nail, it would be very painful and could puncture the skin, but the even distribution of weight over a large surface area means you can lie on a bed of nails without pain. Visitors can even lie down to see for themselves.

360-Degree Immersive Digital Gallery

In 2021 TELUS Spark introduced a 557-square-metre, 360-degree immersive gallery that is unique in Canada. The gallery immerses visitors in sight and sound, telling a story with multiple projectors, music and words. The first presentation was developed by Olivier Goulet, a former director of Cirque du Soleil, and uses the voice talents of Isabella Rossellini. The five-room gallery is a first for a Canadian science centre, and there are plans to change the 15-minute multimedia presentations featured in the gallery so that there will always be something new at the centre.

Brainasium — One of the Longest Metal Slides in Canada

Brainasium is a huge year-round outdoor playground that helps kids train their brains and their bodies. There are giant molecules, a teeter-totter that uses levers to accommodate six children at the same time, musical chimes and many more attractions that help children develop problem-solving skills while they play. One unique attraction designed to get kids to consider the power of gravity is an 11-metre tower with a 19-metre metal tube slide. Surprisingly it is not Canada's longest metal slide (the Malahat Sky-walk in Malahat, British Columbia, has a 20-metre-long metal slide), but it is really long and really fun.

70 HanGar FLIGHT MUSEUM

Address 629 McCall Way Northeast, Calgary, AB, T2E 8A5 | Telephone (403) 250-3752 | Website thehangarmuseum.ca

See Restored Historic Airplanes and a Parachute Dress

An Avro Lancaster Mark X, one of the stars of the Hangar Flight Museum.

Calgary's Hangar Flight Museum is located in the former drill hall of a World War II Royal Air Force (RAF) flying school that opened in 1941. The location is unique, but it's the collection that makes this aviation museum unusual. The museum contains a variety of civilian and military aircraft spanning an entire century of Canadian flight. There are also interpretive displays, uniforms and scale models. The two most unique items in the museum are both from World War II: a Lancaster bomber and a parachute wedding dress.

The Avro Lancaster Bomber — One of 17 Left

The Lancaster bomber was known as the "Lanc" to most Canadian pilots and crew who served with Bomber Command during World War II. It had a large bomb bay that could handle bombs weighing up to 5,400 kilograms and was the primary heavy bomber used by the Royal Air Force (RAF). During the war Lancasters carried out more than 156,000 missions and dropped more than 550,000 tonnes of bombs.

The Avro Lancaster is best known for its role in Operation Chastise, later known as the Dambusters

The museum houses a collection of over two dozen military and civilian aircraft.

This wedding dress was made from parachute silk.

raid. On the night of May 16, 1943, the RAF No. 617 Squadron bombed the Möhne and Edersee dams in Germany, causing catastrophic flooding and damaging or destroying two hydroelectric power stations as well as several factories and mines. The aircraft also played an important part in sinking the German battleship *Tirpitz* on November 12, 1944. The Lancaster could also carry the single largest and heaviest bomb used by the RAF during the war — a 10,000 kilogram bomb that was so large it hung below the aircraft because it would not fit in the bomb bay.

Of the 7,400 Lancasters built, only 17 remain in the world. The one at the Hangar Flight Museum was built in Ontario and flown to England in June 1945. In 1961 it was purchased by Lynn Garrison, a collector and pilot with the Royal Canadian Air Force, and put on display in 1962 at the entrance of the McCall Field, which is now the Calgary International Airport. It was a memorial to those who trained under the British Commonwealth Air Training Plan. The plane was transferred to the Calgary Aerospace Museum in 1992, and in 2016 the museum's name was changed to the Hangar Flight Museum.

Parachute Dress

In addition to an impressive array of aircraft, the Hangar Flight Museum has a collection of aviation artifacts. One of the most unique is a parachute wedding dress. Silk was used in parachutes, and as a result there was a shortage of the fabric during World War II. In some cases, resourceful people repurposed the silk from parachutes to make other items, including wedding dresses.

Near the end of the war, a B-24 Liberator crashed in a field near the village of Zoeterwoude in the Netherlands. Wilhelm Van Niekerk, a local resident, was given the parachute by one of the airmen, who hid in nearby haystacks to evade capture and escaped with the help of the Dutch underground. Niekerk passed the parachute onto his then girlfriend Wilhelmina Van Berg, who stored it. When the couple got married after the war, Wilhelmina made her wedding gown out of the parachute silk and later made christening gowns for their children. When the couple moved to Calgary, the dress made the journey with them. The wedding dress and the sewing machine she used to make it are on display at the Hangar Flight Museum.

PUTTING
THEIR LIVES
ON THE LINE

Patrol officers are on the front line of fighting crime and helping people in Calgary.

They put their lives on the line, often responding to danger when others are running from it. Every patrol officer wears body armour, and never knows what he or she will encounter when arriving first on scene.

Ask Patrol officers why they joined the Calgary Police Service and they will say they want to make a difference.

Today's youth are our future. YouthLink helps build a better tomorrow by teaching kids to make smart choices in an ever changing and often confusing world..."

Exhibits and hands-on displays highlight the challenges and importance of police work.

71 YOUTHLINK CALGARY POLICE INTERPRETIVE CENTRE

Address 5111 47th Street Northeast, Calgary, AB, T3J 3R2 | **Telephone** (403) 428-4530 | **Website** youthlinkcalgary.com

Discover What It Takes to Solve and Prevent Crime

The exterior of Youthlink Calgary Police Interpretive Centre.

YouthLink Calgary Police Interpretive Centre is not your average museum. Geared toward youths aged 10 to 14, this museum has a mission to empower kids and build trust and a positive connection between police and the community. Even though it's aimed at kids and families, the museum is fascinating for anyone who is interested in how police officers solve crimes.

The museum features more than 50 modern policing exhibits, fascinating true crime stories, a forensic lab and hands-on activities and displays. Visitors can examine actual evidence and photos from some of Calgary's most notorious crimes and try to solve them. There are also exhibits on personal safety, bullying and crime prevention to help kids make safe, informed choices.

Visiting the museum is an opportunity to see what work is like for Calgary police officers. Visitors can try on riot gear, see a display of guns, a police car and a replica police helicopter, and go into the forensics lab and experiment with the science that

supports police work. The museum also operates summer camps in July and August.

This unique police interpretive centre also demonstrates how challenging police work can be. Some of the crimes featured in the museum were never solved. The centre also addresses police tragedies like Black Friday, which happened on December 20, 1974. Following a complaint that a shopkeeper was being threatened by a deranged man, a chase and shootout ensued, and more than 130 police officers responded to the scene. Seven officers were wounded, and Detective Boyd Davidson died from shots fired by Philippe Laurier Gagnon. The display explains how police procedures have changed as a result of this tragedy.

While it is true that YouthLink Calgary Police Interpretive Centre is unlike any other museum in Alberta, it is the centre's unique mission that really sets it apart and makes it worth visiting.

Don't Forget to Go to the Biffy

It would be a crime to miss out on using the cellblock-style bathrooms at YouthLink Calgary Police Interpretive Centre.

unusual festivals and events

I f you're on the lookout for entertaining local experiences, look no further than Alberta's unique and sometimes quirky festival scene. Choose from festivals that celebrate food, the arts, snow, sand or bull testicles — just to name a few.

January

High Performance Rodeo, Calgary: Established in 1987 by Michael Green of One Yellow Rabbit Performance Theatre, this unique festival of the arts has grown into the largest festival of its kind in Western Canada. For three weeks starting in mid-January, the High Performance Rodeo takes over downtown Calgary with performances featuring theatre, music, dance and multidisciplinary art. (hprodeo.ca)

SnowDays, Banff National Park: Celebrate the joy of snow with this annual festival in Banff National Park. Larger-than-life snow sculptures are scattered around downtown Banff, while ice sculptures from the annual Ice Magic ice carving competition transform Lake Louise. There are many events throughout the 12-day festival, including skijoring demonstrations (skijoring is a winter sport in which a person on skis is pulled by an animal or machine), a kids' play zone and a craft beer festival. (banfflakelouise.com/snowdays)

Ice on Whyte, Edmonton: The Ice on Whyte Festival was founded in 2003, and it has grown into one of Canada's top winter festivals. The festival features professional ice carving competitions with artists from all over the world. Besides viewing beautiful ice sculptures, visitors can enjoy a drink at an ice bar, get some ice carving lessons and savour good food. (iceonwhyte.ca)

SNOW DAYS

JUNE

PONOKA STAMPEDE

Honey Festival, Falher: The annual Falher Honey Festival celebrates summer in the Peace Country and the town's favourite pollinator, the bee. The event features a parade, a ball tournament, a car show and shine, a vendors market, bee beard demonstrations, games, live music, BEEr gardens and many other events. (honeyfest.ca)

Vikings in the Streets Festival, Viking: Every summer the town of Viking celebrates its Scandinavian heritage at the Vikings in the Streets Festival. There's a viking village with viking re-enactments that display viking crafts, trades and food. There are face painters, storytellers, live music, a market, a parade and a lutefisk eating contest. Lutefisk is a traditional Nordic dish made by soaking dried cod in a lye solution for several days. In the annual event, 10 brave souls try to down as much of the gelatinous food as they can in a timed contest. (facebook.com/VikingAlberta)

Wanham Plowing Match, Wanham: Located 106 kilometres north of Grande Prairie, the tiny hamlet of Wanham has been hosting plowing competitions since 1971. The original event was designed to preserve the skill of competitive plowing and pulling, but today it has grown to feature many events, including plowing, heavy horse pulls, barrel racing, pole bending, show jumping, trick riding, monster trucks, tractor pulls, lawn tractor races, live music and much more. (wanhamplowingmatch.com)

Ponoka Stampede, Ponoka: The town of Ponoka is not a very big place, but the annual Ponoka Stampede has grown to become one of the five-largest rodeos in the world for payouts. Established in 1936 it hosts the largest single-day bull-riding event in the world and attracts competitors from across Canada, the United States and Australia. Besides traditional rodeo events, there are chuckwagon races, a parade, a midway, dances, concerts and beer gardens. (ponokastampede.com)

JULY

Badlands Passion Play, Drumheller: Every summer a cast of over 100 performers portrays the life of Jesus Christ in a spectacular 2,500 seat natural amphitheatre that is surrounded by incredible badlands scenery. The epic story of faith, hope and love is portrayed on Canada's largest outdoor stage. The award-winning play features original music, real animals and amazing costumes, and it's been held for more than 25 years. (badlandsamp.com)

Calgary Stampede, Calgary: This 10-day rodeo, exhibition and festival is billed as the Greatest Outdoor Show on Earth, because it is. The Calgary Stampede attracts over a million visitors each year. Events include one of the world's largest and most lucrative rodeos, agricultural competitions, chuckwagon racing, a parade, a midway, stage shows, concerts and First Nations and Métis exhibitions. Calgary is transformed

CALGARY STAMPEDE

Canadian Death Race, Grande Cache: The Canadian Death Race is one of the world's toughest ultramarathons, and it's been an annual event in Grande Cache for over 20 years. The 125-kilometre course passes over three mountain summits and includes over 5 kilometres of elevation change and a major river crossing. The Canadian race is a qualifier for the prestigious Western States 100-Mile Endurance Run. (sinistersports.ca /deathrace)

Spock Days, Vulcan: There's no guarantee that you will live long and prosper if you attend Spock Days in the Town of Vulcan, but it can't hurt. The town considers itself the Star Trek Capital of the World, and it even has its own landed starship. Spock Days features a parade, a ball tournament, a fair, a pancake breakfast, barbecues, beer gardens, food concessions and other activities. (spockdays.com)

SPOCK DAYS

during the stampede with decorated storefronts, western wear fashions, evening events, pancake breakfasts and barbecues. (calgarystampede.com)

Testicle Festival, Calgary: The Testicle Festival at Bottlescrew Bills Pub has been a running event since 1993. Festival attendees get bragging rights if they can swallow prairie oysters (bull testicles) cooked into appetizers, desserts and the classic Prairie Oyster Caesar salad. At least three unique dishes are served each year. Great Balls of Fire is a spicy crowd favourite that has made its way onto the menu more than once. The festival coincides with the annual Calgary Stampede. (bottlescrewbill.com)

Sand Blast, Devonshire Beach at Lesser Slave Lake: For more than a decade the annual sand sculpture competition on Devonshire Beach at Lesser Slave Lake has been one of the most anticipated events of summer in this region of Alberta. Family-friendly activities, entertainment and sand sculpting competitions are part of the fun. (slavelakeregion.ca/in-the-community /community-events)

Edmonton International Fringe Festival, Edmonton: There are more than 200 Fringe Festivals around the globe, but the Edmonton International Fringe Festival is the oldest and largest of the 23 held in North America. True to the spirit of fringe, there is no jury or censorship of the performances. An unbiased lottery system is used to select the artists, and participating artists receive 100 percent of the ticket revenue from their performances. (fringetheatre.ca)

Calgary Medieval Faire & Artisan Market, Calgary: It's okay to dress up in your best armour for this medieval faire event. There is storytelling, magic shows, music, face painting, sword fighting knights, a market, costumes, food and more. (calgarymedievalfaire.com)

Taber Cornfest, Taber: Every year Taber celebrates the corn harvest with the largest free family festival in Western Canada. There's a parade, live music, entertainment, midway rides, live entertainment, a chili cookoff, beer gardens, bull riding, a show and shine, fireworks and more. There is also a corn-eating contest, of course. If you can eat 10 large cobs of corn clean in two minutes, you might have a shot at winning the title of Corn King. In 2017 Kelly Hatch beat out his son, who previously held the title, by eating 10 large cobs of corn vertically instead of horizontally. (taberchamber.ca/cornfest)

SEPTEMBER

Pyrogy Festival, Glendon: This annual festival is held in Pyrogy Park in the village of Glendon under the shadow of the world's largest perogy. The annual event celebrates the community's Ukrainian heritage and history. Festival highlights include a perogy-eating contest, Ukrainian dancers and live music. (villageofglendon.ca/special-events)

Beakerhead Festival, Calgary: Beakerhead is a weird, wild and wacky outdoor festival that highlights the wonders of art, science and engineering. Science takes to the streets with bizarre public art installations and crazy creations like a giant inflatable dung beetle or a flame-shooting octopus. It's a huge spectacle that puts human ingenuity on display. (beakerhead.com)

OCTOBER

Jasper Dark Sky Festival, Jasper: The annual Jasper Dark Sky Festival celebrates the night sky with a host of events and activities in the world's second-largest dark-sky preserve. There are guided star-viewing events, concerts under the stars, dining, live music, kids activities, presentations from scientists and much more. (jasperdarksky.travel)

NOVEMBER

Canadian Finals Rodeo, Red Deer: The national professional rodeo championship in Canada is held in early November and is the final event of the Canadian Professional Rodeo Association's season. The event features some of the best athletes and some of the richest purses offered in a Canadian rodeo. (cfrreddeer.ca)

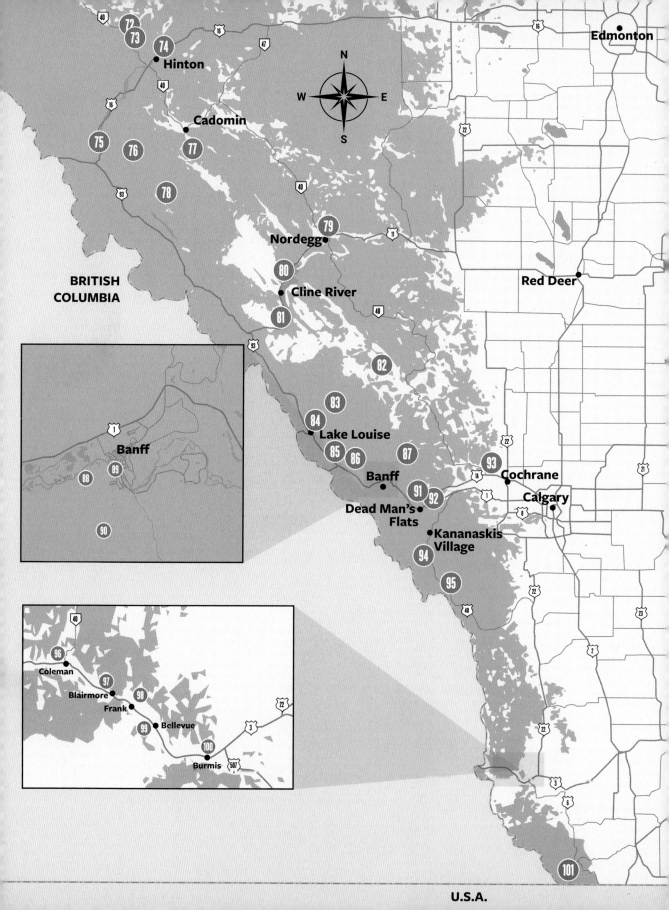

THE ALBERTA ROCKIES

72 Beaver Ranch in William A. Switzer Provincial Park

Address Highway 40 near Hinton, AB | **Telephone** (780) 865-5600
Website albertaparks.ca/parks/central/william-a-switzer-pp

How to Deal with Nuisance Beavers

William A. Switzer Provincial Park is a beautiful place to explore beyond the park's beaver ranch.

When you think of ranching in Alberta, you typically picture cattle and horses, but there was a short period of time when beaver ranching became a thing. Sadly, beaver rodeo events never really took off. In William A. Switzer Provincial Park, you can view the remains of a commercial beaver ranching operation.

The first attempts at beaver ranching occurred in the 1920s. Beavers were nearly wiped out by hunting and trapping, and population numbers were extremely low in the early 19th century. The provincial government instituted the first Alberta Game Act in 1907 and issued a five-year moratorium on beaver trapping. By the early 1920s the beaver population was soaring and beavers began destroying trees in city parks.

At that point the Alberta government made an amendment to the legislation allowing for the trapping of nuisance beavers. Farmers were also having problems with beavers, and some came up with their own solution — in the form of beaver ranching. Farmers with beaver problems got permission to fence in the beaver dams on their land and harvest the beavers as a ranching operation and another source

A short walking trail leads you to the cement beaver pens, where you'll also find interpretive signage.

of revenue. Some of the largest beaver ranches had as many as 100 animals, but the ranches were still subject to the regulations of the Alberta Game Act.

One of the most interesting and ill-fated beaver ranching operations was attempted in 1946 near Jarvis Creek in what is now William A. Switzer Provincial Park. At that time beaver numbers were low and fur prices were high. Newly returned from the war, Lieutenant Colonel Alan Innes-Taylor received veteran assistance funding to start a beaver ranch. He planned to sell the pelts for profit and to sell live animals to the government so that they could be released in other locations.

Innes-Taylor built concrete pens to house the beavers. It was a labour-intensive operation that required him to cut tree branches for food and pipe in water for the animals — even in winter. The biggest problem with the business was a basic misunderstanding of beaver behaviour. It's possible that the beavers did not appreciate the concrete pens. Innes-Taylor also randomly paired beavers in the pens, not realizing that beavers mate for life. As a result, the mismatched beavers never reproduced, and the business went under in about a year's time. Another beaver ranch nearby met with the same fate.

If you want to see the remains of the beaver ranch in William A. Switzer Provincial Park, head to the Beaver Ranch Group Camp. You'll find the cement pens and interpretive signage along a short walking trail in the group camping area.

DID YOU KNOW?

There were an estimated six million beavers in Canada before the fur trade, and by the mid-19th century they were close to extinction. At the peak of the fur trade, more than 100,000 beaver pelts per year were exported from Canada to Europe, mostly to make fur hats. Beavers were saved from extinction in part by conservation efforts and in part because silk hats became more fashionable than beaver hats. The beaver was given official status as the emblem of Canada on March 24, 1975.

73 JOACHIM VALLEY TRAIL

Address Jarvis Lake Campground, William A. Switzer Provincial Park, Highway 40 near Hinton, AB
Telephone 1 (877) 537-2757 | **Website** n/a

A Hike to an Abandoned Airplane

The abandoned airplane on the Joachim Valley Trail.

A trail leading to an abandoned aircraft is no ordinary trail. The Joachim Valley Trail is a relatively easy hike that passes through meadows and forests to an abandoned airplane for a fun photo op or a memorable picnic. The trailhead is located about 26 kilometres northwest of Hinton at the Jarvis Lake Campground in William A. Switzer Provincial Park.

Most airplane hikes lead to crash sites, but this plane never really crashed. The army used it to train search and rescue teams, and they eventually abandoned it in the provincial park. Over time it became a beloved landmark.

A Métis burial ground with distinctive A-frame structures.

This trail is beautiful in all seasons. You can see wildflowers in spring and summer, colourful foliage in fall and snow-capped peaks in winter. Be bear aware, carry bear spray and make noise as you explore the trail. You can make your way along the trail on foot or on bike in warm weather or on skis or a fat bike in winter. The trail is relatively flat with only about 168 metres of elevation gain in total. Partway along the trail, you'll pass a historic Métis burial ground. The graveyard has gravesites with wooden A-frame structures that are sometimes referred to as "spirit houses." They are meant to protect the loved one's remains.

At about 3.6 kilometres along the trail, you'll reach the abandoned airplane. There's a picnic table not far away, and it's a great spot to stop for lunch or dinner. Take a peek inside the plane and get some pictures before heading back the way you came. The Hanington Ski Hut, just past the airplane, is open in winter for skiers to warm up before skiing back.

North York Creek Plane Crash Hike

In 1946 a Royal Canadian Air Force DC-3 Dakota crashed in bad weather on a mountainside near the headwaters of North York Creek, south of Coleman. All seven soldiers on board died in the crash. Remnants of the wreckage are still on the mountainside. A moderately difficult 20-kilometre return hike or quad trail leads to the crash site. If you do this hike, remember to be respectful at the memorial site.

The Beaver Boardwalk winds past an active beaver dam, where you might catch a glimpse of the industrious rodents for which this boardwalk is named.

74 THE BeaVer BoarDWaLK

Address 408 Collinge Road, Hinton, AB, T7V 1L1
Telephone (780) 865-6066 | **Website** hinton.ca/852/Beaver-Boardwalk

The World's Longest Freshwater Boardwalk

The Beaver Boardwalk in Hinton is about 3 kilometres long, and according to the town and several websites, that makes it the longest freshwater boardwalk in the world. It winds through marshland and fens and brings you close to the active beaver dam and lodge that give the boardwalk its name. There are lookouts, benches, interpretive signs, beavers, birds and other wildlife to see along the way. The boardwalk is a lovely family walk that highlights the wetland ecosystem that surrounds Maxwell Lake.

The idea for the boardwalk was conceived by Rick Bonar, a biologist at West Fraser Timber. The idea was to provide public access to a fascinating natural area for both recreation and education. In 2006 West Fraser Timber sponsored the construction costs of the boardwalk in commemoration of the 50th anniversary of the company and the town of Hinton. In addition to West Fraser Timber, the Town of Hinton, Whiskey Jack Bird Club, Forest Resources Improvement Association of Alberta, Fisheries and Oceans Canada, Hinton Rotary Club, Hinton Communities in Bloom, Teck and the Alberta Lottery Fund also contributed to the costs.

More than 150 local people donated their time over several years to help build the Beaver Boardwalk. One local Hinton resident named Rocky Morin, earned the nickname Mr. Boardwalk by donating over four months of his time to the project. More than 20,000 two-by-six treated deck boards and 120,000 screws were used in the project.

The wetlands that surround the boardwalk are a good place for birdwatching, and more than 120 species of bird have been seen in the area. The number of beavers varies from year to year but includes up to about a dozen. Your best chance to see the beavers at work is in the early morning or later in the evening.

It's difficult to manage a recreational facility near beavers, but the town of Hinton mitigates the hazards by feeding the beavers each fall. In the fall beavers gather large amounts of food for their winter cache. Trembling aspen logs are brought in by the truckload so that the beavers can fill their cache before the water freezes. This prevents the beavers from taking down trees near the boardwalk, which could be hazardous to pedestrians. The rest of the year, beavers eat aquatic vegetation that grows in the wetlands and leave the trees surrounding the world's longest freshwater boardwalk untouched.

DID YOU KNOW?

The beaver is Canada's largest rodent and the second-largest rodent in the world next to the capybara from South America. And speaking of rodents, did you know that Alberta is a rat-free province? A rat control program has been in place in Alberta since the 1950s. If you see a rat, email 310rats@gov.ab.ca.

75 PATRICIA LAKE

Address Pyramid Lake Road, Jasper National Park, AB
Telephone (780) 852-6176 | **Website** pc.gc.ca/en/pn-np/ab/jasper

The Site of Operation Habbakuk

You would never know the beautiful waters of Patricia Lake are hiding a war-time secret.

When you gaze out at the tranquil waters of Patricia Lake in Jasper National Park, it's hard to imagine that this peaceful spot in the Canadian Rockies could be hiding anything. But there is a secret sunk beneath the surface of Patricia Lake. It was classified as "Top Secret" during World War II and for many years it was forgotten.

At the bottom of the lake are the remains of an unfinished, top-secret British World War II aircraft carrier codenamed Operation Habbakuk. English journalist, spy and inventor Geoffrey Pyke conceived the idea to build an aircraft carrier out of ice. Since ice is unsinkable, he reasoned that the vessel would be virtually impervious to bomb and torpedo attacks

An archival photo showing the scale model of Habbakuk in Patricia Lake. It was given a roof to appear like a boathouse in the lake.

DID YOU KNOW?

Emerald Bay is one of the prettiest spots on Upper Waterton Lake and it also has a secret. Deep below the surface of the turquoise waters is a sunken turn-of-the-century steam paddlewheeler that was christened the *Gertrude* when it was built in 1907. First used in a sawmill operation that operated on the lake, it later became an excursion vessel and was finally turned into a tea room and restaurant. In 1918 Parks Canada officials in Waterton ordered that the boat be removed or scuttled, so the owners sunk it in the deep waters of Emerald Bay — right behind the famous Prince of Wales Hotel. This wreck is also popular with scuba divers.

and could be easily repaired by pouring water into any holes or cracks and freezing it.

With the approval of British Prime Minister Winston Churchill and with some support from the United States, naval architects and engineers began to build a scale model of Habbakuk on remote Patricia Lake in 1943. The vessel was built from a substance called pykrete, which is made from a mixture of frozen paper pulp and sea water and was said to be almost as strong as concrete.

Since ice is inexpensive to make, especially during the winter in Jasper, the entire budget for the project was limited to £5,000. Unfortunately, the budget had not accounted for the large quantities of steel that were required for the skeleton of the ship. With spiralling steel costs and other technical issues,

the British eventually realized that the budget was unrealistic and the ship would not be ready in time. In late 1943 they decided to scuttle the project and left the ship to sink in place.

In the 1970s the remains of the ship were discovered in Patricia Lake, and in 1989 a plaque commemorating the Habbakuk was placed on the shore.

You don't picture the cold lakes of the Canadian Rockies as great diving sites, but today the Habbakuk is one of the more interesting and popular dive sites in Alberta. For some, standing on the shoreline near the small plaque that commemorates the project's existence is close enough. You can also rent a canoe or kayak and paddle across the lake.

76 MEDICINE LAKE

Address Maligne Road, Jasper National Park, AB
Telephone (403) 721-3975 | **Website** albertaparks.ca/parks/central/medicine-lake-pra

Jasper's Mysterious Disappearing Lake

In the sunny summer months, Medicine Lake looks like an ordinary alpine lake. But when the weather turns cold, this 7-kilometre-long lake drains and becomes a muddy flat with a stream running through it. This is partly because Medicine Lake isn't really a lake. Indigenous Peoples noticed that the lake disappeared each year and believed it to be the work of "big medicine," which is how the lake got its name.

One of the World's Largest Underground Cave Systems

Medicine Lake is a geologic anomaly. It is technically an area where the Maligne River backs up during the warm summer months when snow and glacial meltwater is at its peak. There is an extensive underground cave system the river flows into. It has been estimated that about 24,000 litres of water drain through the cave system every second. It is like a bathtub that is constantly draining. When the water flows

In the summer, Medicine Lake appears to be an ordinary alpine lake.

By the winter, much of Medicine Lake's water has drained, and it better resembles a frozen muddy flat.

in faster than it drains out, the tub fills up and the lake appears.

In the 1970s researchers tried to determine how extensive the underground cave system was using biodegradable dye. They discovered that the dye began resurfacing about 17 kilometres downstream from where it drained. It found its way into many lakes and rivers in the area, indicating that the underground cave drainage system is likely one of the most extensive in the world.

DID YOU KNOW?

In 1927 Medicine Lake was stocked with eastern brook trout, and the fish have managed to survive even though the lake drains every winter.

Watch for wildlife when you visit the lake. You may see bald eagles, bears, bighorn sheep, mule deer, caribou, ospreys and other wildlife nearby. The lake is located about 20 kilometres southeast of the town of Jasper and is approximately 7 kilometres long. There is a viewing platform with interpretive signage near the parking area and some steps that lead you to a rough trail near the shoreline.

Attempts to Plug the Drain

In the 1950s someone got the idea to start a ferry service across Medicine Lake. They decided if they could stop the lake from draining, this would make the ferry service viable. They tried plugging the drain with old mattresses and two truckloads of newspapers, but were unsuccessful.

This peaceful cemetery is nearly all that's left of the town of Mountain Park.

MOUNTAIN PARK CEMETERY

Address Mountain Park, AB | **Telephone** (780) 865-2154 | **Website** albertaparks.ca/parks/central /whitehorse-wpp/information-facilities/trails/mountain-park-cemetery-historic-mining-townsite

Canada's Highest Cemetery Is in a Ghost Town

At 1,890 metres above sea level, Mountain Park Cemetery is not only the highest cemetery in Canada but also the highest cemetery in the British Commonwealth. Even though it is part of a ghost town, it has been lovingly restored by former residents, friends and family members of those buried there. It's a beautiful cemetery on a hillside near the ghost town of Mountain Park, and it is fascinating to explore.

Mountain Park was once a thriving coal mining town of 1,500 residents. Mountain Park Coal Company Limited began operations between 1912 and 1914, producing steam coal for railroad use. As railroad companies began replacing steam locomotives with diesel, the demand for steam coal went down. This, combined with a flood of the McLeod River, which washed out the railroad bed used to transport coal, marked the end of the Mountain Park mine. When the mine closed in 1950, the town was soon abandoned.

Little remains of Mountain Park today besides the cemetery, some abandoned rail lines and a few remnants of the mine. Mountain Park Cemetery is about 15 kilometres southeast of Cadomin, near Whitehorse Creek Provincial Recreation Area. It's marked on Google Maps, but not entirely accurately. When you're travelling from Cadomin, the cemetery is actually before the point where Google Maps says it is. Look for a side road going up a hill on the left side of Grave Flats Road.

Mountain Park Cemetery is the final resting place for people who once lived in the ghost town of Mountain Park. This includes men who worked in the mines as well as their families and other members of the community.

Approximately 20 veterans who served in World War I and World War II are buried in the cemetery, and there is a special veterans memorial at the site.

The road is a gravel mining road that is very rough — especially between Cadomin and the cemetery. A four-wheel drive vehicle with good tires is recommended, and the road is not plowed in winter. It is, however, worth the effort to get to Mountain Park Cemetery to take in the views from Canada's highest cemetery and to see what's left of the community that was once Canada's highest town.

DID YOU KNOW?

The elevation of Lake Louise is 1,750 metres, making it the highest community in Canada.

78 MALIGNE LAKE and SPIRIT ISLAND

Address Jasper National Park, AB | **Telephone** (780) 852-6176
Website pc.gc.ca/en/pn-np/ab/jasper/activ/itineraires-itineraries/lac-maligne

The Largest Natural Lake in the Canadian Rockies

A view of Maligne Lake in the Alberta Rockies.

At 22 kilometres long, Maligne Lake is one of the world's largest glacier-fed lakes and the largest natural lake in the Canadian Rockies. The beautiful turquoise lake in Jasper National Park also has ties to one of the only female explorers of the early 20th century.

Who Discovered Maligne Lake?

Let's be honest, Indigenous Peoples were well acquainted with all the lakes and mountains in the Canadian Rockies. These places had been

Spirit Island is one of the most photographed spots in Canada.

found and named long before Europeans came along and began "discovering" them — often with the assistance of Indigenous guides. The Stoney Nakoda name for Maligne Lake was *Chaba Imne*, which means "Beaver Lake." The first European known to see the lake was Henry MacLeod, a surveyor looking for a possible route for the Canadian Pacific Railway. In 1875 he was on a high mountain and saw the lake from a distance. In 1907 Mary Schäffer, a wealthy Quaker widow from Philadelphia, led an expedition to the lake and explored the area. She followed a map drawn by an Indigenous man named Samson Beaver. She wrote about her adventures, and her popular book *Old Indian Trails of the Canadian Rockies* inspired others to travel

to what is now Jasper National Park. Schäffer returned to survey the lake a few years later for the Geographic Board of Canada. Her work was instrumental in getting the lake included as part of Jasper National Park.

There are three backcountry campgrounds at Maligne Lake that can only be reached by boat. There are also many hiking trails near the lake, including the Skyline Trail, an epic backpacking trail. Cycling, canoeing, kayaking and fishing are popular summer activities on the lake. Cross-country skiing and snowshoeing are favoured in the winter. Wildlife is abundant near the lake; watch for moose, bears, deer, bighorn sheep and rare appearances by woodland caribou.

In the summer you can rent boats at the historic Maligne Lake Boathouse or book a boat cruise to see more of the lake. There is also a gift shop and three restaurants at the head of the lake.

Spirit Island

Spirit Island is the undisputed photographic highlight of Maligne Lake. In 1960 an image of Spirit Island taken by Peter Gales hung in Kodak's Colorama showcase in New York's Grand Central Terminal. For many, it represents the Canadian Rockies. Despite its name, Spirit Island isn't really an island; most of the year it's connected to the shore. It lies 14 kilometres from the docks at the head of the lake and can only be reached by boat — either a boat cruise or a long paddle.

79 BRAZEAU COLLIERIES and NORDEGG NATIONAL HISTORIC SITE

Address David Thompson Highway (Highway 11), Nordegg, AB | **Telephone** (403) 845-4444
Website clearwatercounty.ca/p/nordegg-heritage-centre

One of the Largest Historic Industrial Sites in Canada

The blocked entrance to the coal mine at Brazeau Collieries.

Brazeau Collieries was established in 1911, and the town of Nordegg was established 1914 by a German entrepreneur named Martin Nordegg. The collieries provided coal for the Canadian Northern Railway and are now part of both a provincial and national historic site. It is one of the largest historic industrial sites in Canada. Guided tours are offered during the summer months and lend some insight into both the operation of the coal mine and the lives of the miners who worked there.

A major coal producer in the Rocky Mountain region, Brazeau Collieries operated from 1911 to 1955, producing more than 10 million tonnes of coal. The latest surface preparation techniques were used to produce coal and briquettes for railway and household use. The site is the best-surviving

The Brazeau Collieries mine site, now part of a national historic site of Canada.

Abandoned cars lend a ghostly feeling to this once-productive industrial site.

example of a surface plant in this mountainous region.

In 2001 the Government of Canada recognized the important role this site played in steam coal development and the coal industry of Alberta by creating the Nordegg National Historic Site of Canada. It includes all the coal mining related resources at the Brazeau Collieries site as well as what remains of the company town. There are many buildings on the site, including a power plant, repair workshops, a wash house, a lamp house, an administrative building and residences. The earliest structures were built of wood, but in time more fire-resistant materials were used, such as brick, concrete and steel. The 1951 steel-framed and aluminum-sided coal-processing complex is fully equipped with all the original machinery.

The town of Nordegg was built to be a forward-thinking community for those who worked at the mine. A tour of this national historic site helps you understand what life was like in a busy coal community in the early 1900s to 1955. Since the industrial site is largely intact, you can see where the miners hung up their gear and where they processed the coal and loaded the briquettes into railcars. The actual mine site is blocked off, so you cannot enter it.

The Nordegg Name Change

In 1909 Martin Cohn legally changed his last name to Nordegg. He was originally from Germany, and the name Nordegg translates very roughly to "north corner" in German. If not for the name change, the town of Nordegg and the Nordegg Coal Basin that is located nearby would have had different names. World War I broke out in July 1914, the same year the town of Nordegg was established. Canada's German immigrants were not trusted during the conflict. Brazeau Collieries had been running since 1911 and, at first, Martin Nordegg was permitted to remain and supervise mining operations. But in the summer of 1915 he was asked to leave Canada. He was allowed to return in 1921, but he was eventually voted out of the company that he started.

80 ABRAHAM LAKE

Address David Thompson Highway near Cline River, AB | **Telephone** n/a
Website explorenordegg.ca/guide/see-do/winter-adventures/abraham-lake-ice-bubbles

The World's Most Beautiful Ice Bubbles

There was a time when Abraham Lake was not well known, but those days are long gone. Gorgeous pictures of ice bubbles at Abraham Lake have been making their way around social media sites for a few years. Hundreds of thousands of people around the world have seen the posts, and the lake is now an Instagram-famous tourism phenomenon.

Each winter, pockets of methane gas freeze in layers in the lake's ice, and when the sun shines just right they look like jewels glistening under the surface. Methane gas bubbles are formed when bacteria break down organic matter at the bottom of the lake. As the gas slowly rises, it freezes in ice bubble layers. The phenomenon is found in other lakes, but it's more visible in Abraham Lake because high winds in that area keep the ice clear of snow. When you put the bubbles in the foreground of a photograph and the mountains in the background, you get an incredibly beautiful photo op.

A frozen Abraham Lake with its exquisite ice bubbles.

How to See the Ice Bubbles

You can either go see the ice bubbles on your own or book a tour. The nice thing about a tour is your guide will know the safest and best places to access the ice. There are several companies that offer guided tours. There are even helicopter ice bubble tours.

Abraham Lake is a human-made reservoir that was created when the Bighorn Dam was constructed. It is Alberta's largest reservoir and it takes a long time to freeze. January and February are the best months to go see the ice bubbles. If you want the best photographs, don't go when it's snowing or after a fresh snow. Bring a snow shovel and a broom as a precaution in case the ice is covered with snow when you get there. You can use them to clear a portion of the ice if necessary. Be aware that there are some places on the lake where the ice can be unstable. It's important to be cautious and careful that the ice is thick enough to support your weight.

The bubbles are actually pockets of methane gas frozen in layers.

One of the best access points to the lake in winter is near the sign for Hoodoo Creek. That's the place where most guided tours access the lake. You can either pull over to the side of the David Thompson Highway or drive down the side road that's near Hoodoo Creek. Some people try to access the lake at Preacher's Point, but the ice can be steep there and if you manage to get down to the ice, you might find it difficult to get back up. The ice tends to be flat and stable near the Hoodoo Creek area. Ice cleats or shoes with good grips can be very helpful when you're walking out on the frozen lake.

With or without bubbles, Abraham Lake is breathtaking in winter. If you're fortunate to see the lake on a clear, snow-free day, you'll get a memorable ice bubble experience you are unlikely to find anywhere else.

More Winter Fun in David Thompson Country

Crescent Falls is beautiful in winter. If you wear ice cleats, you can hike to the base of the frozen waterfall for a spectacular image. Crimson Lake Provincial Park is also wonderful in winter, with skating rinks, winter camping, cross-country ski trails and "Snowy Saturdays" events.

81 WHIRLPOOL POINT LIMBER PINE

Address David Thompson Highway (Highway 11), 21 kilometres northeast of Saskatchewan River Crossing, AB
Telephone n/a | **Website** n/a

The Oldest Tree in Alberta

The oldest living thing in Alberta predates the birth of Jesus Christ. The Whirlpool Point Limber Pine is estimated to be 2,500 to 3,000 years old, according to a website called monumentaltrees.com. The age estimation is based on trunk core samples, trunk measurements and height measurements from the presumed point of germination. The tree has multiple trunks and this makes it difficult to accurately determine its age. Some experts have differing age estimates, but if monumentaltrees.com is correct, it is the oldest living limber pine in the world.

The limber pine (*Pinus flexilis*) is a species of the pine tree family that is found in the mountains of Canada, the Western United States and parts of Mexico. A number of limber pines around the world have been documented to live hundreds and, in some cases, thousands of years.

Limber pines grow in subalpine environments. You'll typically see single trees or spaced groups of trees on rocky terrain. The tree roots work their way into the spaces between the rocks and often survive in harsh conditions. This partly explains why they tend to be scrubby twisted trees that grow slowly and look like a set piece from the *Lord of the Rings* film series.

There are no signs identifying the location of this tree and finding it is part of the fun. The tree is not on Google Maps and neither is Whirlpool Point. Whirlpool Point is a point of land that projects into a bend along the North Saskatchewan River between Saskatchewan River Crossing and the Cline River.

The Whirlpool Point Limber Pine, on the banks of the North Saskatchewan River.

DID YOU KNOW?

Alberta has many unique old trees. You'll find a comprehensive list in the book *Heritage Trees of Alberta*, which was published in 2008 and is available in most public libraries. Some fascinating trees include the ancient plains cottonwood trees in Medicine Hat's Police Point Park, the Holowach Tree in downtown Edmonton and the old Douglas firs along the Douglas Fir Trail in Calgary. Interestingly, the book lists the Whirlpool Point Limber Pine simply as "1000 plus years of age."

The twisted trunk of this ancient limber pine.

Directions to Whirlpool Point

From Saskatchewan River Crossing, drive northeast on Highway 11 for about 21 kilometres. You are close when you reach a roadside pullout on the right side with an interpretive sign about Kootenay Plains Ecological Reserve. There is a map on the sign that shows the location of Whirlpool Point. Drive a little farther up the road and you will see a metal guardrail near the top of a hill. There is an old road on the hill on the other side of the guardrail. Farther along Highway 11 is a larger highway pullout on the left side of the road. Park there and walk back to the old road near the guardrail.

As you walk along the old road and trail, you will come to a cairn in honour of "The Original Trail Blazers." If you find the cairn, you're in the right place. It was built in 1980 to honour the first trip by car from Rocky Mountain House to Saskatchewan River Crossing, which took place in 1940. The dangerous journey took 10 days back then. Today it takes less than two hours. The cairn sits near Whirlpool Point, where you will find many ancient limber pines.

You'll know the oldest limber pine when you see it. The ancient, twisted tree is near the North Saskatchewan River, almost hanging over the water. Be gentle in this ancient tree's presence and keep back from its roots to help protect it.

82 YA HA TINDA RANCH

Address Bighorn Campground, Banff National Park, AB
Telephone (403) 770-3085 | **Website** pc.gc.ca/en/pn-np/ab/banff/activ/cheval-horse/YaHaTinda

The Only Federally Operated Working Horse Ranch in Canada

Visitors can ride along trail routes within Ya Ha Tinda Ranch.

Ya Ha Tinda is not a national park, but this beautiful 3,945-hectare site is open to the public, with some restrictions. It is the only federally operated working horse ranch in Canada. There are spectacular mountain views, 27 kilometres of riverfront, abundant wildlife, a campground and trails that can be enjoyed on foot or horseback.

Why Does the Federal Government Need a Working Horse Ranch?

There are thousands of kilometres of trails inside the national parks, and some places in the backcountry of the Rockies are particularly difficult to access. Since the establishment of Canada's first national park in 1885, park wardens have patrolled the backcountry of specific mountain parks on horseback. Even today there is no better way to do the job than from atop a horse. Ya Ha Tinda Ranch is the place where Parks Canada patrol horses spend the winter months and where they are trained.

History of Ya Ha Tinda Ranch

The ranch was originally established by the Brewster Brothers Transfer Company in the early 1900s. The

176

company used the ranch to raise and break horses for their outfitting business. At that time the ranch was inside what was then called Rocky Mountains National Park, but the boundaries of the park changed over the years, and the ranch is now west of the official park boundaries of Banff National Park.

In 1917 Parks Canada took over the ranch to use as a winter range, breeding and training facility for park horses. In 2003 the breeding program was discontinued. The ranch now purchases weanlings each year, raising them and training them over four years before assigning them to the various mountain parks. The horses return to the ranch each winter.

With plenty of varied terrain, Ya Ha Tinda provides the perfect conditions for training park horses. It also has an abundance of wildlife. Grizzly bears, black bears, wolves, cougars, moose, deer, elk and bighorn sheep can all be found here. You may also see domestic bison at the ranch. Bison were brought in to train the horses prior to the reintroduction of wild bison to Banff National Park in 2017.

Indigenous Use and the Meaning of Ya Ha Tinda

Ya Ha Tinda means "Mountain Prairie" in the Stoney Nakoda language. This area has been used by Indigenous Peoples for over 9,400 years. Archaeologists have

A view of the horse barn at Ya Ha Tinda Ranch.

Interpretive signage at the Bighorn Campground.

discovered many camps, tipi rings and other artifacts, including the remains of prehistoric bison. It has been speculated that the Red Deer River was a major trading route since more camps exist along the river toward the Continental Divide.

Visiting Ya Ha Tinda

Ya Ha Tinda is private deeded land, owned by the federal government and managed by Parks Canada. Hikers and horse owners are welcome to use and enjoy the area and its incredible scenery. The on-site Bighorn Campground

is equipped with tie stalls and high lines. The campground is maintained by the Friends of the Eastern Slopes Association and funded by donations and voluntary memberships. There are rules for using the campground and riding inside the ranch. The most important of these is to stay on designated trails and not to travel within fenced pastures. There are 10 trail routes through the site that can be enjoyed on foot or horseback. Tours of the ranch buildings area are available, with schedules posted at the campground.

83 SKOKI LODGE NATIONAL HISTORIC SITE

Address 11 km northeast of Lake Louise Ski Area, Banff National Park, AB
Telephone (403) 522-1347 | **Website** skoki.com

One of North America's Oldest Backcountry Ski Lodges

The rustic exterior of Skoki Lodge.

Commercial alpine skiing began in the Lake Louise region of Banff National Park with the establishment of Skoki Lodge. When the lodge opened in 1931, skiing had just begun to emerge as a popular form of winter recreation in the Rockies. Today, there are three downhill ski resorts in Banff National Park, several backcountry lodges and many cross-country ski trails. The key role Skoki Lodge played in the development of ski tourism in Banff National Park played a part in it being declared a national historic site in 1992.

Skoki Lodge is a backcountry ski lodge that was built by a group of backcountry ski enthusiasts from logs harvested near the site. It hasn't changed much since the 1930s. There are six heritage buildings linked by a series of footpaths. Rustic outhouses serve as bathroom facilities.

The lodge is situated on the banks of Little Pipestone Creek in the Skoki Valley north of Lake Louise. Winter guests can catch a shuttle to the trailhead or ride the gondola at Lake Louise Ski Resort and ski down to the start of the trail near Temple Lodge. Either way, it's an 11-kilometre, three-and-a-half-hour cross-country or ski touring trek over two mountain passes with a 500-metre elevation gain to reach the lodge in winter. In summer, guests hike to the lodge.

There is no electricity or running water available to guests, but Skoki Lodge is famous for providing

The breathtaking alpine scenery surrounding Skoki Lodge.

delicious meals, beautiful scenery and access to incredible backcountry for skiing, snowshoeing, climbing and hiking. At an elevation of 2,165 metres, the lodge is one of the highest-elevated overnight accommodations in the Alberta Rockies. Inside the main lodge is a small library, historical photos and ski equipment dating to the 1930s. Skoki Lodge is a special place that beckons modern travellers for the same reasons today as it did when it first opened.

Prince William and Kate's Rustic Honeymoon Hideaway

In 2011, barely two months after their wedding, Prince William and Catherine, the Duke and Duchess of Cambridge, made their first royal tour as a married couple. The whirlwind nine-day royal tour of Canada saw the newlywed couple visit Ontario, Quebec, Prince Edward Island, Northwest Territories and Alberta. There were many firsts, including the first use of the Duke of Cambridge's personal Canadian flag, the first Canadian citizenship ceremony attended by royalty and the first-time royalty had slipped away for a romantic escape to a rustic backcountry lodge. Unlike most guests who hike or ski to Skoki Lodge, the Duke and Duchess of Cambridge were flown in by helicopter. The couple stayed in the riverside cabin and enjoyed the magnificent mountain scenery — surely a welcome respite from the 1,300 accredited media who followed their first royal tour.

What Is Halfway Hut and Is It Really Haunted?

Halfway Hut is a refuge cabin located at the midway point between the Canadian Pacific Railway station at Lake Louise and Skoki Lodge. It was built as an overnight shelter along the uphill trail for ski tourists travelling to the lodge, but it functions today as a day shelter. The rustic log building is in the Ptarmigan Valley of Banff National Park. Many locals believe the hut is haunted, but they can't agree on which ghosts are doing the haunting. In the 1930s and '40s, three separate avalanches in the region killed a renowned mathematician, a ski guide and two brothers. It's also said that a Calgary painter wasted away in the cabin while trying to create the perfect painting of the Rockies. According to legend, he found the scenery so magnificent that he never wanted to leave. One thing is certain — if you're skiing or hiking to Skoki, you'll want to stop at Halfway Hut.

84 ICEFIELDS PARKWAY

Address Icefields Parkway (Highway 93), AB
Telephone n/a | **Website** pc.gc.ca/en/pn-np/ab/banff/visit/les10-top10/glaciers-icefields

Alberta's Drive of a Lifetime

Parker Ridge Trail.

The Icefields Parkway, otherwise known as Highway 93, is one of the most scenic roadways on the planet. National Geographic called it the drive of a lifetime because it is so staggeringly beautiful. Soaring mountain peaks, glaciers, waterfalls and impossibly blue lakes fill your windshield, and there's wildlife to be seen along the way, too.

The fascinating landscape along the Icefields Parkway dates back millions of years, but the roadway itself was an economic project by the Government of Canada during the Great Depression. In 1931 construction began to turn what was known as the "Wonder Trail" into a roadway. Because of the rugged terrain and the simple tools available for the job, it took 600 men 10 years to complete the project. The road made this incredibly beautiful and

Tangle Creek Falls.

Columbia Icefield Skywalk.

The Athabasca Glacier.

rugged wilderness accessible to all. In 1961 the road was paved and realigned. In a typical year more than 1.2 million people travel the Icefields Parkway — most of them in summer.

It's a 233-kilometre drive between Lake Louise and Jasper on the Icefields Parkway, and if you wanted to, you could make the drive in under three hours. But why rush the tour of a lifetime? If you get the chance to drive it, take your time and enjoy every minute of it. With Lake Louise as the starting point, here are some of the top scenic stops on this road trip and where you'll find them:

KM 39: Bow Lake – scenic pullout.

KM 46: Peyto Lake/Bow Summit Viewpoint – short trail to viewpoints (at 1.5 kilometres and 6 kilometres).

KM 56: Mistaya Canyon – 1.8-kilometre loop trail through a beautiful canyon.

KM 80: Saskatchewan River Crossing – fuel, bathrooms and food services.

KM 107: Weeping Wall Viewpoint – scenic pullout.

KM 121: Parker Ridge Trailhead – 5.1-kilometre steep trail to views of the Saskatchewan Glacier.

KM 127: Wilcox Pass Trailhead – 9.3-kilometre steep trail to a viewpoint over the Athabasca Glacier.

KM 130: Columbia Icefield Discovery Centre – interpretive centre with food and bathrooms. It is a booking and departure point for Athabasca Glacier and Skywalk tours.

KM 131: Athabasca Glacier – 1.4-kilometre roundtrip to the toe of the glacier and back.

KM 136: Columbia Icefield Skywalk – glass walkway tours.

KM 137: Tangle Creek Falls – scenic pullout.

KM 147: Beauty Creek to Stanley Falls – 3.9-kilometre trail passing many waterfalls.

KM 179: Sunwapta Falls – short walk to the upper falls and a 3.2-kilometre trail to the lower falls.

KM 202: Athabasca Falls – 1-kilometre paved trail to the most powerful waterfall in the Canadian Rockies.

KM 233: Town of Jasper

85 CASTLE MOUNTAIN INTERNMENT CAMP

Address Bow Valley Parkway (Highway 1A), Castle Junction, AB | **Telephone** n/a | **Website** n/a

Reliving Dark Moments in Canada's History

Most people who drive along the Bow Valley Parkway are unaware that part of this beautiful road was constructed by "prisoners of war" held in internment camps during World War I. More than 600 internees at the Castle Mountain Internment Camp were forced to work eight hours a day, six days a week with axes, picks and wheelbarrows. They had to walk long distances to get to the worksite, and this often stretched the workday to 13 hours. A small memorial with interpretive signs sits at the edge of the road. It's worth a stop.

In 1914, during World War I, Canada implemented the War Measures Act. Between 1914 and 1920 more than 8,500 settler immigrants from countries at war with Canada were classified as enemy aliens and interned as prisoners of war. Most immigrant prisoners were of Ukrainian, Austrian, Hungarian and German descent. Ukrainian immigrants were by far the largest group interned and used as military

A view of Castle Mountain.

conscript labour for government work projects.

The Castle Mountain camp was the first of the camps located in one of the dominion parks, now known as national parks.

The camp was open from July 1915 to July 1917. In addition to building the road, prisoners of war worked on a variety of other projects, including quarrying stone for the Banff Springs Hotel and constructing the hotel's tennis courts and golf course.

Unfortunately, the Canadian government did not learn from its mistakes. During World War II, over 21,000 Japanese Canadians were interned as prisoners of war under the War Measures Act. Their homes, possessions and businesses were sold by the government to pay for their detention.

There are dark moments in Canadian and Albertan history. It's important to remember them so that they won't be repeated.

What's in a Name?

Castle Mountain has long been one of the most striking peaks between Banff and Jasper, but it hasn't always been called Castle Mountain. From 1949 to 1979 the iconic peak was renamed Mount Eisenhower. Scottish geologist James Hector named the peak Castle Mountain in 1858 because the 11-kilometre-long mountain resembles an ancient fortress with steep walls. When U.S. General Dwight D. Eisenhower, Supreme Commander of the Allied Expeditionary Force in Europe, visited Canada in 1949, Prime Minister William Lyon Mackenzie King ordered the Geographic Board of Canada to officially change Castle Mountain to "Mount Eisenhower." Eisenhower had been given a castle in Scotland and Canada would not be outdone.

Unfortunately, the prime minister did not consult or inform the Alberta government until after the name had been changed. The provincial government created its own Geographical Names Program to discourage the federal government from renaming any other famous sites. Over the years there was a great deal of controversy and opposition over the mountain's new name. In 1979, 10 years after Eisenhower passed away, the name was changed back to Castle Mountain. A pinnacle on the southeastern side of the mountain is still named Eisenhower Tower.

Archival photos of the Castle Mountain Internment Camp and its internees.

This small memorial is a solemn reminder of Canada's dark history.

The Ink Pots in winter.

The Johnston Canyon hike takes you past breathtaking waterfalls and geological formations.

86 THE INK POTS

Address Johnston Canyon Day-Use Area, Banff National Park, AB
Telephone (403) 762-1550 | **Website** pc.gc.ca/en/pn-np/ab/banff/activ/randonee-hiking/banff

Don't Go Wading in These Cool Springs

Hot springs get a lot of attention in the Canadian Rockies, but no one gets excited about cool springs. Maybe they should. The Ink Pots are a group of seven gorgeous springs in the Johnston Creek Valley in Banff National Park. The springs maintain a constant temperature between 1 and 4 degrees Celsius year-round, which means they are cool on hot summer days and the faster-flowing springs never really freeze over in winter. Many people who visit Johnston Canyon only hike as far as the lower or upper waterfalls and miss seeing the Ink Pots, but they are missing out on something special.

The Ink Pots are classified as karst springs, which are found all over the world. Karst springs form because of an outflow of water through an underground cave system. What makes the Ink Pots unique is that at least two of the ponds have a distinct greenish-blue colour. This is what led to the springs being named the Ink Pots. The brilliant colour of the water is caused by fine silt that is dislodged as water flows up from the spring.

Another interesting thing about these ponds is that some of them have quicksand in the bottom. The upward movement of water and air through the sand-covered bottom of the ponds leads to quicksand conditions, which can extend over a large area of the bottom. In some cases, you can see the water and air bubbling up through the quicksand. The takeaway message here is this: if it's a hot summer day and you want to cool off your feet, sit on the edge and dip them — *don't go wading.*

In the warmer months, the greenish-blue water of the Ink Pots really comes to life.

You can reach the Ink Pots on the Johnston Canyon hike, starting at the Johnston Canyon Day-Use Area. It's 1.2-kilometres to the lower falls, 2.5-kilometres to the upper falls and 6.9-kilometres to the Ink Pots — all one way. If you hike all the way to the Ink Pots, you'll pass both waterfalls along the way. Ice cleats are recommended in winter. There are benches near the Ink Pots and it's a beautiful place to relax and enjoy a picnic.

The pristine waters of Lake Minnewanka contain a sunken town, which can explored by divers.

87 Lake Minnewanka and Minnewanka Landing

Address Lake Minnewanka Scenic Drive, Banff National Park, AB
Telephone (403) 762-1550 | **Website** pc.gc.ca/en/pn-np/ab/banff/visit/les10-top10/minnewanka

The Sunken Ghost Town in Banff

Lake Minnewanka is the largest lake in Banff National Park, and it has a rich history that dates back thousands of years. It has long been recognized for its picturesque beauty. The Stoney Nakoda originally called it *Minn-waki*, which means "Lake of the Spirits." They respected the lake and believed it was home to resident spirits. While it may have spirits, the lake definitely has a sunken town deep under its glassy surface.

Shortly after the establishment of Banff National Park, the area became a popular tourist destination. In 1888 the resort village of Minnewanka Landing was developed, and the first hotel was built. Eventually, more hotels and restaurants were constructed, and cottage lots were made available for lease.

While the lake remains incredibly popular with tourists, the present-day lake is vastly different from its original form. Over the years three dams have been constructed on the lake: the first in 1895, the second in 1912 and the third in 1941. The third dam was built under the War Measures Act by the Calgary Power Company, which argued that the power generated from the dam project would be essential to the war effort.

The third dam raised the water level 30 metres and flooded the townsite of Minnewanka Landing, the 1912 dam and a bridge. Today the lake is 21 kilometres long and 142 metres deep, and these sites are sunk far beneath the water's surface. Scuba divers can enjoy exploring the sunken town — especially during the early spring and late fall, when boat

A day spent paddling Lake Minnewanka can be just as memorable as seeing its sunken town.

traffic is reduced on the lake and the clarity of the water is better. The lake's cold, clear waters have preserved house and hotel foundations, sidewalks, wharfs, an oven, a chimney, a cellar, bridge pilings and the footings for two other dams built in 1895 and 1912.

If you are not a diver, the closest you can get to the sunken townsite is by passing over it on a Lake Minnewanka boat tour. These one-hour tours run from late May to early October.

88 Cave and Basin National Historic Site

Address 311 Cave Avenue, Banff, AB, T1L 1K2 | **Telephone** (403) 762-1566 | **Website** pc.gc.ca/en/lhn-nhs/ab/caveandbasin

The Birthplace of Canada's First National Park

An interior view of Cave and Basin National Historic Site.

Indigenous Peoples knew about the hot springs in what is now Banff National Park for thousands of years and considered them to be sacred, but the springs weren't discovered by European explorers until the mid-1800s. The first recorded reference to hot springs in Banff was by James Hector of the Palliser Expedition in 1859, who was likely led to the site by an Indigenous guide. In 1883 Frank McCabe and brothers Tom and William McCardell, who were all working for the Canadian Pacific Railway, stumbled upon a cave with hot mineral springs when they noticed steam venting from a crack in the rocks on the side of a mountain. The three railway workers descended into the cave using a felled tree, and the

A family takes in the sensory experience of the cave.

following year they built a small cabin nearby with the intention of commercializing the hot springs. When they applied for ownership of the site, there were conflicting claims from other parties. In 1885 the Canadian government settled the dispute by reserving 26 square kilometres around the cave as the Banff Hot Springs Reserve. This was the beginning of Canada's national parks system. Today the site is known as Cave and Basin National Historic Site.

When you visit Cave and Basin, you are visiting the birthplace of Banff National Park and Canada's national parks system. You can see the hot water seeping from the rocks and view excellent interpretive signs and displays. There are also some wonderful outdoor trails to enjoy. Cave and Basin is a fascinating site situated in one of the most dazzling parks on the planet.

The Banff Springs Snail: Banff's Most At-Risk Species That Almost Nobody Knows About

The Banff Springs snail (*Physella johnsoni*) was first identified in 1926, but it took 70 years before any serious research was done on the species. The tiny snail lives in a handful of hot springs in Banff National Park and has been found nowhere else in the world. The largest snails are about the size of an adult's pinky fingernail, but most are about half that size. In April 1997 this small snail made history by being the first mollusc species to be classified by the Committee on the Status of Endangered Wildlife in Canada (COSEWIC). It was originally classified as "threatened," but in 2000 it was reassessed as "endangered." An endangered classification means that a species is "facing imminent extirpation or extinction." There are other species in Banff that are classified by COSEWIC, but none are at greater risk than the Banff Springs snail.

Every species on the planet is important — even a tiny snail. Parks Canada has taken steps to protect existing habitat for the Banff Springs snail and to reintroduce the snail into hot springs it previously occupied. Some of the wild hot springs in Banff have been fenced off to prevent people from disturbing the snail's habitat.

89 THE BANFF TRADING POST

Address 101 Cave Avenue, Banff, AB, T1L 1A9 | **Telephone** (403) 762-2456 | **Website** banfftradingpost.com

The Mystery of Banff's Merman

The exterior of the Banff Trading Post.

For over 100 years a mysterious creature of unknown origin has been on display in the Banff Trading Post. The merman specimen was acquired by Norman Luxton, the original proprietor of the trading post, around 1915. There are conflicting stories about its origins, with some saying it was crafted by Luxton himself, others saying it was purchased from a Javanese salesman and other reports saying it was caught in Lake Minnewanka by a local fisherman and is in fact a genuine merman that originated in Banff.

Admittedly, Banff's merman is a little scary looking. Most North Americans envision mermaids as beautiful creatures thanks to Disney's 1989 animated feature *The Little Mermaid*, based on the fairy tale of Danish author Hans Christian Andersen that was first published in 1837. Legends of mermaids and mermen date back hundreds of years and span many cultures. The oldest legends describe mermaids as sirens who lured fishermen to watery graves. In European folklore, mercreatures had magical

The Banff merman, which can be found in a display at the Banff Trading Post.

Mercreatures were a novelty of interest at the time the Banff merman was first put on display. In 1923 J.E. Standley, founder of Ye Olde Curiosity Shop in Seattle, Washington, presented a mercreature that he said he received from a fisherman named Smith. Seattle newspapers covered the story and further legitimized it. The mercreature is still on display in that shop.

Luxton owned and ran the Banff Trading Post from 1903 to 1961. It was then passed to the Garbert family, who have operated it ever since. Luxton requested that the family never change the store, and the promise has been kept.

There is no charge to visit the Banff Trading Post or to see the merman. You'll find him in a glass cabinet near the back of the store. While you can find other mummified mercreatures in other places around the world, most of them are mermaids or are of unidentified sex. Banff has one of the rare examples of a mummified merman.

powers, and though they were mortal, they were soulless.

We owe the phenomenon of fake mummified mermaids in large part to P.T. Barnum and his sideshow circuit. In 1845 Barnum presented the Feejee Mermaid, which was supposedly caught by a sailor in the tropical waters off Fiji. The specimen was an elaborate hoax created by sewing the top half of a monkey to the bottom half of a large fish and adding some papier mâché details. After Barnum's success showing a monstrosity of questionable origins, other similar creatures began appearing in sideshows and wonder cabinets.

The views are wonderful from the top of Sulphur Mountain, and you can climb a boardwalk to see the cosmic ray station up close.

SULPHUR MOUNTAIN COSMIC RAY STATION NATIONAL HISTORIC SITE

Address Sulfur Mountain Trail, Banff National Park, AB
Telephone (403) 762-1550 | **Website** pc.gc.ca/en/pn-np/ab/banff/culture/cosmic

The Most Important Cosmic Ray Station in Canada

The most important cosmic ray station in Canada was located on the top of Sulphur Mountain in Banff National Park. Between 1957 and 1958, Canadian geophysicists participated in the International Geophysical Year by constructing nine sites to study cosmic rays. The National Research Council built a cosmic ray station laboratory on the top of Sulphur Mountain as one of the sites. The station was run by Dr. B.G. Wilson and two research assistants. Because it was located at an altitude of 2,383 metres, this site was considered the best of the Canadian stations. It ceased operations in 1978 and was dismantled in 1981. The following year it was designated a national historic site, and a bronze plaque was placed near the remains of the building's concrete foundation along with several interpretive signs.

Cosmic rays are atom fragments that enter Earth's atmosphere from outside the solar system. They were first discovered in 1912, and even after over a century of study there are still many mysteries associated with these particles. Most scientists believe cosmic rays originate from supernovas (star explosions), but even that has not been indisputably proven. One thing is certain, Sulphur Mountain Cosmic Ray Station contributed to the world's understanding of cosmic rays and their effect on the Earth's environment.

If you want to visit this national historic site, you have two options: you can hike to the top of Sulphur Mountain or you can take the easy way and ride the Banff Gondola to the top. Either way, it's a journey worth making.

Sulphur Mountain Weather Station – A Recognized Federal Heritage Building

The Sulphur Mountain Weather Station is another interesting historical site at the top of Sulphur Mountain. Constructed in 1902 this meteorological observatory was built on a high point on the northern end of Sulphur Mountain. It was constructed out of limestone that was gathered from the mountain. Norman Bethune Sanson was the meteorologist in charge of the weather station from 1903 to 1945. Sanson climbed the peak regularly in all seasons to visit the weather observatory. His weather reports were printed in the local newspaper under the pseudonym "Seer Altudinus." On July 1, 1931, at the age of 69, he was awarded the Freedom of Sulphur Mountain medal in honour of his 1,000th ascent of the mountain.

In 1948 the peak on which the weather station sits was officially named Sanson Peak. Norman Sanson was the curator for the Banff Park Museum for 35 years, and he had a collection of more than 5,000 botanical samples from the Canadian Rockies. He was a remarkable person who contributed to Banff National Park in many ways. A commemorative plaque marks his home at 110 Muskrat Street in the town of Banff.

91 RAT'S NEST CAVE

Address Bow Valley Trail (Highway 1A), near Canmore, AB
Telephone (403) 678-8819 (Canmore Cave Tours) | **Website** canmorecavetours.com

A Fascinating and Unusual Provincial Historic Site

There are many unique geological formations inside Rat's Nest Cave.

On the south slope of Grotto Mountain, not far from Canmore, is one of Alberta's most unique and interesting provincial historic sites. A cave is not your typical historic site, but this one is special. Rat's Nest Cave is one of Canada's longest and deepest caves, with 4 kilometres of cave explored and documented. The cave reaches depths of 245 metres and is home to stalagmites, stalactites, primitive pictographs, ancient bones and incredibly beautiful geological formations. Though many caves are inaccessible to all but experienced speleologists, this cave can be accessed by complete novices on a guided tour.

A young cave explorer climbs down a narrow passage.

Rat's Nest Cave is a limestone cave that was formed millions of years ago. It began as a fracture in the limestone that became an underground waterway. As the Bow Glacier retreated, massive amounts of water flowed through Rat's Nest Cave and expanded the fracture in the limestone. About 12,000 to 13,000 years ago, the Bow Glacier made its final retreat, and the water slowly emptied from Rat's Nest Cave. Spectacular travertine formations were created when calcium carbonate in the limestone was precipitated as the cave dried out.

Once the cave was dry, it provided shelter to a wide variety of animal species. The cave contains the skeletal remains of more than 30 mammalian species as well as palaeontological specimens of birds, snakes, fish and amphibians. It also contains prehistoric tools that are about 3,000 years old as well as ancient pictographs — evidence that it was also used by humans.

Rat's Nest Cave has been a provincial historic site since 1987. Access is restricted to protect the cave and its delicate environment. In 1992 Charles "Chas" Yonge, an experienced speleologist, started Canmore Cave Tours, the only company that offers guided tours through Rat's Nest Cave. Though this cave has been extensively explored, a new passage was discovered in 2019 by members of a local caving club. The discovery led to the cave being remapped and may lead to additional areas for cavers to safely explore.

Experienced and novice speleologists will love exploring Rat's Nest Cave.

92 HEART CREEK BUNKER

Address Highway 1 (Trans-Canada Highway) at Lac des Arcs, AB
Telephone (403) 678-0760 | **Website** albertaparks.ca/parks/kananaskis/heart-creek-pra

Hiking Inside a Cold War Remnant

If hiking inside a partially completed nuclear shelter in the Canadian Rockies isn't unusual, nothing is. Heart Creek Bunker began as a Cold War-era business idea by a Calgary-based company called Rocky Mountain Vaults & Archives Ltd. The plan was to construct a facility where businesses and the government could keep important records safe in the event of a nuclear disaster. To be effective, the site needed to be in a relatively isolated location that was unlikely to be bombed.

The company decided to build a cave on the side of Mount McGillivray, and after getting government approval, construction began in 1969. A 50-metre main tunnel was built along with a 40-metre side tunnel before construction stopped.

It's uncertain why the business failed and the vault was never completed. Some have speculated that construction was halted because moisture was discovered inside the limestone cave — a situation that is not ideal for document storage. It's also possible there was not enough demand for the service being offered or that the company simply ran out of money.

Regardless of the reasons, a huge humanmade cave was left on the side of Mount McGillivray near Heart Creek in Kananaskis Country. For years it was a secret party location for local youths. Today Heart Creek Bunker has become a popular hiking destination where visitors can explore caves that are a visible reminder of the Cold War and the crumbled dreams of a business that hoped to capitalize on it.

The hike to Heart Creek Bunker is not difficult.

The entrance to Heart Creek Bunker, a partially completed nuclear shelter.

A headlamp or flashlight is useful to explore Heart Creek Bunker.

It begins from the Heart Creek Day-Use Area, which is also the starting point for another family-friendly 2.8-kilometre return hike known as the Heart Creek hike. If you have enough time and energy, you could do both hikes in one day. The day-use area is in Bow Valley Provincial Park on the south side of the Trans-Canada Highway across from Lac des Arcs. It is accessible whether you are coming from the east or west on the highway, and there are pit toilets at the day-use area.

The Heart Creek Bunker hike is not as well marked as the Heart Creek hike, but it's an easy 4-kilometre return hike with 218 metres of elevation gain. From the parking lot, take the path leading west. You'll pass a washed-out gravel area, and then you'll reach a wide trail that gradually switchbacks up the side of the mountain to the cave's entrance.

A cellphone light will be enough to light up the first tunnel of the cave, but you really should bring a headlamp or a flashlight for each hiker in your group. As you get deeper inside the cave, it gets very dark. Not surprisingly, there is a lot of graffiti inside. A flashlight lets you see the graffiti and also the blast marks that helped to create the cave.

The Heart Creek hike and the Heart Creek Bunker hike are both very popular — especially in summer. The parking lot and the trails get busy. If you want to beat the crowds, arrive earlier in the day. As with any hike in the Canadian Rockies, carry bear spray and make plenty of noise as you hike along the trails.

DID YOU KNOW?

In the 1950s and '60s the Government of Canada built nuclear fallout shelters across the country to ensure continuity of government in the event of a nuclear attack. These facilities were officially called Emergency Government Headquarters, but opposition politicians nicknamed them "Diefenbunkers," because Prime Minister John Diefenbaker authorized the construction.

Alberta's Diefenbunker was located at Canadian Forces Base Penhold. It consisted of two nuclear fallout shelters. In 1994 the base and the Diefenbunker were decommissioned, and in 1999 the bunker was sold privately. When the new owners advertised the facility for resale, rumours began that a criminal motorcycle gang, possibly the Hells Angels, was interested in purchasing the bunker. The federal government bought the Penhold Diefenbunker back in 2001 and demolished it.

Wolfdogs, exotic pets which are the result of breeding domestic dogs with wolves, are often brought to the sanctuary because they can be difficult to handle as they get older.

Guests on the Interactive Tour can spend one-on-one time with some of the sanctuary's ambassador wolfdogs.

The sanctuary has 11 enclosures protecting 33 permanent wolfdogs, which includes 10 ambassador wolfdogs.

93 Yamnuska WOLFDOG Sanctuary

Address 263156 Range Road 53, Cochrane, AB, T0M 2E0
Telephone (587) 890-9653 | **Website** yamnuskawolfdogsanctuary.com

A Howling Good Time at Alberta's Only Wolfdog Sanctuary

Established in 2011 Yamnuska Wolfdog Sanctuary was created to educate visitors about wolfdogs and wolves. Alberta's only wolfdog sanctuary is located 14 kilometres northwest of Cochrane on 65 hectares of land. As the name implies, wolfdogs are the result of breeding domestic dogs with wolves. They are typically bred by backyard breeders as exotic pets. People who buy wolfdog puppies can usually manage them at first but may have difficulty as they grow older and become more aggressive. Wolfdog traits can vary depending on the breed of domestic dog, the amount of wolf content in the animal and the treatment the animal receives. Sadly, many pet wolfdogs end up euthanized or in shelters.

At Yamnuska Wolfdog Sanctuary, visitors can enjoy an up-close experience with wolf-dogs and learn about their characteristics. It's an opportunity to gain a better understanding about wolf behaviour and how it fundamentally differs from domestic dogs. Visitors also learn about the importance of wolves in nature and why they should be protected in their natural environment.

There are currently three tours at the Yamnuska Wolfdog Sanctuary: the Interactive Tour, the Introductory Tour and the Sanctuary Walk. The Interactive Tour is a semi-private guided sanctuary experience that gives you one-on-one time with the sanctuary's ambassador wolfdogs and plenty of photo ops. You can go inside animal enclosures, but you must be at least 15 years of age to do this tour. The Introductory Tour is a guided tour that provides you with information about the wolfdogs and wolves. The minimum age is 10 for this tour. The Sanctuary Walk is a self-guided walk through the refuge. The minimum age is 6 and there are 11 enclosures to explore. Besides age restrictions for specific tours, the sanctuary has other rules designed to protect both the wolfdogs and visitors. Visit the website so that you know the rules and are dressed appropriately before you visit the sanctuary.

Wolfdogs are beautiful animals that are challenging to raise and need to be better understood. Since wolfdogs are animals that are intentionally bred as exotic pets, there isn't a need to conserve them, but there is a tremendous need for education and awareness about responsible ownership so that fewer wolfdogs end up in sanctuaries. Such education could be helpful for dog owners as well.

94 BLACKSHALE CREEK SUSPENSION BRIDGE

Address Smith Dorrien Trail (Highway 742), Peter Lougheed Provincial Park, AB, T0L 2C0 | **Telephone** n/a | **Website** albertaparks.ca/parks/kananaskis/kananaskis-country/advisories-public-safety/trail-reports/spray-valley/high-rockies-summer

A Thrilling Hike in Peter Lougheed Provincial Park

Hiking across a suspension bridge is exciting — so much so that you have to pay to hike across the Capilano Suspension Bridge or the Golden Skybridge in British Columbia. In Peter Lougheed Provincial Park in Kananaskis Country, you can experience the thrill of hiking across a suspension bridge without a fee.

The Blackshale Creek Suspension Bridge was completed in 2017 as part of the High Rockies Trail. It is 73 metres long and sits 30 metres above Blackshale Creek. Like all suspension bridges, it sways a bit as you walk across it, and that is part of what makes the experience so thrilling.

The High Rockies Trail is a real gem. At 80 kilometres long, the trail connects Goat Creek at the Banff National Park boundary to Elk Pass at the Alberta/British Columbia boundary. It is the westernmost Alberta section of the Trans Canada Trail and is very popular with mountain bikers and hikers. Some sections of the trail are also used by snowshoers

The suspension bridge can sway as you cross it, which makes the experience that much more thrilling.

and skiers, though the suspension bridge is not one of those areas. The bridge is closed in winter.

The High Rockies Trail travels through three provincial parks, but you don't have to hike the entire trail in order to reach the suspension bridge. The trail can be hiked or cycled in small sections and is accessible from the road in many places as well as from several day-use areas.

Alberta TrailNet Society was responsible for creating and building the High Rockies Trail and the Blackshale Creek Suspension Bridge. This non-profit trail organization works to promote and build trails in Alberta. It led the project, organized funding, consulted with Alberta Parks staff and worked with consultant McElhanney Limited to plan and build the trail. Trail design and routing was a complex process that had to address environmental concerns while providing a diverse and beautiful trail for visitors.

A view of Blackshale Creek Suspension Bridge, which lies 30 metres above Blackshale Creek.

DID YOU KNOW?

Alberta's only vehicle suspension bridge is located near Dunvegan, where Highway 2 crosses the Peace River. The 750-metre-long bridge was built in 1960 and is the fourth-longest vehicle suspension bridge in Canada.

If you want to hike the Blackshale Creek Suspension Bridge only, it can be done in a 1-kilometre loop trail with about 53 metres of elevation gain. Though the suspension bridge is closed in winter, there is a detour that keeps the trail accessible in all seasons and provides an option for those who are uncomfortable with crossing the bridge. There is a small parking area near the bridge on the Smith Dorrien Trail (Highway 742). After turning off Kananaskis Trail (Highway 40), the bridge is a little more than 8 kilometres along Highway 742.

The Smith Dorrien Trail is a gravel road and it can be a rough drive in places. Also, cellphone reception can be sketchy. If you plan to use Google Maps to get there, load the map while you have a cellular signal.

From the small parking area, there is a trail to the left and the right, and either option will get you to the bridge. If this parking area is full, you may need to drive to the Black Prince Day-Use Area and do a longer hike from there.

The trail passes through old-growth forest and climbs up to the bridge. Trees block views along the trail, but there are nice views from the bridge if the weather is clear.

95 HIGHWOOD PASS

Address Highway 40 (Kananaskis Trail), Kananaskis Country, AB | **Telephone** n/a | **Website** n/a

Canada's Highest Paved Pass

Breathtaking scenery along Highwood Pass.

Highwood Pass is no ordinary road. At 2,206 metres above sea level, this road through Kananaskis Country is Canada's highest paved pass and one of the prettiest drives in the province. Highwood Pass, found along Highway 40, takes you through the glorious scenery found in the front ranges of the Canadian Rockies. It's common to see wildlife on this drive, and a wide variety of campgrounds, trails and recreation areas lie just off the road. This road is so spectacular that it has been the host site of the ATB Financial Gran Fondo bike race multiple times.

Views along the Ptarmigan Cirque hike, which is one of the many amazing hikes accessed by Highwood Pass.

Bighorn Sheep along Highwood Pass.

Highwood Pass is an elevating ride for hardcore cyclists, but sections of it are very doable for the average weekend warrior. The easiest way to cycle this road would be to start at the gate near

DID YOU KNOW?

Cyclists and runners who go in early June get the road all to themselves. Highwood Pass isn't open to cars until June 15. Be bear aware and carry bear spray if you are hiking, running or cycling in this part of the Rockies.

Longview, cycle 37 kilometres to Highwood Pass and then descend 17 kilometres on the steep road to the King Creek Ridge Trailhead. If you go in the other direction from King Creek, part of the road is Category 1, which is the steepest grade bikers on the Tour de France climb.

For those who are not into cycling, Highwood Pass is also beautiful on four wheels. The drive is punctuated with wonderful day-use areas, great mountain views and an abundance of wildlife. Watch for elk, deer, moose, bighorn sheep and grizzly and black bears as you make your way along the pass.

Because of its high elevation,

many larch trees are visible along Highwood Pass. They are hard to distinguish from other conifers most of the year, but in the fall the needles on larch trees turn golden yellow, and they make a drive along the pass or a hike on the trails near the road stunningly beautiful. Larch season only lasts for a couple of weeks starting in mid-September. After that the larches drop their needles and regrow them the following spring.

Adverse weather conditions are common on this road because of its high elevation. Highwood Pass is closed annually from mid-December to mid-June due to heavy snowfall and to protect wildlife in the area.

96 ALBERTA PROVINCIAL POLICE BARRACKS

Address 7809 18th Avenue, Coleman, AB, T0K 0M0 | **Telephone** (403) 563-5434 | **Website** appbarracks.com

Canada's Most Infamous Rum-Running Murder

The exterior of the Alberta Provincial Police Barracks, which is now a museum.

The Alberta Provincial Police Barracks museum in Coleman isn't very large, but it tells fascinating stories about a police force that only existed for a short time, prohibition, rum-running and murder. The building was constructed in 1904 and was originally used by the Coleman detachment of the North-West Mounted Police before it was turned over to the Alberta Provincial Police (APP). Although it looks like an ordinary house, it was the place where Constable Steven Lawson worked, lived and was murdered. Visitors to the museum are invited to go back to the scene of the crime and decide who did it. Two people were convicted: Emilio Picariello and Florence "Filumena" Lassandro. They were both executed, and Lassandro became the only woman ever executed in Alberta.

Prohibition laws were in place in Alberta from 1916 to 1924. During that time the sale and consumption of liquor was illegal in the province. The APP was established in 1917 with the primary role to combat illegal imports of alcohol from British Columbia and Montana, where alcohol sales were still legal. This activity was referred to as "rum-running," and it became big business in the Crowsnest Pass, where thirsty coal miners were willing to pay well for the privilege of enjoying a drink after a hard day in the mines.

Picariello was one of the most powerful and notorious rum-runners in Alberta. He owned several legitimate businesses in the Crowsnest Pass, including the Alberta Hotel in

Emilio Picariello.

A police photograph of Florence "Filumena" Lassandro.

Constable Steven Lawson.

Filumena, the Opera

Canadian composer John Estacio and Canadian librettist John Murrell created an opera based on Florence "Filumena" Lassandro's life and death. The opera premiered in Calgary in 2003 and was performed by the Calgary Opera. It was also performed at the Banff Centre for Arts and Creativity and by the Edmonton Opera company in 2006.

Blairmore and several ice cream parlours. Though he had been convicted on two occasions for illegally importing liquor, he was a respected alderman in Blairmore and a notable community philanthropist. "Emperor Pic," as he was locally known, was very wealthy and respected. Lassandro and her husband both worked with Picariello in his bootlegging operations.

On September 21, 1922, Picariello's son was involved in a police chase and was shot. Not knowing the whereabouts of his son, Picariello drove to the APP barracks with Lassandro and confronted Constable Lawson. There was a skirmish and Constable Lawson was fatally shot in front of his home.

Both Picariello and Lassandro were arrested and were convicted of Lawson's murder — even though it was never clear which one pulled the trigger. Both were hanged on May 2, 1923, despite Lassandro proclaiming her innocence to the end. At the Alberta Provincial Police Barracks museum, you can revisit the evidence and decide for yourself who was responsible for the crime.

Rapunzel's Cottage takes inspiration from Giambattista Basile's fairytale *Petrosinella* (1634), which inspired the story of Rapunzel.

97 CHARMED RESORTS

Address 13029 25th Avenue, Blairmore, AB, T0K 0E0
Telephone 1 (844) 543-9273 | **Website** charmedfamilyresorts.com

North America's Only Play Cottage Resort

Elvyn's Cottage, which features a rustic interior.

If you've ever dreamed of staying in a whimsical fairy-tale cottage in the woods, Charmed Resorts in the Crowsnest Pass might be for you. The resort is owned and built by Tyson Leavitt. Since 2015 Leavitt has been building luxury playhouses. He and his wife, Audrey Leavitt, even had a reality television show called *Playhouse Masters* that ran on TLC for a season. Some of the playhouses they built for rich and famous clients cost up to half a million dollars.

In 2020 the Leavitts started a new passion project. It's a resort of luxury playhouse-style cottages. Each cottage has a different theme and the Leavitts are slowly adding more. All of the cottages are whimsical, and the resort is a combination of rustic camping and luxury cottages.

Some of the themed cottages include Rapunzel's Cottage, Elvyn's Cottage, Midsummer Cottage and Rumpelstiltskin's Tower. This quirky Alberta resort is ideal for families and couples who like the idea of escaping reality and stepping into a fairy tale.

Other Unusual Accommodations in Alberta

If you want to stay someplace unusual in Alberta, you've got options. You can stay overnight in a tipi at Blackfoot Crossing or pretend you're a fur trader and stay overnight in a trapper's tent at Rocky Mountain House National Historic Site. Those who love trains would enjoy an overnight stay in a caboose cabin on the train tracks at Aspen Crossing near Mossleigh. The exteriors of the caboose cabins are rustic, but the interiors are luxurious and there's even a dining car. Theme rooms at the Fantasyland Hotel in West Edmonton Mall let you live out a multitude of fantasies — everything from sleeping in the back of a truck to staying in an igloo. There are many ways to have an adventurous overnight stay in Alberta.

98 FRANK SLIDE INTERPRETIVE CENTRE

Address Highway 3 (Crowsnest Highway), Blairmore, AB, T0K 0E0 | **Telephone** (403) 562-7388 | **Website** frankslide.ca

The Site of Canada's Deadliest Rockslide

The east face of Turtle Mountain sits beside the Frank Slide Interpretive Centre.

You can't drive the Crowsnest Highway past Frank Slide and not wonder if something unusual happened there. Massive boulders are piled in a vast field of rubble on either side of the highway — evidence left by the deadliest rockslide in Canadian history. On April 29, 1903, at 4:10 a.m., 110 million tonnes of limestone crumbled off the east face of Turtle Mountain, crushing a large part of a mining town called Frank and killing an estimated 92 people. The rockslide covered an area of 3 square kilometres to a depth of up to 45 metres. The exact death toll will never be known for certain because most of those buried were never recovered.

The rockslide on this site killed an estimated 92 people in 1903.

The rockslide only took 90 seconds, but stories about the survivors have become the stuff of urban legend. One of the most famous stories is of a baby girl who was found on top of a boulder. Most versions of the story say that she was the sole survivor of the deadly rockslide. This urban legend is not true, but it is likely based on a true story. Among the survivors were three young girls. One of them, a 15-month-old named Marion Leitch, was thrown from her house and found in a pile of hay. Some believe the boulder baby legend is based on her miraculous survival story.

After the rockslide what was left of the town of Frank was moved to a new location nearby.

Long before the tragedy, the Blackfoot and Ktunaxa Nations called Turtle Mountain "the mountain that moves." According to their verbal history, they believed the mountain was unstable and would not camp near it. As it turns out, those who have occupied this land since time immemorial were right. Turtle Mountain is geologically unstable and that was the primary cause of the rockslide. A major thrust fault runs through the mountain making it weaker. There are also large surface cracks where water can enter and freeze. The thawing and freezing that happened in the spring of 1903 destabilized the mountain further. Coal mining certainly contributed to the instability, but it wasn't the primary cause of the rockslide.

The Frank Slide Interpretive Centre overlooks the rockslide and tells the tragic tale of the night Turtle Mountain crumbled. There are first-hand accounts, geological information, fascinating exhibits and an interesting film. There's also an excellent interpretive walking trail outside the centre.

DID YOU KNOW?

Turtle Mountain is still unstable, and scientists believe there will be another rockslide someday, though it is not likely to happen anytime soon. The Lower South Peak, Upper South Peak and the Lower Third Peak are the most probable sources of rock avalanches in the future, and scientists keep a close watch on them. If those peaks gave way, the rocks would fall to the eastern side of the original rockslide, far removed from where the interpretive centre sits.

99 HILLCREST MINE DISASTER MEMORIAL PARK and CEMETERY

Address 200 4th Avenue, Hillcrest Mines, AB, T0K 1C0
Telephone (403) 562-8833 | **Website** crowsnestpass.com/living-here/operational-services/cemeteries

A Sombre Memorial to Canada's Mining Disasters

If you're driving through the Crowsnest Pass near the community of Hillcrest and you see a sign for "Disaster Park," pull over. The full name of the park is Hillcrest Mine Disaster Memorial Park, but it's hard to fit all of that on a road sign. The park sits next to the Old Hillcrest Cemetery at the north end of the community. Both the park and the cemetery commemorate the worst coal mining accident in Canadian history.

On June 19, 1914, a pocket of methane gas ignited inside the Hillcrest coal mine and set off a coal dust explosion. The exact cause of the accident is unclear, but one theory is that falling rocks might have created a spark that ignited the gas. One hundred and eighty-nine men were killed in the explosion. Those not killed directly by the fire or the explosion died from poisonous gases. Almost every family in the tiny community of Hillcrest was affected in some way by the tragedy. Ninety women became widows, and 250 children were fatherless at a time when it was

A memorial for those who perished in the disaster as well as other coal mining disasters across Canada.

Hillcrest Cemetery, the final resting place for many of the miners who died in the Hillcrest Mine Disaster.

almost impossible for women to gain employment to support themselves and their children. Most of the miners who were killed were buried in one of two mass graves at Hillcrest Cemetery. Many of them were immigrants. You can pick up a brochure at the cemetery and take a short self-guided interpretive walk. The cemetery is recognized as one of Canada's Historic Places.

Outside the cemetery is a memorial to commemorate all the victims of coal mining

A restored coal car in Hillcrest Mine Disaster Memorial Park.

disasters across Canada. The memorial was made from stones native to each province in Canada and contains individual monuments for each of the mining disasters.

In 2016 Hillcrest Mine Disaster Memorial Park was officially opened near the cemetery and the memorial. There's a short walking path and interpretive signage that tells the fascinating history of the mine and the story of the mine disaster. There's also a restored coal car and a picnic table. The park, the cemetery and the memorial are all sites worth stopping for.

DID YOU KNOW?

Three of Alberta's deadliest disasters happened within a few kilometres of each other in what is now known as the Crowsnest Pass. Before the Hillcrest Mine disaster in 1914, the Frank Slide killed an estimated 92 people in 1903 and an explosion at Bellevue Mine in 1910 killed 31 men.

The Burmis Tree, a symbol of the Crowsnest Pass.

100 THE BURMIS TREE

Address Crowsnest Highway (Highway 3), near Bellevue, AB
Telephone n/a | **Website** crowsnestheritage.ca/attractions/burmis-tree

The World's Most Photographed Dead Tree

This beloved tree has been guarded and repaired by locals for decades.

Alberta's most photographed tree has been dead since the late 1970s. That probably makes it the most photographed dead tree in the world, but nobody really keeps track of these things.

The legendary limber pine known as the Burmis Tree is located on the edge of the Crowsnest Highway (Highway 3), near the site of the former town of Burmis, about 10 kilometres northeast of Frank Slide. The tree has been a beloved symbol of the Crowsnest Pass for so many years that even when it lost the last of its needles in the late 1970s, locals took care of it. When the Crowsnest Highway was built, they made sure the road passed safely by it. When the wind toppled the dead tree in 1998, it was moved back to its upright position and braced so that it would stay that way. In 2004 when vandals sawed off one of the tree's branches, the branch was glued back into place and given a crutch to help hold it up. Knowing all that, it's not surprising that there is an interpretive sign and a highway pullout near the dead tree.

Limber pines can live for hundreds of years, and some estimates put this particular limber pine at around 700 years of age before it died. One thing is certain, the Burmis Tree saw a lot of change in its lifetime. It was in place long before the first Europeans arrived in what is now called Canada.

The tree is named for the coal mining town of Burmis, which is now a ghost town. Established in the early 20th century, Burmis had shops, a school and a church. When the mine dried up, the town eventually disappeared, but the tree stayed as a reminder of what once was.

This gnarled tree on a stony ridge near the east entrance of the Crowsnest Pass has become a symbol of a region that, like the tree, has survived against many challenges. This unusual symbol also makes a surprisingly dramatic photo op.

101 WATERTON LAKES NATIONAL PARK

Address Highway 5, Waterton Park, AB | **Telephone** (403) 859-5133 | **Website** pc.gc.ca/en/pn-np/ab/waterton

How to Travel to the U.S. without a Passport

The Prince of Wales Hotel looks out over Waterton Lakes.

The old saying "good things come in small packages" holds true when you look at Waterton Lakes National Park. At 505 square kilometres, Waterton is the smallest of the Canadian Rocky Mountain national parks, but it's also one of the most diverse parks in the national parks system. In 1932 Waterton Lakes National Park was combined with Glacier National Park in Montana to form the world's first international peace park. The Waterton-Glacier International Peace Park was the first park of its kind in the world. The park was established as a symbol of peace and goodwill between Canada and the United States.

Though the border between Canada and the U.S. is technically partway across the lake, you don't need a passport to enjoy a two-hour cruise (via the Waterton Shoreline Cruise Co.) from the Canadian side of Upper Waterton Lake to the American side of the lake. However, if you want to hike on the U.S. side, you must bring a passport and report your entry into the country using the U.S. Customs and Border Protection's CBP ROAM app or by calling the port of Piegan. The boat tour used to stop on the American side of the lake and allow passengers to get out on the shore, but since the U.S. stopped manning the border crossing at Goat Haunt, the cruise no longer stops there. If you want to cross at Goat Haunt and experience the trails in Glacier National Park, you must hike around the lake. It's common to see moose on the 4-kilometre Kootenai Lakes hike that departs from Goat Haunt.

Located in a region known as the Crown of the Continent, this park contains beautiful scenery and a vast array of flora and fauna. Over half of Alberta's plant species can be found inside the park, and there are more than 175 provincially rare plants, such as mountain lady's slipper, pygmy poppy and mountain hollyhock. An annual spring wildflower festival celebrates the diversity of plant life in the park.

There is also an incredible array of wildlife inside the park. More than 60 species of mammal, 250 species of bird, 24 species of fish and 10 species of reptile and amphibian can be found in the park. Large predators include grizzly bears, black bears, wolves, coyotes and cougars. All wildlife, big and small, is important, and so you will see "Salamander Crossing" signs along the roadway in Waterton. In spring and fall, long-toed salamanders migrate across the road. A great deal of research and roadwork went into ensuring these tiny creatures could safely cross on their annual breeding migration. An autumn wildlife festival is held every year to celebrate the diversity of wildlife found in the park.

Wildflowers are plentiful in Waterton Lakes National Park.

There are beautiful mountain views from the shores of the Upper and Lower Waterton Lakes.

Crypt Lake Hike – One of the World's Most Thrilling Trails

Waterton's Crypt Lake Hike is one of the most breathtaking hikes in Canada. National Geographic named it one of the "World's 20 Most Thrilling Trails." This unique hike features a 15-minute boat ride across Upper Waterton Lake to the trailhead at Crypt Landing. You'll pass four waterfalls, climb a steel ladder, crawl through an 18-metre tunnel and manoeuver around a cliff using a steel cable before you arrive at beautiful Crypt Lake. Waterton is a unique and special place, and hiking to Crypt Lake is an experience of a lifetime.

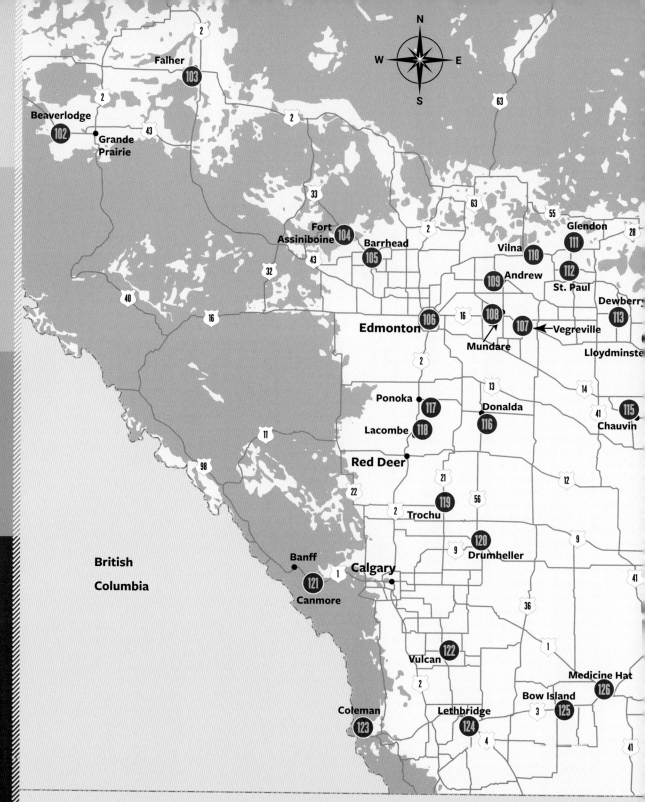

ALBERTA'S ROADSIDE ATTRACTIONS

Alberta has more than 100 gigantic roadside attractions. Drivers can stop in tiny towns and villages across the province to see everything from a giant pinto bean to the world's largest sausage. Among these giant tourist attractions are several Guinness World Record holders. These attractions exist for a number of reasons, whether it's to celebrate a community's identity or simply give people a reason to pull over, marvel and take a selfie with something unusual.

102 WORLD'S LARGEST BEAVER | BEAVERLODGE

It isn't surprising that a town named Beaverlodge would be home to a statue of the world's largest beaver. The town gets its name from the Beaverlodge River, which was known as "temporary lodge" by members of the Beaver First Nation. On July 21, 2004, the town celebrated its 75th year of incorporation, and part of the celebration included the unveiling of a giant beaver sculpture.

The beaver is surrounded by interpretive signage that tells visitors about the town and about beavers. The Beaverlodge Beaver weighs 680 kilograms, as does the log it sits on. It is 5.5 metres long, 3 metres wide and 9.1 metres high, including the log base. It took 340 litres of polyurethane and approximately 49 litres of paint to coat the sculpture.

103 WORLD'S LARGEST HONEYBEE | FALHER

The largest humanmade honeybee is 6.9 metres long and 2.3 metres in diameter, and it sits outside the town of Falher. It was built by a local welder named Richard Ethier in 1990 to celebrate Falher's first honey festival. This small community had a large apiary industry in the 1970s and '80s, and the giant honeybee mascot symbolizes the history of honey production in the region, the honey festival and the industrious hard-working nature of this small northern Alberta community.

104 WORLD'S LARGEST WAGON WHEEL AND PICKAXE | FORT ASSINIBOINE

The world's largest wagon wheel is over 7 metres tall, and the world's largest pickaxe is just over 6 metres tall. They both stand next to the Fort Assiniboine Museum, in the heart of the hamlet. The wagon wheel and pickaxe represent the rich history of this region. Fort Assiniboine was founded as a Hudson's Bay trading post, and it became an important trade centre and a key stopping point on the Klondike Trail. The world's largest wagon wheel and pickaxe were installed in 2005.

105 AARON, THE WORLD'S LARGEST BLUE HERON | BARRHEAD

The world's largest great blue heron is 2.4 metres tall and stands on a 1.2-metre-high pedestal in the middle of the town of Barrhead. The heron was constructed of rebar, wire mesh and concrete in 1984 by Trygve Seland, who also built other Alberta monuments, and it has been dubbed "Aaron the Blue Heron" by locals. Great blue herons are often spotted on the shores of local lakes, and that is part of the reason it was selected as the town's mascot.

106 WORLD'S LARGEST COWBOY BOOT | EDMONTON

The world's largest cowboy boot sits outside the One Stop Biker Shop at 10007 167th Street Northwest in Edmonton. This local landmark went up in 1989, when the store was called the Western Boot Factory. When the Western Boot Factory closed, the big boot stayed. The boot is four storeys (almost 12 metres) tall. It's 2.7 metres wide at the top and 4.9 metres long at the sole. At night the boot is lit up with 183 metres of neon tubing.

was born in the area. Sembaliuk worked with Ronald Resch, a computer science professor from the University of Utah, and his team to design the egg. It was the first physical structure designed entirely with computer-aided geometric modelling software. The pysanka's design achieved nine mathematical, architectural and engineering firsts. It was built out of anodized aluminum, and it has 524-star patterns, 2,208 equilateral triangles, 3,512 visible facets, 6,978 nuts and bolts, and 177 internal struts. The pysanka leans on its support base and is turned by the wind like a weathervane.

107 WORLD'S LARGEST PYSANKA (EASTER EGG) | VEGREVILLE

The world's largest pysanka is in Vegreville. A pysanka is a Ukrainian Easter egg that is decorated with traditional designs using a wax resist (batik) method. Molten beeswax is applied to the egg with a stylus in a writing motion (the word "pysanka" comes from the verb *pysaty*, which means to write).

The Vegreville pysanka was conceived in 1973 when the Alberta government established a committee to coordinate the centennial celebrations of the Royal Canadian Mounted Police (RCMP). The committee funded monuments in Vegreville and several other communities. The Vegreville & District Chamber of Commerce decided to build a giant pysanka to symbolize the community's Ukrainian culture and the peace and security the RCMP provided to immigrants and their descendants.

The pysanka is more than 7.8 metres long, 5.5 metres wide and 9.5 metres tall, and it weighs 2.5 tonnes. The sculpture was designed by Paul Maxum Sembaliuk, a Canadian artist of Ukrainian descent who

108 WORLD'S LARGEST SAUSAGE | MUNDARE

When you look at it from the side, some locals say the 12.8-metre-tall kielbasa sausage statue in Mundare looks like a "giant turd" — their words, not mine. The 5,443-kilogram statue and the accompanying tourist rest area that surrounds it were opened in 2001. The sausage was built as a tribute to Stawnichy's Mundare Sausage, a family-owned Ukrainian food company that opened in Mundare in 1959 and now has multiple locations in Alberta. The company is famous for Ukrainian sausage — including its kielbasa. The Stawnichy family set up a non-profit foundation to raise $120,000 to fund the giant sausage and the rest area. The statue itself was four years in the making. Its heavy weight allows the sausage to withstand high winds of up to 160 kilometres per hour, which the area sometimes receives. If you stop to see the sausage, you should take a walk downtown to Stawnichy's shop, at 5212 50th Street, to buy some of the Ukrainian sausage that has been touted as the best in Canada. Across the street, you can also stop at Baba's Attic and Coffee House for homemade pies and perogies.

109 WORLD'S LARGEST MALLARD DUCK | ANDREW

You'll find the world's largest mallard duck at the junction of Highways 855 and 45 in a community park in the village of Andrew. The bird weighs in at 1 tonne and has a wingspan of 7 metres. It was built in 1992 to recognize local wetlands and duck breeding grounds. The duck is shown in flight, and the sculpture sits on an angled metal support in Centennial Park, a great spot for a picnic. During the COVID-19 pandemic, the duck sported a custom-made mask over its bill.

While in Andrew, you can visit the Andrew Museum and the Andrew Grain Elevator Interpretive Centre and take a stroll down Ed Stelmach Avenue, named in honour of a local boy who became the 13th premier of Alberta. You might also pop over to Whitford Lake, 6 kilometres southeast of the village, to look for live ducks.

110 WORLD'S LARGEST MUSHROOMS | VILNA

The world's largest mushrooms are over 6 metres tall and weigh 8,165 kilograms, and they are located in a community park in the tiny village of Vilna. The statues are a replica of the *Tricholoma uspale* mushroom that grows wild in the area. Mushroom hunting dates to the early 1900s, when the first Ukrainian settlers arrived in Vilna. The mushrooms were harvested and dried and used in traditional dishes. The giant mushrooms were constructed in 1993 at a cost of $28,000 as a symbol of the excellent wild mushroom picking in the area.

If you stop to see the mushrooms, it's also worth visiting the historic main street. The village's 1921 pool hall and barbershop building is a provincial historic site where you can still play a game. There are many other restored shops and buildings to see in the village.

111 WORLD'S LARGEST PEROGY | GLENDON

People who live in the village of Glendon like perogies — a lot. Glendon's main street is called Pyrogy Drive, they hold an annual perogy festival and the world's largest perogy is in a park right in the middle of the community. The perogy was built in 1991 and is the main tourist attraction in town. It is 8.2 metres high and weighs 2,721 kilograms. A giant fork was included as part of the perogy statue to make sure it was recognizable.

WORLD'S LARGEST PEROGY

112 WORLD'S FIRST UFO LANDING PAD | ST. PAUL

You could say St. Paul is out of this world. There has been a UFO landing pad in town since 1967. It was built as part of the Canadian centennial celebration that year and symbolizes the community's openness to visitors from literally anywhere. The concrete splash weighs more than 130,000 kilograms and can support large, heavy alien aircraft — though it's never had to.

The town's museum is across from the landing pad, and there is a spaceship-shaped tourist information centre adjacent to the landing pad. It is conveniently located to provide tourist information to any aliens that land at the site as well as tourists who walk up. The UFO landing pad has become a beloved landmark and an enduring tourist attraction. Aliens have yet to touch down in St. Paul, but when they do, the town is ready.

WORLD'S FIRST UFO LANDING PAD

WORLD'S LARGEST BORDER MARKERS

114 WORLD'S LARGEST BORDER MARKERS | LLOYDMINSTER

If you've ever wanted to be in two places at once, Lloydminster is the city for you. Canada's only border city is partly in Alberta and partly in Saskatchewan. If you stand at the dividing point, you can put one foot in Alberta and one foot in Saskatchewan and be in two places at once. The world's largest border markers delineate the division between the two provinces. The four 30.5-metre-high border markers sit on the crossing of Highway 16 and 17 next to Lloydminster's city hall. The gap between the steel pillars of each monument represents the actual border.

The border markers were erected in 1994. They represent four themes that are important to the history of this region: oil and gas, the Barr Colonists, agriculture, and First Nations and Métis.

113 WORLD'S LARGEST CHUCKWAGON | DEWBERRY

The hamlet of Dewberry has a population of about 200 and a good number of the residents in the hamlet and surrounding area are chuckwagon drivers. It's known as the chuckwagon capital of Alberta. In 2015 the community held an event to honour 11 area chuckwagon drivers and one long-time chuckwagon announcer. Three of the drivers honoured had won the Calgary Stampede Rangeland Derby championship, the pinnacle of success, a total of six times. It's not surprising the hamlet would also be home to the world's largest chuckwagon. It is not as big as you might imagine, but it is reputed to be the world's largest.

WORLD'S LARGEST CHUCKWAGON

115 SUZIE, THE WORLD'S LARGEST SOFTBALL | CHAUVIN

The world's largest softball is about 1.8 metres in diameter and sits outside the softball diamonds in the village of Chauvin. The giant softball was built to recognize a softball tournament held in the town. It was built from an old fibreglass septic tank. Nearby, a collection of decorated fire hydrants sits in the stands.

Dillberry Lake Provincial Park is 22 kilometres southeast of Chauvin and is worth visiting if you are in the area.

WORLD'S LARGEST SOFTBALL

116 WORLD'S LARGEST LAMP | DONALDA

Donalda is well known for its museum's remarkable lamp collection, and on July 1, 2000, the village officially opened the world's largest oil lamp as a millennium project. The lamp is made of steel and fibreglass and is 12.8 metres high and 5.8 metres wide at the base. It sits in a park that overlooks Meeting Creek Coulee, and it lights up every evening at dusk. You can step inside the lamp during museum hours or get a picture outside it anytime. The lamp even has its own Facebook account (@donalda.lamp).

If you stop in the village, a visit to the Donalda & District Museum to see the impressive lamp collection is highly recommended. The village was originally named Eidswold by the Norwegian settlers who founded it. Like many communities, the name was changed when the railway came to town. The village was renamed in 1911 after Donalda Crossway, the niece of Sir Donald Mann, a Canadian Northern Railway official.

WORLD'S LARGEST LAMP

117 *THE LEGACY,* THE WORLD'S LARGEST BUCKING BRONCO AND RIDER | PONOKA

The Legacy is a 9.8-metre-tall statue of a bucking bronco and rider that is in the middle of the Lions Centennial Park (Highway 2A, just north of Highway 53) in Ponoka. The statue was built in 2004 to celebrate the town's 100th anniversary and is the world's largest bucking bronco and rider.

It isn't surprising that the town chose a rodeo statue. The Ponoka Stampede was first held in 1936 and has grown to become the largest Canadian Professional Cowboy Association–approved rodeo. Today the Ponoka Stampede is among the five-largest rodeos in the world for payouts, and the Professional Bull Riders event is the largest single-day bull-riding event in the world, attracting competitors from across Canada, the United States and Australia.

WORLD'S LARGEST BUCKING BRONCO AND RIDER

223

WORLD'S LARGEST FISHING LURE

119 WORLD'S LARGEST GOLF TEE |
TROCHU

In 2009 ATB Financial held a competition called the Teenormous contest, and the first prize was the world's largest golf tee. The town of Trochu worked with the local golf club and community members to produce a video featuring the golf club and local golfers. The communities of Trochu, Marwayne and Camrose were finalists in the contest. Interviews with the entrants and the original videos were posted online, and the public voted online for their favourite entry. Trochu garnered two-thirds of the votes and became the proud winner of a more than 12-metre-tall replica golf tee. The area around the world's largest golf tee is landscaped, and lights were added to enhance the visibility of this unique landmark. You can see it from Highway 585, but you should get a closer look. If you bring your golf clubs, you can enjoy a round at the Trochu Golf and Country Club, where the enormous golf tee is located.

WORLD'S LARGEST GOLF TEE

118 WORLD'S LARGEST
FISHING LURE | LACOMBE

The Five of Diamonds fishing lure was invented by Len Thompson in the 1950s and has remained one of the most popular and bestselling fishing lures in Canada over many decades. The contrast of red diamonds on a yellow background grabs the attention of fish and is the go-to lure for many. Thompson-Pallister Bait Company Limited has been a family-run business in the town of Lacombe since 1929. To celebrate its 90th anniversary, the company joined forces with Echo Energy and Comet Welding to make the world's largest fishing lure.

The world's largest fishing lure is of course a Five of Diamonds. The spoon size of the lure is 8.7 metres tall and measures just over 3 metres across at the widest point. The hook is 2.4 metres wide at the base and 4.3 metres tall. If you visit, bring your fishing rod and lures as the world's largest fishing lure sits near the shores of the Len Thompson Pond, which is stocked with rainbow trout every year.

120 WORLD'S LARGEST DINOSAUR | DRUMHELLER

The World's Largest Dinosaur is a female *Tyrannosaurus rex* located in the town of Drumheller. Her name is Tyra, and visitors can climb 106 stairs to stand inside her gaping jaws and take in the view of the Drumheller Valley and the surrounding badlands. There's a gift shop and a visitor information centre at the base.

The *Tyrannosaurus* was constructed out of steel and fibreglass. She stands at a height of 26.3 metres and a length of 46 metres — making her at least four times larger than any *Tyrannosaurus rex* that ever lived. Tyra holds the Guinness World Record for World's Largest Dinosaur. She took almost three years to complete, and since her unveiling in 2001 more than two million people have visited her. In 2020 Tyra underwent a $300,000 restoration.

Drive around Drumheller and you'll see dinosaur statues all over town. A visit to the Royal Tyrrell Museum just outside town will let you see real dinosaur fossils. The World's Largest Dinosaur has her own website and her own social media accounts (@worldslargestdinosaur).

121 *Ceannmore* (BIG HEAD) | CANMORE

The public art piece known locally as "Big Head" is actually named *Ceannmore* by Alan Henderson, the Alberta artist who created it for the town of Canmore. King Malcolm III of Scotland was also known as Ceannmore, which means "Great Head." The nearly 7-tonne stone head appears to be partially buried and its eyes are closed, as if it is lost in meditation. The blue granite head stands 1.6 metres tall and sits on a bed of river stones near the Policeman Creek Trail. *Ceannmore* was installed in 2008 and has since become a beloved landmark. Locals have been known to accessorize the sculpture throughout the year with a scarf and hat in winter and a pirate costume at Halloween.

BIG HEAD

122 VULCAN TOURISM AND TREK STATION | VULCAN

The town of Vulcan was named by a surveyor for the Canadian Pacific Railway after the Roman god of fire, Vulcan. It was incorporated as a village in 1912, and all of the streets were named after Roman gods and goddesses, such as Juno, Mars and Jupiter. When the *Star Trek* television series became popular and the planet Vulcan became widely known, the town's name took on a new meaning. At one time the entire town council had replica *Star Trek* uniforms complete with plastic pointed ears that they wore to various events.

Today the town has the most unique visitor information centre in Alberta. Opened in 1998 it was built to look like a landed space station with clever landscaping and fibre optic lighting on the exterior. Inside there is a collection of over 800 pieces of *Star Trek* memorabilia, life-sized *Star Trek* character cut-outs for photo ops, the Galaxy Souvenir Gift Shop and tourist information about the town. Friendly Trek Station crew members greet you on entry to this unusual visitor centre and *Star Trek* attraction.

123 POSSIBLY THE WORLD'S LARGEST PIGGY BANK | COLEMAN

A sign above Ten Ton Toots in the community of Coleman says it is the biggest piggy bank in the world, but Guinness World Records says otherwise. According to them, the world's largest piggy bank is in Ludwigsburg, Germany, but the one in Coleman is interesting nonetheless. Ten Ton Toots is a 0-4-0 type of locomotive that was used to pull

coal cars in mines. (A 0-4-0 locomotive has two axles and four coupled wheels.) Between 1904 and 1954 Toots hauled over 4.5 million tonnes of coal. It is a compressed air locomotive that could pull loads of almost 200 tonnes at a time. Rather than scrap the locomotive after the mines closed, Coleman turned Toots into a giant piggy bank, though it has very little money in it.

WORLD'S LARGEST WIND GAUGE

124 WORLD'S LARGEST WIND GAUGE | LETHBRIDGE

The world's largest wind gauge is in the parking lot of the official visitor centre located at 2805 Scenic Drive South in Lethbridge. For the city's centennial in 1985, the Royal Canadian Legion funded the erection of the giant wind gauge. It was originally designed to be a working wind gauge, but the strong winds in the area raised concerns that it might whip the giant ball around and hurt someone, so it was welded in place. It's an appropriate landmark for the city of Lethbridge, which is the windiest city in Alberta.

WORLD'S LARGEST PIGGY BANK

125 WORLD'S LARGEST GOLF PUTTER | BOW ISLAND

The Bow Island Golf Club opened in 1955 and it is an excellent nine-hole course. In the 1990s club member George Thacker built a large blade-style golf putter that was placed on the sign for the golf course on the north side of Highway 3 near the eastern edge of town. It is reputed to be the world's largest golf putter.

While you're in the town of Bow Island, you should also get a picture of the town's official mascot, Pinto MacBean. The statue of Pinto is 5.5 metres tall and located adjacent to Highway 3. Bow Island is known as the bean capital of Western Canada. About 20,000 hectares of beans grow in the area annually.

126 WORLD'S TALLEST TEPEE | MEDICINE HAT

Originally constructed for the Calgary 1988 Winter Olympics, the Saamis Tepee is as tall as a 20-storey building and sits next to the Trans-Canada Highway near the tourism information centre in Medicine Hat. The massive tepee is 65.5 metres tall, has a diameter of 49 metres and weighs 800 tonnes. There are 10 large storyboards in each of the masts that depict different aspects of Indigenous culture and history. The tepee overlooks the Seven Persons Coulee, the site of one of the most important archaeological sites on the Northern Plains. Experts estimate that there are more than 83 million artifacts buried at the Saamis Archaeological Site. Interpretive signage inside the Saamis Tepee tells the story of how Medicine Hat got its name and other local history.

NORTH OF EDMONTON

The shoreline of Lake Athabasca,
near Fort Chipewyan.

127 Lake Athabasca

Address Fort Chipewyan, AB | Telephone n/a | Website n/a

Alberta's Largest Lake

A snowmobiler on Lake Athabasca, near Fort Chipewyan.

With a surface area of 7,850 square kilometres, Lake Athabasca is the eighth-largest lake in Canada. A little more than one-quarter of this massive water body is in Alberta and the rest is in Saskatchewan. However, even if you only count the portion of the lake that is in Alberta, it is still Alberta's largest lake.

Lake Athabasca is in the northeast corner of Alberta, and it is one of the deepest lakes in the province, with a maximum depth of 124 metres. There are 23 species of fish in the lake, including lake trout, Arctic grayling, northern pike, walleye and whitefish. Fort Chipewyan, Alberta's first European settlement, is located on the western shore. Fort Chipewyan is still probably the best place in Alberta to visit if you want to see the lake.

Lake Athabasca, Great Slave Lake and Great Bear Lake are all remnants of a large proglacial lake known as Lake McConnell. It existed from about 12,000 to 8,000 years ago and covered a maximum surface area of 210,000 square kilometres. As this ancient lake drained, it left behind daughter lakes that are still some of the largest lakes in Canada.

Water from Lake Athabasca flows through the Slave and Mackenzie rivers into the Arctic Ocean. In 1789 Sir Alexander Mackenzie began his legendary expedition to the Arctic Ocean from Fort Chipewyan on Lake Athabasca.

Peace-Athabasca Delta: The Largest Freshwater Inland Delta in North America

The Peace-Athabasca Delta was formed where the Peace and Athabasca rivers converge with the Slave River and Lake Athabasca. It is the largest freshwater inland river delta in North America and the largest boreal delta in the world. It is located in the southeast corner of Wood Buffalo National Park and is one of the reasons the park was named a UNESCO World Heritage Site. The delta encompasses about 321,200 hectares and was designated a wetland of international importance. It is one of the most important waterfowl nesting and staging areas in North America, with up to 400,000 birds using the delta in spring and more than a million in autumn. Alberta has been divided into 20 distinct natural sub-regions, and the Peace-Athabasca Delta is one of them.

128 FORT CHIPEWYAN

Address Fort Chipewyan, AB | **Telephone** (780) 697-3600
Website rmwb.ca/en/indigenous-and-rural-relations/fort-chipewyan

Alberta's First European Settlement

Located on the western shores of Lake Athabasca, Fort Chipewyan was the first European settlement in Alberta. It was established as a North West Company trading post in 1788, and at one time it was the richest fur-trading post in North America. Today the community has almost 1,000 permanent residents.

Fort Chipewyan was the second fur-trading post established in Alberta. The first was an independent post established in 1778 on the Athabasca River by Peter Pond. It was called Fort Athabasca River and was also known as "Peter Pond's Fort."

In 1779 the North West Company was established with Pond as its agent in Athabasca Country. Alexander Mackenzie, a Scottish fur trader and one of Canada's greatest explorers, ultimately became the man responsible for overseeing operations in the Athabasca region, and when he travelled to Fort Athabasca River in 1787, he decided the fort should be replaced with a new one on Athabasca Lake that would be more conveniently located. The fort was named Fort Chipewyan for the Chipewyan First Nation that lived there at the time of its construction. Mackenzie went on to become the first European to cross North America north of Mexico, reaching both the Arctic and Pacific oceans. The Mackenzie River was named in his honour.

Two-hundred and seventy-eight kilometres north of Fort McMurray, Fort Chipewyan is one of the most northerly communities in the Regional Municipality of Wood Buffalo, and it is a gateway to Wood Buffalo

The Nativity of the Blessed Virgin Roman Catholic Church was built in 1909.

National Park. In the days of the fur trade, the Athabasca River was the main means of transportation, which made Fort Chipewyan convenient to reach. Today it's a relatively isolated community that can only be accessed by plane or boat in summer or an ice road in winter. Travelling on the Fort Chipewyan Winter Road is an unusual experience in itself.

The tiny, resilient community of Fort Chipewyan has a fascinating history and residents with a unique lifestyle. The community has always had a large

An aerial view of Fort Chipewyan.

The Fort Chipewyan Bicentennial Museum has several interesting displays, including this one showing traditional Métis attire.

result, trapping, fishing and hunting are activities locals still use to feed their families.

The Fort Chipewyan Bicentennial Museum is a must-see stop in the community. The museum is a replica of the 1870s Hudson's Bay Company store and it contains interesting artifacts. Fort Chipewyan National Historic Site of Canada is located on monument hill near the museum. It is an archaeological site located at Old Fort Point, which was established in 1788 as the centre of

northern trade. There is a plaque at the site. The Nativity of the Blessed Virgin Roman Catholic Church is another must-see. The church was built in 1909 and is another national historic site. Attend a Sunday service or get a tour of the interior to see stunning well-preserved paintings made with paint fabricated from berries and fish oil. There are also a few local guides who offer dogsledding, fishing, northern lights viewing and other experiences.

Indigenous population. Many of the locals are Mikisew Cree First Nation, Athabasca Chipewyan First Nation and Fort Chipewyan Métis. The isolated nature of the community means that groceries are very expensive compared with other Alberta communities. As a

Alberta's Second European Settlement

Fort Vermillion was also established as a fur-trading post by the North West Company in 1788. Some websites list it as the oldest community in Alberta, but it was technically established after Fort Chipewyan.

129 Beaver Dam in Wood Buffalo National Park

Address Wood Buffalo National Park, AB
Telephone 1 (867) 872-7960 | **Website** pc.gc.ca/en/pn-np/nt/woodbuffalo/decouvrir-discover/beaver_gallery

The World's Largest Beaver Dam

The world's largest beaver dam is so big that it's visible from space. In fact, that's the way it was discovered.

This massive beaver dam was first discovered in 2007 by researcher Jean Thie, who was looking at satellite photos of Wood Buffalo National Park. Thie and some fellow scientists were examining the effects of climate change on the landscape, and finding the beaver dam was coincidental. Parks Canada was notified of the discovery in 2009, and the following year rangers made a site visit and took photos by helicopter to confirm the dam's existence.

How Big Is It?

According to the Guinness World Records website, the beaver dam is 850 metres long, and Parks Canada reports that the entire perimeter of the dam is close to 2,000 metres and the surface area 70,000 square metres. The pond created by the dam is about one metre deep and therefore

An aerial view of the world's largest beaver dam, in Wood Buffalo National Park.

How Can You Visit?

The world's largest beaver dam isn't easy to get to. It's located 80 kilometres from Fort Chipewyan, the closest human settlement. It lies deep within a wetlands area in Wood Buffalo National Park, between the Peace-Athabasca Delta and the Birch Mountain Highlands. It has been seen by helicopter, but the first recorded person to have visited the world's largest beaver dam is an American adventurer named Rob Mark. In September 2014 he travelled about 200 kilometres through marshland, battling mosquitos and bad weather, to reach the dam. For most people, Google Earth or Parks Canada photos are the best ways to see the world's largest beaver dam.

Wood Buffalo National Park

At 44,807 square kilometres, Wood Buffalo National Park is the largest national park in Canada and the second-largest in the world. This UNESCO World Heritage Site is larger in area than Switzerland. Most of the park is in northeastern Alberta, but it also extends into the southern Northwest Territories. Besides being home to the world's largest beaver dam, Wood Buffalo has one of the last remaining free-roaming wood bison herds in the world. It also provides important nesting habitat for endangered whooping cranes.

There's a lot to see and do in Wood Buffalo National Park, including spotting wood bison and other wildlife, hiking trails and canoeing.

holds approximately 70,000 cubic metres of water.

To put those numbers into perspective, the beaver dam is more than twice the length of the Hoover Dam. The front end of the dam is about the length of seven football fields, and the water in the pond would fill 92,000 dump trucks.

An aerial view of the Athabasca
Dunes Ecological Reserve.

130 ATHABASCA DUNES ECOLOGICAL RESERVE

Address Maybelle River Wildland Park, AB
Telephone (780) 743-7437 | **Website** albertaparks.ca/parks/northeast/athabasca-dunes-er

Alberta's Moving Desert

Alberta's largest ecological reserve, the Athabasca Dunes Ecological Reserve, also contains part of the province's largest active sand dune system. This off-the-beaten-path natural site lies 200 kilometres north of Fort McMurray and is one of the most northerly active sand dune systems on Earth.

The dunes were formed about 8,000 years ago during the last glacial period. When the massive ice sheet retreated, the meltwater channels and spillways washed large amounts of sand and sediment into Glacial Lake Athabasca. As the lake retreated, the sand dunes were left.

The sand dune system is about 8 kilometres long and 1.5 kilometres wide. Alberta's moving desert shifts 1.5 metres per year, migrating with prevailing winds and slowly burying forests and lakes. The dunes range in size from 12 to 30 metres tall, and there are large areas of kettles and kames. Kettles are depressions that often fill with water, while kames are large sandhill formations. Both are glacial landforms. The 60-metre-high kames are some of the largest in the world.

The dunes are surrounded by peatlands, forest and kettle lakes that support a variety of unique species. This is the only place where Arctic terns are known to nest in Alberta. Sandhill cranes and woodland caribou have also been sighted in this region.

The Athabasca Dunes Ecological Reserve is a fascinating place that is difficult to access. You can get there by helicopter, ATV or on foot.

Other Sand Dunes in Alberta

Sand dunes are not common in Alberta, but there are several regions in the province where you can see them. The Jasper Lake Sand Dunes are the only sand dunes in the Canadian Rockies. The Brule Lake Sand Dunes are located about 26 kilometres west of Hinton. Brule Lake is a 10-kilometre-long lake with a unique sand dune ecosystem. It is one of the only dune areas in Alberta that allows off-highway vehicles on designated trails. The Brule Lake Sand Dunes have become a popular recreation area for those who own ATVs and dirt bikes.

The sandy shoreline of Jasper Lake, home to the only sand dunes in the Canadian Rockies.

131 FORT CHIPEWYAN ICE ROAD

Address Fort McMurray, AB, to Fort Smith, NWT | **Telephone** 1 (866) 743-6111
Website rmwb.ca/en/roads-and-construction/winter-roads.aspx

Ice Road Trucking on Alberta's Winter Road

A large sign identifies the entrance of the Fort Chipewyan Winter Road.

Direction signs aren't very fancy on the winter road that connects Fort McMurray to Fort Chipewyan and Fort Smith.

There's a reason the reality television series *Ice Road Truckers* ran for 11 seasons on the History Channel. Driving on a road made of ice is a little dangerous and very exciting. You don't have to leave Alberta to experience the thrill of driving an ice road. More than 500 kilometres of ice connect the community of Fort Chipewyan to Fort McMurray to the south (280 kilometres) and Fort Smith, Northwest Territories, to the north (228 kilometres). It is called the Fort Chipewyan Winter Road.

There are places on the ice road where vehicles must travel at a reduced speed for safety reasons.

During the summer months Fort Chipewyan is only accessible by airplane or boat. But when it gets cold enough, large trucks apply water over the muskeg until the surface is about 15 centimetres thick and reasonably smooth. It takes weeks to build the ice road, and when spring comes the road melts. The winter road must be rebuilt every year.

It takes about four-and-a-half hours to drive the 280 kilometres from Fort McMurray to Fort Chipewyan. You need a sturdy four-by-four vehicle with good winter tires, and you need to be prepared with basic emergency gear, enough fuel and oil, a spare tire and jack, a breakdown tool kit, warm clothes and boots, candles and other emergency supplies. There are no roadside services and there is no cellular signal for vast tracts of the route. If you run into trouble, you must be prepared to help yourself or wait in the cold until help comes.

It is expensive to live in the remote north, and the ice road has become a lifeline for the residents of Fort Chipewyan. During the winter months they can drive to Fort McMurray to get groceries, household items and other supplies. Prices for food and fuel are also lower in Fort Chipewyan during the winter, when food can be driven in instead of flown in.

Driving an ice road isn't quite as dramatic as they make it out to be on *Ice Road Truckers*, but it is a completely unique experience that you won't have in many places in the world. Winter is wonderful — especially if you want to visit Fort Chipewyan or Fort Smith.

Alberta's Highway of Death

Surprisingly, there aren't many accidents on the Fort Chipewyan Winter Road. The road to be more worried about is Highway 63, which connects Edmonton to Fort McMurray. That road has been nicknamed the "Highway of Death." Between 2007 and 2012, 46 people died in collisions on the notorious road. The Coalition for Safer Alberta Roads set up a website (fatalities.saferalbertaroads.ca) dedicated to high-lighting the fatalities on Highway 63 (as well as Highway 881), and an annual memorial ride was established in 2011 to remember the lives lost on the highway. The 10th ride was held in 2021. After many accidents and much public outrage, the road was upgraded in 2016, but the long-term plan is to create a divided highway for the entire stretch between Edmonton and Fort McMurray.

132 PHILIP J. CURRIE DINOSAUR MUSEUM

Address 9301 112th Avenue, Wembley, AB, T0H 3S0 | Telephone (587) 771-0662 | Website dinomuseum.ca

Where to See the River of Death

A fossil of *Pachyrhinosaurus lakustai*, a species of horned dinosaur that was discovered by a local teacher named Al Lakusta.

When you stand at the edge of the River of Death near Wembley, it doesn't look very deadly. But millions of years ago, it was a raging torrent that killed hundreds of dinosaurs. It is now known as the Pipestone Creek Bonebed, and it is one of the densest fossil sites in the world. The Philip J. Currie Dinosaur Museum outside Grande Prairie exists because of the Pipestone Creek Bonebed.

The bonebed was discovered in 1974 by a local teacher named Al Lakusta. It's about the size of a football field, and hundreds of dinosaur fossils are buried deep below the surface. Only a fraction of them have been excavated, but among the many fossils unearthed so far was a new species of horned dinosaur that was named *Pachyrhinosaurus lakustai* in honour of Lakusta. Besides the new species, researchers have also found hadrosaurs,

Hadrosaur fossils on display at the Philip J. Currie Dinosaur Museum.

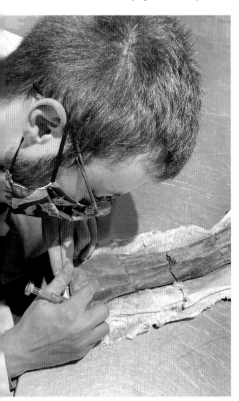

A researcher at work at the museum.

tyrannosaurs, plesiosaurs and pterosaurs.

The Philip J. Currie Dinosaur Museum opened in 2015. It is located 23 kilometres east of Grande Prairie in the town of Wembley and 16 kilometres south of the Pipestone Creek Bonebed. The museum contains displays and information about the dinosaur fossils found in the area. There are many hands-on activities to enjoy as well as excellent programs. Visitors can tour the bonebed and watch researchers as they work to uncover fossils there. They can also tour the fossil preparation laboratory, see the fossils stored there and watch researchers prepare fossils extracted from the Pipestone Creek Bonebed. A variety of special events are held at the museum throughout the year.

Who Is Philip J. Currie?

Dr. Philip J. Currie is one of the top palaeontologists and museum curators in the world. Though he was born in Ontario, he has worked in Alberta since 1976. He helped found the Royal Tyrrell Museum of Palaeontology in Drumheller and has made numerous discoveries in his long career as a palaeontologist — including describing dozens of new species. He was one of the models for palaeontologist Alan Grant in the 1993 film *Jurassic Park*. He has received many accolades during his long career, but having a world-class dinosaur museum named after him might be the greatest tribute of them all.

133 KLESKUN HILL NATURAL AREA

Address Township Road 724, County of Grande Prairie, AB, T0H 0G0
Telephone (780) 538-5350 | **Website** albertaparks.ca/parks/northwest/kleskun-hill-na

Alberta's Northernmost Badlands

A view of Kleskun Hill Natural Area's badlands.

There's a tendency to think that Alberta's badlands all lie in the southern part of the province, but that isn't true. There are badlands in several locations and Alberta's northernmost badlands are found just 30 kilometres northeast of Grande Prairie at Kleskun Hill Natural Area. This preserved natural area is home to stunning badlands, fossil-bearing strata in exposed bedrock and undisturbed native grasslands.

Long before the first European settlers arrived, Kleskun Hill was a favourite Indigenous campsite. The name "Kleskun" is likely of Beaver origin and means "white mud," referring to the bentonite clay found in the area. First Nations valued the area for the abundance of saskatoon berries and the bison that grazed on the

DID YOU KNOW?

The County of Grande Prairie was established in 1951 as the first county in Alberta. A plebiscite was held at Manning House to see if area residents wanted to become a county.

The historical village found at Kleskun Hill.

There are more than 160 flowering plants in this park.

in spring, including prairie crocus, purple onion, wood lily, blue flax and three-flowered avens. Large patches of juniper and kinnikinnick grow in low areas and patches of trembling aspen and shrubs like saskatoon berry, honeysuckle and prickly rose are interspersed throughout the area.

The native grassland supports a variety of bird species, including upland sandpipers, western meadowlarks and vesper sparrows. Prairie butterflies include common branded skippers, Garita's skippers and Alberta arctics.

A small campground with showers, a playground and a historical village where you can learn more about the history of settlement in this area are all operated by the municipality and the local historical society. In the historical village, there are a variety of interesting buildings to explore, including the East Kleskun School, which opened in 1919 and is fully equipped with desks, a school bell and other implements. There's also a log home, a red barn and a bunkhouse that date to the 1920s. The oldest building was built by Herbert Manning in 1914. Manning House served as a post office and a polling station for local, provincial and federal elections. A small fee is charged to visit the historical village.

prairie nearby. Legend has it that a great battle between the Beaver and Sikanni nations took place here, and the remains of several Beaver warriors are buried in a mass grave at the end of the hills.

Alberta's northernmost badlands have been shaped by erosion and include rocks of the same age as fossil-bearing badlands in other regions of the province. The site also protects one of the few remaining areas of undisturbed northern grasslands. As you hike through the area, you'll see a variety of grassland and parkland plants. Prickly pear cactus grows on the dry south exposures, this species being at the northern edge of its range. A variety of wildflowers can be seen

134 GRANDE CACHE LABYRINTH PARK

Address 10406 97th Avenue, Grande Cache, AB, T0E 0Y0
Telephone (780) 827-5099 | **Website** facebook.com/GCLabyrinth

A Meditative Experience West of Edmonton

The labyrinth at Grande Cache Labyrinth Park.

If you're seeking enlightenment, a visit to the Grande Cache Labyrinth Park might help. Walking a labyrinth is meant to be a meditative experience, and this labyrinth has a particularly beautiful background view. The Greek myth of the Minotaur and the 1986 fantasy film *Labyrinth*, starring David Bowie, would have you believe labyrinths are just very complicated mazes. But the ancient practice of labyrinth walking is not about solving a puzzle; it's about walking a long single pathway with a purpose.

Sulphur Gates, near Grande Cache.

The Grande Cache Labyrinth Park contains a unique 21-metre, 11-circuit labyrinth made out of rocks. It can be experienced in every season and it is always open. It's a walking meditation park where you can quiet your mind and take a special kind of reflective journey.

Other Things to See in Grande Cache
Grande Cache is one of the best dinosaur track sites in the world. More than a dozen such sites have been discovered in a 25-square-kilometre area near the community. The tracks were uncovered by coal mining operations and were designated a protected provincial historic site in 2006. You can see replicas of the tracks at the Grande Cache Tourism & Interpretive Centre. While you're in the area, you should also take the short drive to Sulphur Gates and take in the view. It's an impressive cliff-edged viewpoint above the confluence of the Smoky and Sulphur rivers. There's a short trail and viewing platforms along the dramatic cliffs.

Find a Labyrinth

The first labyrinths were built thousands of years ago. One of the oldest was found inside an Egyptian pyramid. Today there are many labyrinths around the world — including close to 50 in Alberta. If you want to find a labyrinth near you, visit labyrinthlocator.com.

135 LESSER SLaVE LaKE PROVINCIAL PaRK

Address Highway 88 Connector, Slave Lake, AB, T0G 2A0
Telephone (780) 849-8240 | **Website** borealbirdcentre.ca; albertaparks.ca/parks/northwest/lesser-slave-lake-pp

North America's Bird Nursery

There's a reason the boreal forest has been referred to as North America's bird nursery. Almost half of all North American bird species breed in Canada's boreal forest. Every spring between 1 to 3 billion migratory birds fly north to raise their young here, and each fall 3 to 5 billion fly south. An astounding number of birds are produced each breeding season. The boreal forest is the largest natural area in Alberta, and one of the best places to experience it is Lesser Slave Lake Provincial Park.

A researcher bands a dark-eyed junco.

The Boreal Centre for Bird Conservation

The Boreal Centre for Bird Conservation is a must-see for those who love nature and birds. Canada's most northerly bird observatory is also the only educational and research facility in the world that studies boreal birds on their breeding grounds. The centre itself has indoor and outdoor exhibits, interpretive programming, a gift shop, office space and research space. Near the centre is a comfort camping facility called The Nest that accommodates up to 10 people. The Songbird Trail is also nearby. The easy 0.6-kilometre loop winds through an aspen poplar forest. You'll want to read the interpretive signs along the trail, but make sure you take the time to stop and listen for birds. During migration season you can watch researchers at work as they band birds and do bird counts.

The Boreal Centre for Bird Conservations acts as the visitor centre for Lesser Slave Lake Provincial Park.

Lesser Slave Lake Provincial Park

When a strong wind blows waves across Alberta's third-largest lake, you can almost believe you're at the edge of the ocean as you gaze out from the sandy shoreline. At nearly 1,200 square kilometres, Lesser Slave Lake is rimmed by some of the finest beaches in the entire province and is a wonderful place to play on a warm summer day. It's also a great place to see sand dunes, hike, watch wildlife and see birds — in every season. It is the largest car-accessible lake in Alberta.

Lesser Slave Lake is a prime fishing lake, and the forests that surround it teem with wildlife. For these reasons, the region is well known to the Beaver and Woodland Cree, two Indigenous groups that traditionally lived and hunted in the region.

A researcher measures the wing of a sharp-shinned hawk.

A researcher retrieves a bird for research and identification.

David Thompson was the first European to reach Lesser Slave Lake, arriving in 1799. He commented on the abundance of moose, bison and waterfowl in the area, and he made detailed observations to map the area. Fur-trading posts were eventually built on the shores of the lake by both the North West Company and Hudson's Bay Company, and Lesser Slave Lake became one of the most productive fur-bearing regions in Canada.

A unique microclimate and the rich habitat of the boreal forest make this area a haven for nesting and migratory birds — especially songbirds. The site has been designated an Important Bird Area, a classification established by BirdLife International for areas deemed crucial to conserving bird populations. Many birds pass through during the spring and fall migrations, and it's estimated that up to 20 percent of the western population of tundra swans stops to feed on the lake. Flocks of up to 3,500 swans have been documented in the spring and fall. Reeds around the lake provide nesting habitat for a globally important western grebe population. The area also has an incredible concentration and diversity of migrant songbirds, including yellow warblers, bay-breasted warblers and red-eyed vireos, to name a few. Visitors with a particular interest in songbirds should attend the Songbird Festival, held in the park each spring.

The cairn at the geographic centre of Alberta.

GRIZZLY TRAIL
PROMOTIONAL ASSOCIATION

CENTRE OF ALBERTA
L.S. 14-33-43-7-W5

HONORARY CHAIRMAN
KEN KOWALSKI M.L.A.

SURVEYED BY
ROY CHIMIUK

JULY 1989

136 THE GEOGRAPHIC CENTRE OF ALBERTA

Address Highway 33 (Grizzly Trail), 36 kilometres southeast of Swan Hills, AB
Telephone (780) 333-4477 (town of Swan Hills) | **Website** townofswanhills.com/lifestyle/tourism/center-of-alberta

Journey to the Centre of the Province

The geographic centre of Alberta is not where most Albertans think it is. The region between Calgary and Edmonton is frequently referred to as central Alberta, but in reality the true geographic centre of Alberta lies 185 kilometres northwest of Edmonton and 36 kilometres southeast of the town of Swan Hills.

For those that live in the Swan Hills area, the misidentification of the geographic centre of Alberta is a bit of a pet peeve. Local resident Roy Chimiuk set out to identify and mark the exact centre of the province. With 20 years of experience as a surveyor, he was uniquely qualified to calculate the measurements both vertically and horizontally. The intersection point was the precise centre.

Once the spot was identified, many hours were spent cutting a 5-kilometre trail through a heavily forested area to reach the true geographic centre of Alberta. The path leads to a clearing where you'll find a stone cairn. There's a statue of a grizzly cub on top of the cairn, a Swan Hills Grizzly pawprint on the back and a plaque on the front that acknowledges the Grizzly Trail Promotional Society, the Honorable Ken Kowalski and Roy Chimiuk.

On September 10, 1989, 100 people made the hike to the geographic centre of Alberta and Kowalski, Member of the Legislative Assembly for the Barrhead-Westlock-Swan Hills riding, dedicated the site. The trailhead is marked with a pullout off Highway 33, about 36 kilometres southeast of Swan Hills. It's marked on Google Maps.

The trail to the centre of Alberta.

Today the trail is fairly easy to traverse on an ATV and a little more challenging on foot. There are some marshy spots along the way that you have to bypass when you're hiking, and this can make the journey take a little longer. The walk will take you through a forested area, and you should keep an eye out for birds and other wildlife along the way (consider carrying bear spray). It's worth the effort to make the trek to the geographic centre of Alberta and take a selfie with the cairn. It's definitely a unique place in the province.

137 GEORGE PEGG BOTANIC GARDEN

Address 56015 Range Road 43, Glenevis, AB, T0E 0X0
Telephone (780) 203-0331 (April to September) | **Website** pegggarden.org

Learn about a Self-Taught Pioneer Botanist

A small boardwalk goes through the botanic gardens.

You can explore the family home where George Pegg lived.

I f you've ever doubted your ability to make a difference in the world, you should visit the George Pegg Botanic Garden and learn about the man who created it. George Pegg was an Alberta homesteader who was passionate about botany. He didn't have the opportunity to attend university, so he studied and researched the subject on his own. Because of Pegg's involvement, more than 100 plant species were included in *Flora of Alberta* when it was published in 1959. His botanical

Some of the flower species found at the George Pegg Botanic Garden.

of land on the original Pegg family homestead just outside the hamlet of Glenevis, about 91 kilometres northwest of Edmonton. The garden is so remarkable that it was the first in Alberta to be declared a provincial historic resource. It is also on the list of Canada's Historic Places.

The garden is an eclectic preserved landscape with historic buildings, wildflowers, shrubs, native and exotic plants, and heritage trees. There are two heritage trees in the garden — a ponderosa pine and a Swedish columnar aspen — which are both marked with plaques. Heritage trees are designated as such because of their size, age, shape, location or history. Some of the other unique trees on the property include a bristle cone pine and rare species of hawthorn, poplar, cedar and juniper.

Besides walking through the gardens and seeing the many living plants, it is interesting to see Pegg's preserved specimens. Pegg had a substantial herbarium, and he was the first to identify several species in Alberta, including a plant known as the bur-reed (*Sparganium glomeratum*), which had previously been found in only four other locations in North America.

The George Pegg Botanic Garden is a special place that is as unique as the man who created it. The garden is open to visitors from June through August.

collection also extended the known ranges of more than 50 plant species. Pegg did not let his limitations prevent him from making a significant contribution to the science of botany.

The George Pegg Botanic Garden is located on 5.13 hectares

138 THE IRON HORSE TRAIL

Address Waskatenau, AB (multiple entry points exist along the trail)
Telephone (780) 645-2913 | **Website** ironhorsetrail.ca

Alberta's Longest Section of the Trans Canada Trail

The Beaver River Trestle Bridge is a definite highlight of the Iron Horse Trail.

The Trans Canada Trail stretches more than 28,000 kilometres across Canada and is the longest network of multiuse recreational trails in the world. Although Canadians celebrated the completion of the Trans Canada Trail in 2017, the trail is not fully connected in Alberta. Existing roadways were designated as interim pathways to allow the province to say the Trans Canada Trail was fully connected in time for the celebration. One bright spot is the Iron Horse Trail. It is Alberta's longest continuous stretch of Trans Canada Trail, running 300 kilometres from Waskatenau to Cold Lake, with a branch to Heinsburg.

The Iron Horse Trail can be explored on foot, by mountain bike, on horseback, by ATV, by snowmobile or even in a Red River cart. Along the way, you can see birds, wildlife, farms, rural communities and historic sites. The trail was built on abandoned Canadian National Railway railbed, and as a result it passes through small rural communities, traversing the transition zone between Alberta's aspen parkland and northern boreal forest biomes. Watch for deer, moose, coyotes, badgers, beavers and bears near the trail, and keep your eye on the skies for bird species — this part of Alberta is a birdwatcher's paradise. You might see cardinals, warblers, grosbeaks,

ATV is a popular means of travelling the Iron Horse Trail.

Hike past the pumpkins in Smoky Lake.

chickadees, owls, geese, nuthatches, orioles, woodpeckers, hawks, bald eagles and many more species.

In Alberta's early years railways were the backbone of transportation, and communities were located near stops along rail lines. Over many years roads and highways were built up, and some rail lines became uneconomical to operate. When the lines in east central Alberta were retired and the rails were pulled up, local stakeholders and community leaders recognized the opportunity for trail development on the abandoned railbeds that were left behind. Local volunteers, businesses, groups, associations, municipalities and government organizations worked together with the support of the Trans Canada Trail Foundation (tctrail.ca) and Alberta TrailNet Society (albertatrailnet.com) to realize their collective vision and develop and maintain the magnificent recreational trail you see today.

The Iron Horse Trail takes multiple days to explore in its entirety. There are 14 communities, 20 trail staging areas and three provincial parks along the way. Most people break the journey up into smaller sections. In the small towns near the trail you'll find municipal campgrounds, motels, hotels and B&Bs. One of the highlights of the trail is the Beaver River Trestle Bridge near Cold Lake. The view from the top of this 1-kilometre-long, 60-metre-high bridge is spectacular.

139 MÉTIS CROSSING

Address 17339 Victoria Trail, Smoky Lake, AB, T0A 3C0 | **Telephone** (780) 656-2229 | **Website** metiscrossing.com

Where to See the Most Sacred Living Creature on Earth

The exterior of Métis Crossing's intepretive centre.

lberta's first Métis cultural destination sits on the banks of the North Saskatchewan River near Smoky Lake on the original river lots of the first Métis settlers in the region. It was a major meeting site for Métis, other Indigenous Peoples and Europeans. The crossing was used to access fishing grounds to the north and buffalo hunting grounds to the south. It was the site of a Methodist mission and located near Victoria Settlement, a Hudson's Bay trading post. Many Métis moved to this region from other parts of Canada to farm and work in the fur trade. That is part of the reason Alberta now has the largest Métis population of any province or territory in Canada.

Métis are of mixed European and Indigenous ancestry and are one of the three recognized Indigenous Peoples of Canada. The Métis Nation originated from the Red River Settlement in Western Canada, where the Métis developed their own language, culture, music, food and traditional ways of living. If you want to experience and understand Métis culture, one of the best places to go is Métis Crossing.

Métis Crossing is open all year and has a large on-site interpretive centre. During the summer months you can follow costumed interpreters through a traditional harvesting camp, explore a river lot farmyard and see traditional gardens and real farm animals. There are also craft and skills

A white bison — the most sacred living creature on Earth.

You can experience an overnight stay in a traditional Métis trapper tent.

demonstrations and many hands-on activities. Winter offerings include cross-country ski trails, snowshoeing and stargazing opportunities. There's also a new wildlife park open year-round. Guests who wish to remain overnight can stay at the 40-room on-site guest lodge or in traditional Métis trapper tents.

White Bison: Vision, Hopes and Dreams at Métis Crossing

In 2021 Métis Crossing opened a new wildlife park with small herds of woods bison, plains bison, white bison, elk and Percheron horses. Bison have not roamed on the land in this region since sometime between 1860 and 1865. Many Indigenous cultures consider bison to be sacred and white bison in particular to be the most sacred living creatures on Earth. White bison are so rare that they are often the stuff of legend. In the wild, it is estimated that one out of every 10 million bison is born white. Many First Nations legends say that seeing a white bison is a sign that prayers are being heard. Some believe that white bison have the power to restore harmony and spirituality to a troubled world. Seeing bison on the land is very moving, but seeing a white bison is a rare privilege. The new wildlife park at Métis Crossing is one of the only places in the world where you can do that.

140 VICTORIA SETTLEMENT PROVINCIAL HISTORIC SITE

Address 58161 Range Road 171A, Pakan, AB, T0B 0C0 | Telephone (780) 656-2333 | Website victoriasettlement.ca

Experience Life in Alberta in the Late 19th Century

Visiting Victoria Settlement is a chance to step back in time to the late 1800s and learn about missionary activity, the fur trade and the settlement of Alberta. Costumed interpreters help tell the stories of this part of Alberta. You can also book a program that includes a canoe ride from Métis Crossing to Victoria Settlement. Métis Crossing is another interesting attraction nearby.

George McDougall, a Methodist minister, first came to the area in 1862 to establish a mission. The region had long been an important site for seasonal camps of Cree. The Victoria Mission was the earliest Methodist mission in Western Canada. McDougall was superintendent of the Methodist missionary work in the Saskatchewan District, and in 1871 he established another mission at Edmonton House, a Hudson's Bay Company outpost located in what is now Edmonton. Both missions were closely tied to the fur trade.

The establishment of Victoria Mission and a Hudson's Bay trading post resulted in an influx of Métis settlers a few years later. By the early 1900s there were 100 residents in the area, and the community changed its name to Pakan. When the Canadian Northern Railway arrived in Smoky Lake in 1918, it was the beginning of the end for the community of Pakan. What is left of it now is a provincial historic site.

Victoria District National Historic Site of Canada

Victoria Settlement is a provincial historic site, but the district that surrounds it is a national historic site of Canada. Soak up the history and the landscape as you drive along Victoria Trail to reach Victoria Settlement. The farmlands are organized in long narrow river lots along the North Saskatchewan River as well as in 800-square-metre sections. The designation recognizes the interesting landscape as well as the historic buildings within the district. The surviving structures illustrate Métis construction techniques as well as Ukrainian settlement

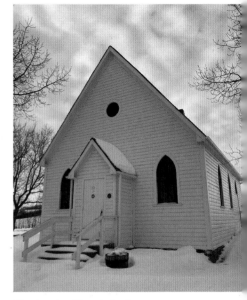

The church at Victoria Settlement Provincial Historic Site.

patterns to the north of Victoria Settlement. There are also historic cemeteries in the area.

Theft of the Sacred Manitou Stone

Reverend McDougall is revered for establishing Alberta's first Methodist mission and for assisting in negotiations that led to the signing of Treaty 6 and Treaty 7. One story that isn't told as often

Costumed intepreters help bring the history of Victoria Settlement to life.

is his role in stealing a large iron stone that many Indigenous nations consider to be sacred. The 320-pound (145-kilogram) meteorite was known by several names. The Plains Cree named the meteorite *papamihaw asiniy*, which means "flying rock." It was also known as the Manitou Stone or the Stone God, because it appears to have the profile of a face when it is viewed from

a certain angle. Many Indigenous nations believe the stone represents the Creator and is a source of strength, power and protection.

The stone was located near Hardisty and many would visit it whenever they passed through the area. McDougall considered the stone to be a pagan symbol, and some have theorized that he saw it as a hindrance to

converting First Nations to Christianity. Whatever his reasons, he took the stone and sent it to Ontario in 1886 to be displayed at the Victoria Methodist College, where he was trained. After the stone was stolen, elders predicted war, disease and starvation would follow. Their predictions, unfortunately, came true.

The Manitou Stone was displayed at the Royal Ontario Museum for many years. At the request of the Alberta Government, Victoria College placed the Manitou Stone on long-term loan with the institution now known as the Royal Alberta Museum (RAM) in 1972. Between 2002 and 2004, RAM held consultations with 33 Alberta and Saskatchewan First Nations and seven Indigenous organizations to find the most appropriate location for the Manitou Stone. The majority believed that it should be returned to its original location in a secure facility; however, there was no consensus on who should build and operate the facility. The stone remains at RAM in the interim, as the space is both secure and accessible to Indigenous Peoples. Discussions about the care and future of the Manitou Stone are ongoing.

The 4.5-billion-year-old stone currently sits on soil from its original location and is displayed in a separate gallery where people can pay homage and leave spiritual offerings.

The church at Lac La Biche Mission

(141) Lac La Biche Mission National Historic Site

Address 67453 Mission Road, Lac La Biche, AB, T0A 2C2
Telephone (780) 623-3274 | **Website** laclabichemission.com

A Hub of Trade, Transport and Early Agriculture

Agriculture has long been one of the most important industries in Alberta, but the province's earliest European settlers had to experiment to determine which crops could be successfully grown. Notre Dame des Victoires, commonly known as Lac La Biche Mission, was established in 1853 and moved to its present site in 1855, a location where the ground was more suitable for agriculture and farther away from the corrupting influence of the nearby Hudson's Bay Company trading post. In 1856 a crop of potatoes, barley and turnips was grown, and five years later so were wheat and barley. The first commercial crop of wheat in Alberta was grown at Lac La Biche Mission. In 1863 the Roman Catholic missionaries built one of Alberta's first flour mills, and in 1871 they built its first water-powered sawmill. Their work revealed that crops such as wheat could be successfully grown in Alberta, and today almost one-third of all the wheat produced in Canada comes from Alberta.

By the 1870s Lac La Biche Mission was one of the most important western Oblate missions and a major transportation hub. The mission became part of a significant portage route that ran overland from St. Boniface to the Lac La Biche Mission and from the Athabasca-Mackenzie River system to Fort Good Hope. Warehouses were constructed to store goods until they could be shipped to missions farther north.

The introduction of steamboats on the North Saskatchewan and Athabasca rivers in the late 1800s changed transportation routes and ended the mission's role as a transportation hub. Some of the Métis settlers in this region relocated to Athabasca Landing to work on the steamboats.

Lac La Biche Mission served Cree, Dene and Métis converts. The first school at the mission was established in 1862 and operated as both a boarding school and a day school for students who lived close enough to travel back and forth between their homes and the school. From 1893 to 1898 an Indian Residential School was officially established at the site. In 1898 students were moved to a residential school built in Saddle Lake First Nation called Blue Quills and later moved again to a residential school near St. Paul. The mission's involvement with residential schools is a dark period in its history that should not be forgotten. There is a display at the site containing information about it.

If you visit this site today, you can see the historic buildings and learn about the history of the mission. Notre Dame des Victoires, or Lac La Biche Mission, was designated a national historic site in 1989. The designation recognizes the Oblate Mission's important role in development of the fur trade and in transportation and communications in Western Canada. The mission also played an important role in demonstrating that agriculture is a viable industry in Alberta.

SIR WINSTON CHURCHILL PROVINCIAL PARK

Address Provincial Park Road, Lac la Biche, AB, T0A 2C0
Telephone (780) 623-7189 | **Website** albertaparks.ca/parks/northeast/sir-winston-churchill-pp

Alberta's Only Island Park

The Boardwalk Trail in Sir Winston Churchill Provincial Park.

In a landlocked province, it's a little surprising to have a provincial park on an island. While Alberta doesn't have an ocean, it does have massive lakes that almost seem like the ocean when you stand on their shores. At 236 square kilometres, Lac la Biche is one of the largest lakes in the province. Sir Winston Churchill Provincial Park includes several islands on the lake, including the largest one, which is fittingly named Big Island. There's a campground and cabins on the island as well as a playground, beaches and other facilities. Located at the east end of Lac la Biche, the island is accessed by a 2.5-kilometre-long causeway, making it one of the most unique provincial parks in the province.

Birding is one of the most popular activities at this park, and the area surrounding the lake has been designated an Important Bird Area. In addition to large populations of red-necked grebes and California gulls, at least 224 of the 330 bird species in Alberta have been observed within the park. Some of the

Visitors can explore old-growth boreal forest.

It's not hard to get a beach all to yourself at this island park.

most sought-after species include warblers (blackburnian, Cape May, black-throated, green and bay-breasted warblers), olive-sided flycatchers, white-winged crossbills, Swainson's and hermit thrushes, sparrows (sharp-tailed, Le Conte's and swamp sparrows), osprey, bald eagles and owls (northern saw-whet, barred, great grey, boreal and great horned owls). There's a platform at Pelican Viewpoint where you can see water birds such as American white pelicans, double-crested cormorants and Franklin's gulls.

The island is criss-crossed with hiking trails. You can walk to the westernmost tip of the island on the 2.5-kilometre Long Point Trail. Along the way you'll pass a remote beach and walk along a lovely forested trail. The 1.2-kilometre Boardwalk Trail goes through old-growth boreal forest that has been untouched by fires for at least 300 years. Old Growth Alley connects the Long Point and Boardwalk trails and goes around the edge of the island, where you have a good chance of seeing birds.

What Difference Does One Capital Letter Make?

Sir Winston Churchill Provincial Park is 11-kilometres away from the town of Lac La Biche. One capital letter distinguishes the name of the town from the name of the lake, Lac la Biche. It's not confusing at all!

A variety of aircraft can be seen outside the museum.

The Cold Lake Museum dome.

Touring the museum is a chance to learn about the Cold War radar facilities that were once used at this site.

143 COLD LAKE AIR FORCE MUSEUM

Address 3699 69th Avenue, Cold Lake, AB, T9M 0B5
Telephone (780) 594-3546 | **Website** coldlakemuseums.org/about/air-force-museum

Inside a Cold War Radar Station

Cold Lake is the only Cold War radar station in Canada that has been transformed into an accredited Air Force Museum. The radar facility was built in the early 1950s and used until 1992, when the 42 Radar Squadron was moved onto Canadian Forces Base (CFB) Cold Lake. The old radar facility was then turned into a museum. It's one of the few Cold War radar facilities you can view, but that's not the only reason to visit this museum. Inside the facility is an incredible collection of artifacts and information about the nearby air force base as well as the 42 Radar Squadron.

There are five airplanes outside the museum, and inside is a massive collection of military artifacts. The Cold Lake Air Force Museum is also connected to other nearby museums: the Oil and Gas Interpretive Centre, the Heritage Gallery and the Aboriginal Gallery. By the time you explore these museums, you'll have a vast knowledge of the history of the Cold Lake area and its military base.

CFB Cold Lake, commonly known as 4 Wing Cold Lake, is where Canadian fighter pilots train. The Cold Lake Air Weapons Range covers an area of 1.17 million hectares and is considered one of the finest facilities of its kind in the world.

DID YOU KNOW?

Alberta is home to Canada's busiest air force base (CFB Cold Lake) as well as Canada's largest military base (CFB Suffield). CFB Suffield occupies over 2,690 square kilometres of land north of Medicine Hat and is one of the largest live-fire training areas in the Western world. The base includes a 45,836-hectare natural area known as Suffield National Wildlife Area. Terrain and wildlife are protected in this natural area. The site also protects the Suffield Tipi Rings and British Block Cairn, which contain many tipi rings, cairns and at least 14 medicine wheels. The location of these national historic sites makes it difficult to visit them, and few people ever get the opportunity to enter the base.

There's no charge to see the airplanes that sit outside the museum.

MUSEUMS THAT CELEBRATE ENERGY PRODUCTION

Alberta has more museums and historical sites that celebrate energy production than any other province in Canada. It's one of the things that makes Alberta unusual.

144 CANADIAN ENERGY MUSEUM

Address 50339 Highway 60 South,
Leduc County, AB, T9G 0B2
Telephone (780) 987-4323
Website canadianenergymuseum.ca

In 1947 an oil strike at Leduc No. 1 changed the course of Alberta history. The Canadian Energy Museum tells the stories of the momentous discovery and Alberta's energy history — including information about the technological advancements, innovations and people who have worked in the energy sector.

Canadian Energy Museum

145 OIL SANDS DISCOVERY CENTRE

Address 515 MacKenzie Boulevard,
Fort McMurray, AB, T9H 4X3
Telephone (780) 743-7167
Website oilsandsdiscovery.ca

The Athabasca Oil Sands are considered the world's largest single oil deposit. At the Oil Sands Discovery Centre in Fort McMurray, visitors can learn about the geology and history of the oil sands and the technology behind extracting crude oil from them. The museum has exhibits and interactive displays. Outdoor exhibits feature retired equipment, including one of the largest land-based artifacts in Canada — a seven-storey bucket-wheel excavator.

146 DIPLOMAT MINE INTERPRETIVE SITE

Address Township Road 410A,
Forestburg, AB, T0B 1N0
Telephone (780) 582-3668
Website flagstaff.ab.ca/tourism/things-to-do
/museums/80-visit/288-diplomat
-mine-interpretive-site

Canada's only surface coal mining museum, the Diplomat Mine Interpretive Site tells the history of surface coal mining in Flagstaff County. The Diplomat Mine was operated by Forestburg Collieries Limited, a division of Luscar Limited, from 1949 to 1986. When the mine was closed, the company donated several pieces of large equipment that can be seen at this reclaimed site. There's a visitor gazebo, picnic tables and washrooms. This site is on the list of Canada's Historic Places.

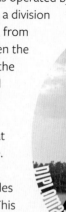

Diplomat Mine Interpretive Site

147 TURNER VALLEY GAS PLANT NATIONAL & PROVINCIAL HISTORIC SITE

Address Sunset Boulevard Southeast,
Turner Valley, AB, T0L 2A0
Telephone (403) 933-6243
Website turnervalleygasplant.ca

Visitors to this site can explore Western Canada's first commercial oil field and processing plant, which is also a national historic site. On May 14, 1914, wet natural gas sprayed out of the well bore at Dingman No. 1 in Turner Valley. This discovery led to the creation of Alberta's first natural gas plant. For many years the Turner Valley Gas Plant was one of Canada's most significant petroleum processing facilities. After the plant closed in 1985 it became a provincially and nationally designated historic resource that offers public tours. Visitors can take a guided tour through some of the historic buildings and the interpretive displays in the exhibit hall.

148 BELLEVUE UNDERGROUND MINE TOUR

Address 2531 213rd Street, Bellevue, AB, T0K 0C0
Telephone (403) 564-4700
Website bellevuemine.com

The Bellevue Mine was active from about 1905 until 1961, and the mine is the reason the town of Bellevue exists. An underground mine tour is a chance to put on a hardhat and see what it was like to work in a coal mine. There are coal mining artifacts inside the mine and near the entrance. Visitors can also learn about the history of the mine on guided tours. On December 9, 1910, an underground explosion claimed the lives of 31 men. Had the explosion happened at another time, it would have taken many more lives.

149 LEITCH COLLIERIES PROVINCIAL HISTORIC SITE

Address 12 km southeast of Blairmore, off Highway 3
Telephone (403) 562-7388
Website leitchcollieries.ca

Interpretive panels, listening posts and walking pathways through the ruins of this coal mine site tell the story of the collapse of the only fully Canadian-owned and operated mining venture in the early 1900s. Leitch Collieries was one of the most sophisticated early coal mines in the Crowsnest Pass. The site is open to the public from mid-June through Labour Day, with knowledgeable interpretive staff available to answer questions and lead guided tours. It's a self-guided experience the rest of the year. There is no trail maintenance in winter and washrooms are closed.

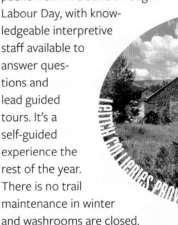

150 FIRST OIL WELL IN WESTERN CANADA NATIONAL HISTORIC SITE

Address 6 kilometres northwest of the Waterton townsite on Akamina Parkway
Telephone (403) 859-5133
Website pc.gc.ca/en/lhn-nhs/ab/puits-well

Alberta's first oil well is not where you think it might be. Lineham Discovery Well No. 1 was drilled in 1902 in what is now Waterton Lakes National Park. Though the well was short-lived, it did ignite a passion for petroleum exploration. Interpretive panels tell the story of this national historic site.

ACKNOWLEDGEMENTS

I wish to acknowledge the First Nations, Inuit and Métis who have lived on and cared for this land since time immemorial. The enduring presence and stewardship of the Indigenous Peoples of Canada has helped to preserve the many majestic and unusual places we enjoy today.

I sought the advice of many experts while selecting, researching, writing and sourcing images for *Top 150 Unusual Things to See in Alberta*. I owe special thanks to Olga Fowler and the staff of the Heritage Division of Alberta Culture and Tourism, Guy Theriault and Eric Magnan with Parks Canada, the staff at Alberta Parks, and the staffs of each of the sites included in this book.

They say a picture is worth a thousand words, but in my experience, it's worth more. A special thank you to my husband, Greg Olsen, who contributed many photographs to this book and travelled with me to many of the sites included in the book. Sincere thanks to the many others who supplied and contributed images.

I had many adventures while researching this book. Special thanks to Shannon Bear Chief and Sam Healy, who guided my husband and me to Iniskim Umaapi (Majorville Medicine Wheel). I don't think we would have found it on our own. Also, special thanks to Jud Overton and his friends who came to our rescue when we got a flat tire while travelling the rough road to get to Mountain Park Cemetery, the highest cemetery in Canada.

A big thanks to the team at Firefly for putting together such a beautiful book. Special thanks to my editor, Julie Takasaki, who spent many hours collaborating and working with me on this project. She is an amazing editor, and her queries and suggestions made the book better. I am also grateful to Hartley Millson for his design work, Ronnie Shuker for his careful copyedit and Margaret de Boer for her index. Special thanks to Barry Cuff for proofreading the manuscript.

And, finally, a big thanks to my family who put up with me while I was engrossed in this project and always love me unconditionally — even when I work too hard. Thanks for all your support.

PHOTO CREDITS

Front cover:
Shutterstock/r.classen.

Back cover (clockwise from top left): Greg Olsen, Shutterstock/ Litwin Photography, Kyla Hornberger, Greg Olsen, Greg Olsen.

Interior:
All photos © Greg Olsen, except as listed below.

Debbie Olsen: 8, 10, 11, 16, 18, 35 (bottom), 44, 50, 51 (top and middle), 53 (left), 63 (bottom), 74, 75 (left), 79 (bottom), 82 (middle inset and bottom), 88 (bottom left and bottom right), 89, 92, 93 (bottom), 99, 105 (top), 109, 126, 127, 129 (top and middle), 137 (bottom), 145 (right), 157, 160, 173, 175, 182, 183 (bottom), 202, 203, 210, 211, 222 (top), 223 (bottom left), 224 (right), 232, 233 (bottom), 237, 238, 239, 240, 241 (top), 243, 249, 250, 251, 253, 255, 256, 260, 261, 262 (inset, bottom left and bottom right), 264 (right).

Photo courtesy of the Art Gallery of Alberta: 77.

Alamy Stock Photo:
Ashley Cooper: 230, 236; Autumn Sky Photography: 177 (bottom); Design Pics Inc: 176; John Elk III: 130; Matthiola: 231; Michael Wheatley: 78, 80 (bottom); Michelle Gilders: 151.

City of Edmonton: 80 (middle inset)

Deanna Noot: 264 (left).

Dustin Creviston: 71.

Photos courtesy of the Government of Alberta: 67.

Photo courtesy of Head-Smashed-In Buffalo Jump World Heritage Site: 24.

Jasper-Yellowhead Museum & Archives, 84.32.251: 163.

Jeff Hinman: 30 (inset).

Joanne Nielson: 26.

Karen Sommerfeldt: 91 (top left).

Keith Payne: 27.

Kelsey Olsen: 198 (bottom left).

Kyla Hornberger: 206, 207.

Larry Michielsen: 98.

Courtesy of Libraries and Cultural Resources Digital Collections, University of Alberta: 183 (top and middle), 205.

Nicole Larson: 51 (bottom).

Nigel Thiessen: 30, 31.

Parks Canada:
Charla Jones: 235; Graham Twomey: 188; Parks Canada: 177 (top), 179; Rob Belanger: 234; Ryan Bray: 90; Scott Munn: 91 (top right, middle right, bottom right), 189.

RCMP Academy: 94, 95.

Photos courtesy of Reynolds-Alberta Museum: 86, 87.

Shutterstock:
achinthamb: 164; Aleksa Georg: 156; Alex JW Robinson: 12; Autumn Sky Photography: 178; Bob Hilscher: 57 (bottom); Carey Jaman: 143 (top); CarruthersCat: 81; Chris Dale: 209, 265 (right); christopher babcock: 114 (top); Danielle royer: 25 (top); Danita Delimont: 198 (top); Edinburghcitymom: 138 (top); EdmontonMartin: 70 (bottom);

i viewfinder: 132; Jeff Whyte: 62, 76, 106, 128, 129 (bottom), 133, 136, 137 (top), 142 (top), 144, 198 (bottom right); Josef Hanus: 208; Jukka Jantunen: 45 (right); Justin Hetu: 242; Karynf: 53 (right); LisaBourgeault: 125; Litwin Photography: 28; Nalidsa: 265 (left); nednapa: 111 (right); NelzTabcharani316: 184 (bottom); Pecold: 25 (bottom); Pixels by Tina: 226 (bottom); ravensfoot: 52; Ritu Manoj Jethani: 61 (top); Ronnie Chua: 20, 48, 80 (top); Rush Photography Calgary: 212; Russ Heinl: 233 (top); Scott Prokop: 29; Sean Ferguson: 245; Shawn.ccf: 150; Steve Boer: 120; Tessa Chou: 185; TetyanaT: 70 (top); Todamo: 32, 33 (right), 43, 118 (middle inset), 181 (top right); Vincent JIANG: 114 (bottom); Wang Sing: 124.

Photo courtesy of Stephansson House: 93 (top).

TELUS World of Science – Edmonton: 60, 61 (bottom).

Tourism Lethbridge: 226 (top).

Town of Vulcan: 152 (middle right).

Photos courtesy of the Ukrainian Cultural Heritage Village: 84, 85.

Photos courtesy of the University of Alberta Museums: 68, 69.

Photos courtesy of University of Alberta Botanic Garden, photos by Paul Swanson: 56, 57 (top).

Photos courtesy of Victoria Settlement Provincial Historic Site: 257.

Youthlink Calgary Police Interpretive Centre: 148, 149.

INDEX